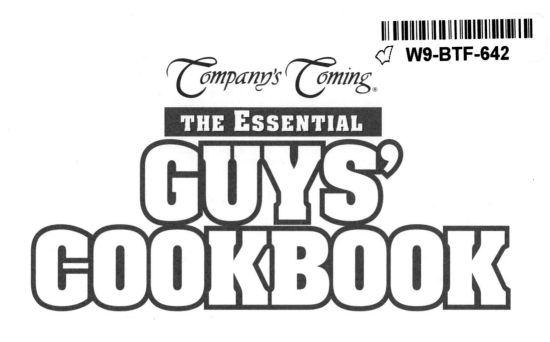

Company's Coming

THE ESSENTIAL

GUYS' COOKBOOK

Morrison · Smoliak · Paré · Darcy

The Essential Guys' Cookbook

First Printing May 2014

Library and Archives Canada Cataloguing in Publication

Morrison, Jeff, 1967-, author

The essential guys' cookbook / Jeff Morrison, Brad

Smoliak, Jean Paré, James Darcy.

(Essential collection)

Includes index.

ISBN 978-1-927126-44-8 (bound)

1. Cooking. 2. Cookbooks. I. Smoliak, Brad, 1966-, author II. Paré,

Jean, author III. Darcy, James, author IV. Title.

TX652.M675 2014   641.50811   C2013-907153-9

Image Credits: © Company's Coming Publishing: 4, 15, 17, 18, 35, 36, 53, 54, 71, 72, 89, 90, 107, 108, 125, 126, 143, 144, 161, 162, 179, 180, 197, 198, 215, 216, 226, 233, 234, 240, 251, 252, 269, 270, 287, 288. © Photos.com: Anastasia Fisechko, 60c; Andrew Howe, 7b; Anthony Oshlick, 135; BONNINSTUDIO, 39; Comstock Images, 6; DamianPalus, 60d; Dynamic Graphics, 8, 9; Elena Elisseeva, 60b, 261; ep_stock, 13c; George Doyle, 76, 77; goce, 123; grafvision, 13b; Hemera Technologies, 5; ivan_baranov, 10abc; IvonneW, 220; jamesbin, 33a; Jon Schulte, 33b; jumadinur 85, 60a, 60e; Jupiterimages, 110, 208; katkov, 285; lightstock, 87; Lisa F. Young, 13d, 194; lisafx, 146; Matthew Hart, 59b; michaeljung, 277; monticelllo, 231; nito100, 59a; Photos.com, 254; Planet Flem, 170; ron sumners, 96; scorton, 188; shuchun ke, 13a; Stockbyte, 50; sunemotion, 7a; SZE FEI WONG, 74; tatniz, 59c; Uros Petrovic, 181; YekoPhotoStudio, 44
Cover Image: Sandy Weatherall, Jinsei Photographics

Recipes on pages 221, 225 and 229 are taken from *Canadian Culinary Olympic Chefs Cook at Home* by Culinary Team Canada (Company's Coming, 2012).

Published by
Company's Coming Publishing Limited
2311 – 96 Street
Edmonton, Alberta, Canada T6N 1G3
Tel: 780-450-6223   Fax: 780-450-1857
www.companyscoming.com

Company's Coming is a registered trademark owned by Company's Coming Publishing Limited

We acknowledge the financial support of the Government of Canada through the Canada Book Fund for our publishing activities.

Printed in China

PC: 21

TABLE OF CONTENTS

THE COMPANY'S COMING STORY

Jean Paré (pronounced "jeen PAIR-ee") grew up understanding that the combination of family, friends and home cooking is the best recipe for a good life. From her mother, she learned to appreciate good cooking, while her father praised even her earliest attempts in the kitchen. When Jean left home, she took with her a love of cooking, many family recipes and an intriguing desire to read cookbooks as if they were novels!

"Never share a recipe you wouldn't use yourself."

When her four children had all reached school age, Jean volunteered to cater the 50th anniversary celebration of the Vermilion School of Agriculture, now Lakeland College, in Alberta, Canada. Working out of her home, Jean prepared a dinner for more than 1,000 people, launching a flourishing catering operation that continued for over 18 years. During that time, she had countless opportunities to test new ideas with immediate feedback—resulting in empty plates and contented customers! Whether preparing cocktail sandwiches for a house party or serving a hot meal for 1,500 people, Jean Paré earned a reputation for great food, courteous service and reasonable prices.

As requests for her recipes increased, Jean was often asked the question, "Why don't you write a cookbook?" Jean responded by teaming up with her son, Grant Lovig, in the fall of 1980 to form Company's Coming Publishing Limited. The publication of *150 Delicious Squares* on April 14, 1981 marked the debut of what would soon become one of the world's most popular cookbook series.

The company has grown since those early days when Jean worked from a spare bedroom in her home. Nowadays every Company's Coming recipe is *kitchen-tested* before it is approved for publication.

Company's Coming cookbooks are distributed in Canada, the United States, Australia and other world markets. Bestsellers many times over in English, Company's Coming cookbooks have also been published in French and Spanish.

Familiar and trusted in home kitchens around the world, Company's Coming cookbooks are offered in a variety of formats. Highly regarded as kitchen workbooks, the softcover Original Series, with its lay-flat plastic comb binding, is still a favourite among readers.

Jean Paré's approach to cooking has always called for *quick and easy recipes* using *everyday ingredients.* That view has served her well. The recipient of many awards, including the Queen Elizabeth Golden Jubilee Medal, Jean was appointed Member of the Order of Canada, her country's highest lifetime achievement honour.

Jean continues to share what she calls The Golden Rule of Cooking: *Never share a recipe you wouldn't use yourself.* It's an approach that has worked—*millions of times over!*

INTRODUCTION

I am man, hear me roar!

Welcome to the male mentality—loud, boisterous and always something to prove. These inherent traits we have enjoyed throughout much of our lives, although they prove somewhat of a thorn in our sides at times. When it comes to men, little has really changed over the years. Bigger is always better. My dad is stronger than your dad. My truck is higher than your truck. My sister is prettier than your sister. Sorry, that went too far. But the point is well taken. "Y" chromosomes lean towards bold and brash, often lacking any real sense of refinement, class or taste. Our emotions are tempered and our patience is often on the verge of being lost, but we carry these characteristics with pride, much to the detriment and frustration of others around us.

Okay then, so how do we keep our "machismo" under wraps long enough to prepare a decent meal?

Well, quite honestly, men are for the most part an epic failure when it comes to cooking, cleaning or any other kitchen-related task. Fortunately, we seem to share one redeeming quality which we hope will resonate across the pages of this cookbook.

Men of today are eager and willing to learn!

Sure, we may not all be gifted with the culinary skills of Wolfgang Puck or Chef Gordon Ramsey, or even know what a Michelin star is, but we'll try anything once, and if it isn't a complete flop we might considering giving it a second chance. Knowing our limitations and working within

them is our key to success, and being open-minded enough to attempt something out of our comfort zone for dinner doesn't hurt either. A decade and a half ago when Jeff and his lovely bride were first married, meal preparation was considered "her job" and now 15 years later the tables have turned, to where he shares the bulk of the cooking duties in their household. With young children and a busy lifestyle, the men of today have become a more evolved species than those produced back in 1955 when Jeff's parents were married. "Honey, I'm home, what's for dinner?"—once a standard phrase throughout North American households—is now a cliché of the past.

Today's man is every bit as masculine as the males from generations gone by, but we are just slightly more well-rounded—in our cooking knowledge (and our waistlines, in some cases). Gender lines have since blurred and stereotypes no longer exist when it comes to cooking and meal preparation. Whipping up a well-balanced meal is every bit a man's responsibility as it was once deemed a woman's job. With a network of eager male beavers out there, the recipes and variety of dishes at our disposal are staggering. Here in

The Essential Guys' Cookbook, you will quickly see that being a man in the kitchen is nothing to be ashamed of; in fact, it is a thing of grace and beauty (in some cases; you've never seen Jeff in his camouflage apron).

The following recipes and helpful hints truly run the gamut and are prepared with a masculine flair that even your buddy from the auto body shop, or that fellow you golf with every Saturday, would be proud of.

Here within these pages, we not only embrace our male gender, we rejoice in the newfound skills unleashed. Peppered amongst these fabulous yet easy to prepare recipes are tips, pointers and quotes that every guy out there will appreciate.

Okay boys, pull up a chair and be prepared to expand your horizons. Male cooking (like the man himself) is here to stay, so if you ladies can't stand the heat, get out of the kitchen!

Nutrition Information Guidelines

Each recipe is analyzed using the most current versions of the Canadian Nutrient File from Health Canada, and the United States Department of Agriculture (USDA) Nutrient Database for Standard Reference.

- If more than one ingredient is listed (such as "butter or hard margarine"), or if a range is given (1 – 2 tsp., 5 – 10 mL), only the first ingredient or first amount is analyzed.
- For meat, poultry and fish, the recommended serving size per person is 4 oz. (113 g) uncooked weight (without bone), which is 2 – 3 oz. (57 – 85 g) cooked weight (without bone)—approximately the size of a deck of playing cards.
- Milk used is 1% M.F. (milk fat), unless otherwise stated.
- Cooking oil used is canola oil, unless otherwise stated.
- Ingredients indicating "sprinkle," "optional" or "for garnish" are not included in the nutrition information.
- The fat in recipes and combination foods can vary greatly depending upon the sources and types of fats used in each specific ingredient. For these reasons, the amount of saturated, monounsaturated and polyunsaturated fats may not add up to the total fat content.

BIGGER
IS BETTER

Bigger is better. Bigger is bigger. We're all about the show. We like to grow big tomatoes, heft big turkeys, turn a whole pig on a spit—picture Fred Flintstone toting a rack of Brontosaurus ribs to the dinner table. What a spectacle! To accomplish this performance, you need big serving platters. Be careful, though, if the platter is too big, the food will look small and you will feel inadequate.

BARBECUES & SMOKING

If it's not grilled, it's not food

Men and grilling go together in perfect harmony like Simon and Garfunkel, the classic duo from the '70s. The average male has a great natural affinity for his barbecue and will approach grilled dishes with vim and vigor. As much as we enjoy grilling and excel at it, we could use a few more recipe choices in our repertoire. Here you will find a handful of simple yet delicious grilling ideas that will make you shine like a grill master! Pull up your favourite zero-gravity deck chair, pop open a brew, and get ready for some intense grilling action. Things are about to heat up, boys!

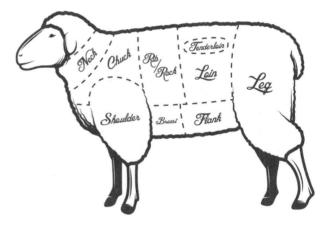

MEAT CUTS

Meat sold in Canada has to follow federal labelling guidelines on identification of the various cuts, and this information is useful in determining how that chunk of meat on your counter needs to be cooked. In other words, get to know your butcher.

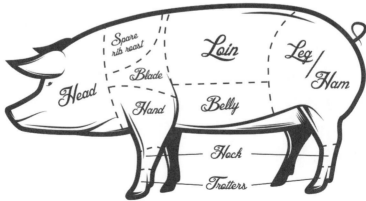

SMOKY GRILLED BEEF JERKY

MAKES: ABOUT 35 PIECES **DIFFICULTY: ★ ★**

A tasty appetizer for your guests to munch on with cold beer while the main course is on the grill. A fragrant hickory aroma and savoury spice flavours make these hard to resist.

1/3 cup	75 mL	soy sauce
1/4 cup	60 mL	bourbon whisky
1/4 cup	60 mL	brown sugar, packed
1/4 cup	60 mL	white vinegar
2 Tbsp	30 mL	Worcestershire sauce
1 Tbsp	15 mL	chili powder
1 Tbsp	15 mL	garlic powder
2 tsp	10 mL	Louisiana hot sauce
2 tsp	10 mL	pepper
1 lb	454 g	flank steak, trimmed of fat, thinly sliced across the grain (1/8 inch, 3 mm, slices)
2 cups	500 mL	hickory wood chips, soaked in water for 4 hours and drained

For the marinade, combine first 9 ingredients in a medium bowl.

Put beef into a large resealable freezer bag and pour marinade over top. Seal bag and turn until coated. Marinate in fridge for at least 6 hours or overnight, turning occasionally. Remove beef and discard any remaining marinade.

Put wood chips into a smoker box and place it on 1 burner. Turn burner to high. When smoke appears, adjust burner to maintain interior barbecue temperature of medium-low. Arrange beef evenly on a sheet of heavy duty (or a double layer of regular) foil and place it on an ungreased grill over unlit burner. Close lid and cook for about 1 hour until darkened. Blot dry with paper towel. Turn beef and rotate foil 180°. Close lid and cook for about 2 hours, rotating foil 180° at halftime, until beef is dried but still flexible. Cool completely.

1 piece: 35 Calories; 1 g Total Fat (0 g Mono, 0 g Poly, 0 g Sat); 5 mg Cholesterol; 2 g Carbohydrates (0 g Fibre, 2 g Sugar); 3 g Protein; 170 mg Sodium

To slice meat easily, place it in the freezer for about 30 minutes until it is just starting to freeze. If you are using frozen meat, partially thaw it before cutting.

SMOKED APPLE MAPLE CHICKEN

MAKES: 4 SERVINGS   **DIFFICULTY: ★ ★**

Golden chicken is subtly infused with apple and maple. Marinating makes the chicken juicy and tender.

4	4	chicken legs, backs attached
1	1	12 1/2 oz (355 mL) can of frozen concentrated apple juice, thawed
3/4 cup	175 mL	dry (or alcohol-free) white wine
1/2 cup	125 mL	maple syrup
6 Tbsp	90 mL	soy sauce
4	4	cloves garlic, minced
1 1/2 tsp	7 mL	pepper
2 cups	500 mL	maple wood chips, soaked in water for 4 hours and drained

Place chicken in a large resealable freezer bag.

Combine next 6 ingredients in a small bowl and pour over chicken. Seal bag and turn until coated. Marinate in fridge for 4 hours, turning occasionally. Remove chicken and blot dry. Transfer marinade to a small saucepan and bring to a boil. Reduce heat to medium. Boil gently, uncovered, for about 30 minutes until reduced by half. Reserve 3/4 cup (175 mL).

Put wood chips into a smoker box and place it on 1 burner. Place a drip pan on opposite burner. Turn burner under smoker box to high. When smoke appears, adjust burner to maintain interior barbecue temperature of medium. Place chicken on greased grill over drip pan. Close lid and cook for about 30 minutes per side, brushing occasionally with remaining apple juice mixture, until internal temperature reaches 170°F (77°C). Serve with reserved marinade.

1 serving: 440 Calories; 7 g Total Fat (2 g Mono, 2 g Poly, 2 g Sat); 110 mg Cholesterol; 57 g Carbohydrates (trace Fibre, 54 g Sugar); 30 g Protein; 1520 mg Sodium

BBQs

Little Green Egg

Hibachi

70 million BTU 6 burner BBQ
with several burners and grills
and warmers? In your dreams!

MONGOLIAN BEEF

MAKES: 4 SERVINGS   **DIFFICULTY:** ★

Serve this spicy, Asian-inspired beef as is, or slice thinly and serve over a bed of rice noodles and stir-fried veggies.

1/2 cup	125 mL	hoisin sauce
1 Tbsp	15 mL	granulated sugar
1 Tbsp	15 mL	sherry vinegar
1 Tbsp	15 mL	rice vinegar
1/4 cup	60 mL	chili sauce
1 Tbsp	15 mL	sambal olek
1 Tbsp	15 mL	crushed garlic
1 Tbsp	15 mL	crushed ginger root
1/4 cup	60 mL	sesame oil
1 lb	454 g	flank steak

Whisk together first 9 ingredients. Pour into a resealable freezer bag.

Add beef and marinate in fridge for 3 hours. Preheat barbecue to medium-high. Grill for about 5 minutes per side for medium-rare or until steak reaches desired doneness. Cover with foil and let stand for 10 minutes before serving.

1 serving: 450 Calories; 24 g Total Fat (10 g Mono, 6 g Poly, 6 g Sat); 30 mg Cholesterol; 33 g Carbohydrates (0 g Fibre, 25 g Sugar); 25 g Protein; 1160 mg Sodium

Kill a cow. Start a fire.
The magic begins.
—Anonymous

SPICY GRILLED PORK TENDERLOIN

MAKES: 6 SERVINGS   **DIFFICULTY: ★**

This crowd favourite is sure to please even the most finicky guest but does require a little finesse on the grill to get it just right. As any good grill master knows, you can't rush perfection when it comes to tenderloin. Slow and steady is the way to go.

3 Tbsp	45 mL	chili powder
1 tsp	5 mL	garlic powder
4 Tbsp	60 mL	brown sugar
1 tsp	5 mL	salt
3	3	1 lb (454 g) pork tenderloins

In a large bowl combine chili powder, garlic powder, brown sugar and salt. Place tenderloins in bowl and coat thoroughly with mixture. Marinate in fridge for 1 hour. Preheat grill to medium heat and coat with cooking spray. Place tenderloins on grill, making sure to space them evenly, and cook for 15 to 20 minutes or until slightly pink in middle, turning meat often so as not to burn. Remove from grill and let stand for 5 minutes. Cut in 3/4 inch (2 cm) slices before serving.

1 serving: 130 Calories; 2.5 g Total Fat (0 g Mono, 0 g Poly, 1 g Sat); 40 mg Cholesterol; 11 g Carbohydrates (1 g Fibre, 9 g Sugar); 15 g Protein; 660 mg Sodium

Rediscover the ancient rituals that show how truly heroic men are. The rotisserie is a man's job for a good reason—it's hard work to turn a big piece of meat by hand over an open firepit. You'll have days of wrist pain afterward, but you'll also get to do a lot of manly whining  about what a hero you are. Just think about the mouthwatering celebration of a successful hunt and receiving enthusiastic praise for the bountiful display of food.

DIJON PRIME RIB

MAKES: 12 SERVINGS   **DIFFICULTY:** ★ ★

The barbecue adds a distinctive smokiness to the roast, and the garlic cloves roast as the meat cooks, infusing it with fabulous flavour. When you buy the roast, have the butcher cut off the ribs then tie them back in place. While the meat is roasting, it will take on the delicious flavour of the bones, but they can be removed easily from the roast just before carving.

1	1	6 lb (2.7 kg) bone-in prime rib roast
4	4	cloves garlic, halved lengthwise
1/3 cup	75 mL	Dijon mustard (with whole seeds)
3 Tbsp	45 mL	mayonnaise
2 Tbsp	30 mL	prepared horseradish
1 tsp	5 mL	liquid honey
1 tsp	5 mL	salt
1 tsp	5 mL	coarsely ground pepper

Cut 8 slits randomly in roast with a small, sharp knife. Push garlic clove halves halfway into each slit.

Combine remaining 6 ingredients. Spoon over roast, spreading evenly over top and sides. Prepare grill for indirect medium heat with a drip pan. Cook, bone side down, for 1 hour, then rotate roast 180°. Cook for about 1 1/2 hours until internal temperature reaches 145°F (63°C) for medium-rare or until roast reaches desired doneness. Cover with foil and let stand for 15 minutes. Cut roast into slices.

1 serving: 690 Calories; 57 g Total Fat (25 g Mono, 2.5 g Poly, 2.5 g Sat); 160 mg Cholesterol; 2 g Carbohydrates (0 g Fibre, trace Sugar); 38 g Protein; 403 mg Sodium

Pictured on page 17.

Helpful Tips

Be sure to let roasts rest for 15 to 30 minutes after coming off the barbecue (the bigger the roast, the longer the stand time). Letting it stand will give the meat a chance to finish cooking (it will come up several degrees) and the juices will be reabsorbed into the meat, making your roast more moist and succulent.

Dijon Prime Rib, page 16

Teriyaki-glazed Ribs, page 19

TERIYAKI-GLAZED RIBS

MAKES: 4 SERVINGS   **DIFFICULTY: ★ ★**

Ribs are one of the hardest things to master on the grill. There are a few different methods you can try. You can boil the ribs first and then finish them on the barbecue, as we have in this recipe. You can cook them entirely on the barbecue, keeping the heat low and slow—no higher than 250ºF (120ºC)—and spray or mist them every 30 minutes with an acidic liquid such as apple cider to keep them moist. Or you can bake them in the oven at 300ºF (150ºC) for an hour on each side, then just finish them on the grill.

4 lbs	1.8 kg	back ribs
1/2 cup	125 mL	teriyaki sauce
1/2 cup	125 mL	liquid honey
1/3 cup	75 mL	Dijon mustard
1/4 cup	60 mL	Worcestershire sauce
1 Tbsp	15 mL	hot pepper sauce
15	15	cloves garlic, minced

Fill Dutch oven with 8 cups (2 L) of water and bring to a boil. Add ribs. Turn heat down and let ribs simmer for 20 minutes. Transfer to a shallow dish.

Combine teriyaki sauce, honey, mustard, Worcestershire sauce, hot pepper sauce and garlic in a small pot. Simmer, uncovered, for about 10 minutes until sauce is reduced to a glaze-like consistency. Preheat barbecue to medium. Brush ribs with sauce and place, meat side down, on greased grill. Flip every 5 minutes, brushing with sauce, for a total of 20 minutes. Remove from barbecue and cut into 3-bone portions.

1 serving: 740 Calories; 54 g Total Fat (24 g Mono, 4.5 g Poly, 20 g Sat); 185 mg Cholesterol; 27 g Carbohydrates (0 g Fibre, 22 g Sugar); 37 g Protein; 710 mg Sodium

Pictured on page 18.

Spare rib, anyone?

—Adam

BEST-EVER RIBS

MAKES: 4 SERVINGS   **DIFFICULTY:** ★

This old family favourite will have the meat falling off the bone and your dinner guests falling off their chairs when they eat it—especially when it's served with a big keg of beer.

2 cups	500 mL	clam tomato beverage
1 cup	250 mL	water
4 lbs	1.8 kg	pork back ribs
2 cups	500 mL	bottled barbecue sauce

Add clam tomato beverage and water to cover bottom of a large roasting pan with lid. Place ribs on rack inside roasting pan so that they are not sitting in juices and cover. Cook in a 250°F (120°C) oven for 3 hours. Remove ribs from oven and allow to cool (or meat will fall off the bone and it will be hard to remove from roasting pan). Recipe can be made ahead to this point.

Brush ribs with barbecue sauce. Preheat grill to medium. Re-coat ribs with barbecue sauce and place on grill. Cook for 5 minutes per side. Remove from grill and serve.

1 serving: 1440 Calories; 107 g Total Fat (48 g Mono, 9 g Poly, 40 g Sat); 365 mg Cholesterol; 45 g Carbohydrates (1 g Fibre, 4 g Sugar); 75 g Protein; 2360 mg Sodium

Helpful Tips

If you don't want to grease your grill with cooking spray, hold a piece of bacon with tongs and rub it over the grill. Don't use butter because it will scorch.

SAUSAGES ON THE GRILL

MAKES: 4 SERVINGS   **DIFFICULTY:** ★

Nothing beats sausages cooked on the grill, but they can be tricky to get right and require a little extra attention so as not to overcook.

1/4 cup	60 mL	honey mustard
1 tsp	5 mL	cider vinegar
1	1	egg yolk
1 Tbsp	15 mL	chopped fresh dill
1 1/2 lbs	680 g	sausages

In a small saucepan, combine honey mustard, cider vinegar and egg yolk. Cook over low heat until thickened. Remove from heat and stir in dill. Set aside to cool.

Preheat grill to high. Pierce sausages with a fork and arrange on grill.

Cook for 8 to 12 minutes, turning occasionally, until lightly browned. Remove from heat, cut into bite-sized chunks and serve with dip.

1 serving: 620 Calories; 51 g Total Fat (0.5 g Mono, 0 g Poly, 18 g Sat); 185 mg Cholesterol; 8 g Carbohydrates (0 g Fibre, 3 g Sugar); 29 g Protein; 1680 mg Sodium

Helpful Tips

An easy way to check the temperature of your barbecue is to hold your hand above the flames at the height the food will sit while it is cooking. If you can comfortably hold it there for 5 seconds or more, you have low heat (about 300°F, 150°C); 3 to 4 seconds is medium (about 350°F, 175°C); 1 to 2 seconds is hot (400°F, 200°C, or more).

LARRY'S GRILLED LAMB

MAKES: 4 SERVINGS **DIFFICULTY: ★**

Every man should have a few good lamb recipes in his culinary tool box. Impress family and friends with this quick, easy grilled lamb.

2 Tbsp	30 mL	extra virgin olive oil
1/2 cup	125 mL	white vinegar
1 Tbsp	15 mL	minced garlic
1	1	onion, chopped
2 tsp	10 mL	salt
		pepper to taste
2 lbs	900 g	lamp chops

In a medium bowl, blend oil, vinegar, garlic, onion, salt and pepper. Add lamb and turn until well coated. Marinate in fridge for 2 hours. Preheat grill to medium. Slowly remove chops from marinade, being careful to keep them well coated. Place on grill and cook 5 to 7 minutes per side. Chops are done when outside is firm to the touch and inside is only slightly pink.

1 serving: 700 Calories; 57 g Total Fat (25 g Mono, 2.5 g Poly, 26 g Sat); 185 mg Cholesterol; 4 g Carbohydrates (0 g Fibre, 1 g Sugar); 39 g Protein; 670 mg Sodium

Helpful Tips

To cut back on the labour when cleaning your grates, lay a sheet of foil over them when you are preheating the barbecue. The charred bits will easily lift off.

SWEET GLAZED LAMB CHOPS

MAKES: 4 CHOPS   **DIFFICULTY: ★**

The glazed goodness of these lamb chops warrants extra napkins at the dinner table. If you run low on napkins, the tablecloth will also work.

1/4 cup	60 mL	brown sugar
2 tsp	10 mL	ground ginger
1 tsp	5 mL	ground cinnamon
1 tsp	5 mL	pepper
1 tsp	5 mL	garlic powder
1/2 tsp	2 mL	salt
4	4	lamb chops

Combine first 6 ingredients in a small bowl. Rub lamb chops with seasoning mix and place on a plate. Cover and refrigerate for 1 hour.

Preheat grill for high heat and brush grill grate lightly with oil or spray with a grill non-stick spray. Arrange chops on grill. Cook 5 minutes on each side, or to desired doneness.

1 chop: 230 Calories; 14 g Total Fat (5 g Mono, 0.5 g Poly, 7 g Sat); 50 mg Cholesterol; 15 g Carbohydrates (trace Fibre, 13 g Sugar); 11 g Protein; 320 mg Sodium

...While a man's best friend might be a dog, his best culinary toy is most definitely his grill.

—Julia Child

HONEY CHICKEN BROCHETTE

MAKES: 4 SERVINGS   **DIFFICULTY: ★**

The word "brochette" refers to food that is cooked on a skewer. What is the difference between a kabob and a brochette? Nothing really—both are yummy and are great reasons to eat with your fingers. Serve these skewers on a bed of rice along with a fresh salad.

1/4 cup	60 mL	cooking oil
1/3 cup	75 mL	liquid honey
1/3 cup	75 mL	soy sauce
1/4 tsp	60 mL	pepper
8	8	skinless, boneless chicken breast halves, cut into 1 inch (2.5 cm) cubes
2	2	cloves garlic, minced
3	3	medium onions, cut into 2 inch (5 cm) pieces
1	1	medium red pepper, cut into 2 inch (5 cm) pieces
1	1	medium green pepper, cut into 2 inch (5 cm) pieces
8	8	bamboo skewers (8 inches, 20 cm, each), soaked in water for 10 minutes

Combine oil, honey, soy sauce, and pepper in a large bowl and whisk to mix well. Pour into resealable freezer bag.

Add chicken, garlic, onions and peppers and mix well. Marinate in fridge for at least 2 hours (the longer the better). Preheat grill for high heat and brush grill grate lightly with oil or spray with a grill non-stick spray. Thread chicken and vegetables alternately onto skewers and place on grill. Cook for 12 to 15 minutes, turning frequently, until chicken juices run clear.

1 serving: 390 Calories; 10 g Total Fat (2.5 g Mono, 4.5 g Poly, 2 g Sat); 135 mg Cholesterol; 18 g Carbohydrates (1 g Fibre, 14 g Sugar); 57 g Protein; 770 mg Sodium

JERK CHICKEN

MAKES: 4 SERVINGS   **DIFFICULTY:** ★

Here's a spicy grilled chicken that's easy and fast. Make sure you preheat your grill and clean it off before you cook on it. Increase the chopped jalapeño if you would like this dish to be hotter.

1/2 cup	125 mL	chopped green onion
1 Tbsp	15 mL	crushed garlic
1 Tbsp	15 mL	chopped jalapeño pepper
2 Tbsp	30 mL	lime juice
2 Tbsp	30 mL	olive oil
1 tsp	5 mL	dried thyme
1/2 tsp	2 mL	allspice
1/2 tsp	2 mL	coarsely ground pepper
1/2 tsp	2 mL	ground cinnamon
2 tsp	10 mL	soy sauce
1 Tbsp	15 mL	brown sugar
1	1	whole chicken (cut into 8 pieces)

Process first 11 ingredients in a blender or food processor. Pour over chicken and marinate in fridge for 2 to 3 hours.

Preheat grill for medium-high heat and brush grill grate lightly with oil or spray with a non-stick spray. Cook chicken for 12 to 15 minutes, turning frequently, until chicken juices run clear.

1 serving: 280 Calories; 12 g Total Fat (6 g Mono, 2 g Poly, 2.5 g Sat); 115 mg Cholesterol; 5 g Carbohydrates (trace Fibre, 3 g Sugar); 36 g Protein; 280 mg Sodium

ROADHOUSE GRILLED FAJITAS

MAKES: 2 SERVINGS   **DIFFICULTY: ★**

Every man needs a special fajita recipe to call his own, and this is it—a roadhouse favourite that's even more fun when cooked at home. Just don't forget your cowboy hat and chaps.

2	2	**4 oz (113 g) boneless, skinless chicken breasts**
1	1	**medium onion**
1	1	**medium green pepper**
2 Tbsp	30 mL	**chili powder**
1 Tbsp	15 mL	**salt**
1 Tbsp	15 mL	**granulated sugar**
1 tsp	5 mL	**onion powder**
1 tsp	5 mL	**garlic powder**
1/2 tsp	2 mL	**cayenne pepper**
1/2 tsp	2 mL	**cumin**
4	4	**bamboo skewers (8 inches, 20 cm, each), soaked in water for 10 minutes**
4	4	**tortilla shells**
		diced tomatoes, optional
		sour cream, optional
		salsa, optional

Cut chicken into 1 inch (2.5 cm) cubes. Cut onion and green pepper to a similar size.

In a medium bowl, mix chili powder, salt, sugar, onion powder, garlic powder, cayenne and cumin. Roll chicken cubes in mixture. Alternately thread chicken, pepper and onion on skewers. Preheat grill to medium. Grill for about 15 minutes, turning often, until chicken is cooked and no longer pink inside. Remove meat and vegetables from skewers and wrap with tortilla shells.

Top with tomatoes, sour cream and salsa, if using.

1 serving: 360 Calories; 9 g Total Fat (6 g Mono, 1.5 g Poly, 1.5 g Sat); 70 mg Cholesterol; 37 g Carbohydrates (7 g Fibre, 6 g Sugar); 34 g Protein; 1200 mg Sodium

BEER CAN CHICKEN

MAKES: 6 SERVINGS   **DIFFICULTY: ★ ★**

Feel free to indulge in a can of "inspiration beer" while preparing this dish. Why should the chicken have all the fun?

1 cup	250 mL	butter
2 Tbsp	30 mL	garlic salt
2 Tbsp	30 mL	paprika
		salt and pepper to taste
1	1	12 1/2 oz (355 mL) can beer
1	1	3 lb (1.4 kg) whole chicken

Melt butter in a small saucepan. Add garlic salt, paprika, salt and pepper. Pour half of mixture into a small bowl and set aside.

Drink or pour half of beer out of can and pour other half of butter mixture into can. Set chicken on beer can, inserting can into cavity of chicken, and place on a disposable baking sheet. Preheat barbecue or grill. Baste chicken with remaining butter mixture and place on prepared grill. Cook over low heat for about 3 hours, or until chicken is no longer pink and juices run clear.

1 serving: 430 Calories; 20 g Total Fat (9 g Mono, 2 g Poly, 20 g Sat); 160 mg Cholesterol; 3 g Carbohydrates (trace Fibre, 0 g Sugar); 24 g Protein; 2010 mg Sodium

Barbecue naked and show
off your buns.

—Anonymous

GRILLED PACIFIC SALMON

MAKES: 4 SERVINGS   **DIFFICULTY: ★ ★**

Finding the right salmon in the grocery store can be a daunting task. Chinook is the largest and usually the most expensive, with the highest fat content, while coho is generally milder and leaner. You can also go with pink or chum salmon, but they are smaller fish and are often not marketed in fillet form.

2 lbs	900 g	Pacific salmon fillets
1/4 tsp	1 mL	pepper
1/4 tsp	1 mL	garlic powder
1/2 cup	125 mL	soy sauce
1/2 cup	125 mL	cooking oil
1/2 cup	125 mL	brown sugar
1/2 cup	125 mL	water
1/4 tsp	1 mL	salt

Season fillets with pepper and garlic powder.

Blend together soy sauce, cooking oil, brown sugar and water in a large resealable freezer bag. Add fish and turn to coat. Marinate in fridge for 1 hour.

Preheat barbecue grill to medium. Place salmon on grill and cook for 5 to 7 minutes on each side. When meat flakes easily with a fork, remove salmon from grill and season with salt.

1 serving: 470 Calories; 25 g Total Fat (11 g Mono, 9 g Poly, 3 g Sat); 125 mg Cholesterol; 11 g Carbohydrates (0 g Fibre, 11 g Sugar); 47 g Protein; 990 mg Sodium

GRILLED NEW ENGLAND LOBSTER TAILS

MAKES: 4 SERVINGS   **DIFFICULTY:** ★ ★

Lobster is one of those meals that epitomizes summer, and when cooked to perfection it is one of the best-tasting types of seafood. Some people think the world's best lobster hails from New England, be it Maine, New Hampshire or Massachusetts; others think Canada's East Coast has the best lobster.

1/2 cup	125 mL	extra virgin olive oil
1 tsp	5 mL	sea salt
1 tsp	5 mL	paprika
1/4 tsp	1 mL	pepper
1/4 tsp	1 mL	garlic powder
4	4	10 oz (285 g) New England lobster tails

In a medium bowl mix olive oil, salt, paprika, pepper and garlic powder. Set aside.

With a large knife or cleaver, split lobster tails up the middle and open slightly. Brush marinade mixture over flesh side. Preheat grill to medium-high. Place tails on grill, meat side down, and cook for about 5 to 7 minutes. Brush meat side with more marinade, then turn tails over and cook for 5 to 7 minutes on shell side. Lobster is cooked when meat turns opaque and firm to the touch.

1 tail: 310 Calories; 16 g Total Fat (12 g Mono, 1.5 g Poly, 2.5 g Sat); 265 mg Cholesterol; trace Carbohydrates (0 g Fibre, 0 g Sugar); 43 g Protein; 2460 mg Sodium

Pictured on page 54.

COMPANY'S COMING PIZZA

MAKES: 10 PIZZAS   **DIFFICULTY: ★**

Need to feed a crowd but don't want to spend the whole time in the kitchen? Prep and pre-grill individual crusts before your guests arrive and then let everyone add their own favourite toppings to finish on the barbecue. Great for a hot summer day when you just don't want to turn the oven on!

1 1/2 cups	375 mL	warm water
1 tsp	5 mL	granulated sugar
1	1	1/4 oz (8 g) package of active dry yeast
1 Tbsp	15 mL	olive (or cooking) oil
3 1/2 cups	875 mL	all-purpose flour
1 cup	250 mL	whole wheat flour
2 tsp	10 mL	Italian seasoning
2 tsp	10 mL	salt
2/3 cup	150 mL	pizza sauce
2 1/2 cups	625 mL	grated Mexican cheese blend

Stir water and sugar in a medium bowl until sugar is dissolved. Sprinkle yeast over top. Let stand for 10 minutes. Stir until yeast is dissolved, then stir in olive oil.

Combine next 4 ingredients in a large bowl. Add yeast mixture and mix until a soft dough forms. Turn out onto lightly floured surface. Knead for about 8 minutes until smooth and elastic. Place in a large greased bowl, turning once to grease top. Cover with greased waxed paper and a tea towel. Let stand in oven with light on and door closed for about 1 hour until doubled in bulk. Punch dough down. Turn out onto lightly floured surface. Knead for about 1 minute until smooth. Divide into 10 equal portions. Roll out each portion on lightly floured surface to 6 inch (15 cm) circle. Preheat barbecue to high. Place pizza crusts, 2 or 3 at a time, on greased grill. Cook for about 2 minutes per side until light grill marks appear. Cool. Poke several holes randomly with fork into each pizza crust.

Spread 1 Tbsp (15 mL) pizza sauce over each pizza crust and top with whatever you like. Sprinkle with 1/4 cup (60 mL) cheese. Preheat barbecue to medium. Place pizzas, 2 or 3 at a time, on greased grill. Close lid. Cook for 8 to 12 minutes until toppings are heated through and cheese is melted.

1 pizza: 320 Calories; 9 g Total Fat (1 g Mono, 0.5 g Poly, 4.5 g Sat); 25 mg Cholesterol; 43 g Carbohydrates (3 g Fibre; 4 g Sugar); 12 g Protein; 800 mg Sodium

DRESSED VEGGIE SKEWERS

MAKES: 8 SKEWERS   **DIFFICULTY:** ★

Grilling vegetables enhances their flavour, and the addition of bottled Italian dressing adds a complementary sweetness.

1	1	large red onion, quartered
2	2	small green zucchini (with peel), cut into 8 slices (about 3/4 inch, 2 cm, thick)
2	2	small yellow zucchini (with peel), cut into 8 slices (about 3/4 inch, 2 cm, thick)
24	24	small fresh whole white mushrooms
8	8	bamboo skewers (8 inches, 20 cm, each), soaked in water for 10 minutes
1/2 cup	125 mL	Italian dressing

Peel off top 3 layers in a stack from each onion quarter. Cut each stack lengthwise into 3 equal strips. Save remaining onion for another use.

Thread onion and next 3 ingredients alternately onto skewers.

Brush skewers with dressing. Preheat barbecue to high. Place skewers on greased grill and close lid. Cook for 12 to 15 minutes, turning often and brushing with remaining dressing, until zucchini is tender.

1 skewer: 80 Calories; 4.5 g Total Fat (0 g Mono, 0 g Poly, 0 g Sat); 0 mg Cholesterol; 8 g Carbohydrates (2 g Fibre, 5 g Sugar); 2 g Protein; 260 mg Sodium

GARLIC AND HERB BREAD ON THE GRILL

MAKES: 8 SERVINGS   **DIFFICULTY:** ★

This refined twist on traditional garlic bread will draw you one slice closer to ecstasy. To add earthiness, use wild garlic instead of regular garlic. You will be greatly impressed.

1 cup	250 mL	butter
4	4	cloves garlic, minced
1 Tbsp	15 mL	salt
1/2 cup	125 mL	chopped parsley
		pepper to taste
2	2	loaves fresh crusty bread, halved horizontally

Preheat barbecue to low. Melt butter in a small pot (or use your microwave) and add garlic and salt. Transfer to a bowl and cool. Stir in parsley and pepper to taste.

Brush cut sides of bread with half of garlic butter. Place bread on grill cut sides down, 5 to 6 inches (12.5 to 15 cm) over glowing coals. Cook for about 2 minutes, then turn bread over and brush with remaining garlic butter. Grill until golden brown, 2 to 3 minutes more. Cut each half into 4 slices.

1 serving: 360 Calories; 24 g Total Fat (6 g Mono, 1 g Poly, 15 g Sat); 60 mg Cholesterol; 29 g Carbohydrates (1 g Fibre, 0 g Sugar); 6 g Protein; 1110 mg Sodium

BURGERS, HOTDOGS & SANDWICHES

For most men these days, sandwiches, burgers and dogs compose three of the four essential food groups. No longer are these lunchtime staples resigned to the midday meal menu. The modern male can gorge himself on sandwiches, burgers and dogs morning, noon and night. Even midnight snacks are not off limits when it comes to S, B and D! With a wide range of acceptable eating times in this category, it is imperative that modern guys become aware of some interesting new takes on some favourite old standbys. This section is especially handy for its ease of preparation, which we considered when deciding on which recipes to include; keeping in mind that a new spin on some old classics will go a long way to keeping our comrades happy.

SUPER OZ BURGER

MAKES: 6 BURGERS   **DIFFICULTY: ★ ★**

If you have travelled to Australia, you may have already experienced this burger. Stacked high with sliced beets, bacon, egg, cheese, onions and more, this is a meal in a bun!

1 Tbsp	15 mL	cooking oil
3	3	medium onions, thinly sliced
6	6	large eggs, optional
3/4 cup	175 mL	finely chopped onion
1/3 cup	75 mL	fresh bread crumbs
1	1	large egg, fork-beaten
1/4 tsp	1 mL	salt
1/4 tsp	1 mL	pepper
7 Tbsp	105 mL	barbecue sauce, *divided*
1 lb	454 g	lean ground beef
6	6	hamburger buns, split
1	1	14 oz (398 mL) can of sliced beets (12 to 18 slices)
6	6	Cheddar cheese slices
2	2	medium tomatoes, sliced
6	6	bacon slices, cooked almost crisp
6	6	green leaf lettuce leaves

Preheat barbecue to medium and heat cooking oil on a griddle. Add onion and cook for 5 to 10 minutes, stirring often, until softened. Remove to a medium bowl and cover to keep warm.

Reduce heat to medium-low. Break 3 eggs onto same griddle. When eggs start to set, add about 1 Tbsp (15 mL) water. Cover and cook for about 1 minute until egg whites are set and yolks reach desired doneness, adding more water if needed. Remove eggs to plate and cover to keep warm. Repeat with remaining 3 eggs.

Combine next 5 ingredients and 2 Tbsp (30 mL) barbecue sauce in large bowl. Add ground beef. Mix well. Divide and shape into 6 patties, about 5 inches (12.5 cm) in diameter. Increase heat to medium. Cook patties on greased grill for about 6 minutes per side until no longer pink inside.

Place buns, cut side down, on greased grill. Toast until lightly browned. Spread remaining barbecue sauce on bottom half of each bun. Top each with patty, sliced onion, beets, cheese, egg, tomato, bacon and lettuce. Cover with top half of each bun.

1 Burger: 770 Calories; 44 g Total Fat (16 g Mono, 4.5 g Poly, 1 g Sat); 340 mg Cholesterol; 49 g Carbohydrates (4 g Fibre, 15 g Sugar); 38 g Protein; 1380 mg Sodium

Pictured on page 35.

Super Oz Burger, page 37

Extra-Sweet, Sweet Potato Fries, page 265 • Gentleman's Italian Sausage Sub, page 47
Out-of-the-Park Jalapeño Dawgs page, 37

OUT-OF-THE-PARK JALAPEÑO DAWGS

MAKES: 4 DAWGS   **DIFFICULTY:** ★

A grand-slam dawg like this one needs a big bun and even bigger napkins. Serve this crowd-pleaser with an icy cold pitcher of lemonade or beer.

3 Tbsp	45 mL	mayonnaise
1 Tbsp	15 mL	finely chopped pickled jalapeño peppers
1/4 tsp	1 mL	grated lime zest
5 Tbsp	75 mL	green jalapeño jelly, *divided*
1 Tbsp	15 mL	lime juice
2 tsp	10 mL	cooking oil
2 tsp	10 ml	minced pickled jalapeño peppers
4	4	4 oz (113 g) precooked turkey bratwurst sausages
1	1	large yellow pepper, quartered
1	1	red onion slice, about 1/2 inch (12 mm) thick
4	4	large hoagie buns, partially split

Combine first 3 ingredients and 3 Tbsp (45 mL) green jalapeño jelly in a small bowl. Set aside.

Combine next 3 ingredients and remaining 2 Tbsp (30 mL) jalapeño jelly in a separate bowl.

Make diagonal slashes on both sides of sausages. Grill sausages, yellow pepper and onion slice on direct medium heat for about 15 minutes, turning occasionally and brushing with lime juice mixture, until hot and vegetables are tender-crisp. Chop onion and slice yellow pepper into slivers.

Spread buns with mayonnaise mixture. Serve sausages, topped with onion and yellow pepper, in buns.

1 dawg: 680 Calories; 39 g Total Fat (21 g Mono, 5 g Poly, 11 g Sat); 115 mg Cholesterol; 41 g Carbohydrates (2 g Fibre, 15 g Sugar); 34 g Protein; 1286 mg Sodium

Pictured on page 36.

Helpful Tips

Cutting into the sausage allows it to cook through to the centre faster and keeps it from curling.

BARBECUE BACON CHEESE DOGS

MAKES: 8 CHEESE DOGS   **DIFFICULTY: ★**

Cheese has always been a good friend of the hotdog, and now bacon is invited to the party. Don't limit yourself to Swiss; other varieties of cheese will also work. Be creative and daring.

8	8	**slices bacon**
8	8	**all-beef hot dogs**
8	8	**hot dog buns, split**
8	8	**slices Swiss cheese**
1/2 cup	125 mL	**barbecue sauce**
1	1	**medium red onion, diced**

In a skillet on medium heat, cook bacon until evenly browned.

Place hot dogs on preheated grill and cook until browned.

Grill hot dogs buns until lightly toasted. Add one slice of Swiss cheese, one slice of bacon, one hot dog and 1 Tbsp (15 mL) barbecue sauce to each bun. Top with diced red onion.

1 serving: 570 Calories; 16 g Total Fat (8 g Mono, 3 g Poly, 16 g Sat); 80 mg Cholesterol; 31 g Carbohydrates (1 g Fibre, 5 g Sugar); 20 g Protein; 1320 mg Sodium

Too few people understand a really good sandwich.

—James Beard

MANLY BURGER TOPPINGS
YOU MAY NOT HAVE THOUGHT OF

There is something to be said about a giant man burger you can hardly get your mouth around. Venture beyond the usual lettuce, tomato and processed cheese slice, into some of these ideas:

Eat your vegetables—onion rings, French fries, smashed tater tots, hashbrowns, grilled eggplant, mushrooms or peppers, caramelized onions, alfalfa sprouts (just kidding), coleslaw, pickled okra

More protein is better—bacon, sushi, sliced deli ham, pastrami, mortadella, corned beef

Leftovers—mac 'n' cheese, baked beans, chili, pizza (with bacon, obviously)

Fruit—avocado, mango slices, fruit chutney, pineapple

Cheese—brie, ricotta, feta

Sauces—hummus, tzatziki, wasabi, guacamole, gravy, sriracha mayo, bacon jam, sambal olek, hot sauce, chimichurri

And for a little heat banana, jalapeño, serrano or for the truly brave, pickled habanero peppers

GREAT GUACAMOLE BURGERS

MAKES: 4 BURGERS   **DIFFICULTY: ★ ★**

This Mexican twist on burgers is sure to please any party-goer or lover of Tex-Mex. Join the guacamole craze that is sweeping the nation these days.

2	2	**avocados, chopped**
1/2	1/2	**small yellow onion, diced**
1	1	**jalapeño pepper, minced**
3 Tbsp	45 mL	**cilantro, chopped**
1	1	**lime**
		salt and pepper to taste
1 lb	454 g	**extra lean ground beef**
1/4 cup	60 mL	**bread crumbs**
1	1	**large egg**
1/4 cup	60 mL	**steak sauce**
1/4 cup	60 mL	**shredded Cheddar**
4	4	**hamburger buns, split**

Combine avocado, onion and jalapeño in a medium bowl. Add cilantro and squeeze juice of lime into bowl, then season with salt and pepper. Mix well and refrigerate, covered.

In a large bowl, combine ground beef, bread crumbs, egg, steak sauce and cheese. Shape into 4 patties. Lightly oil grill grate and cook patties for 5 minutes per side, or until desired doneness.

Place burgers on bottom half of buns, add guacamole and top with top half of bun.

1 burger: 550 Calories; 29 g Total Fat (15 g Mono, 3 g Poly, 8 g Sat); 105 mg Cholesterol; 41 g Carbohydrates (9 g Fibre, 4 g Sugar); 34 g Protein; 930 mg Sodium

BURGERS STUFFED WITH BLUE CHEESE

MAKES: 6 BURGERS   **DIFFICULTY: ★**

The blue cheese hidden in the burger is amazing. A little melted, a little gooey—great with the horseradish aioli, which is basically just mayo with horseradish to add a little zing. Tastes great topped with tomato, raw onion and lettuce.

2 tsp	10 mL	pepper, *divided*
1 Tbsp	15 mL	prepared horseradish
1 cup	250 mL	mayonnaise
1 1/2 lbs	680 g	lean ground beef
1/2 cup	125 mL	diced onion
2 tsp	10 mL	kosher salt
6 oz	170 g	blue cheese, formed into little balls
6	6	hamburger buns, split

For the aioli, combine first 2 ingredients and 1 tsp (5 mL) pepper in a small bowl. Set aside.

For the burgers, combine next 3 ingredients and remaining 1 tsp (5 mL) pepper until well mixed. Form into 6 balls and make a well in centre. Stuff 1 blue cheese ball in each well and close meat around cheese. Gently shape into a patty. Grill patties on direct medium heat for about for 5 to 8 minutes or until burger is done. Serve in buns and top with horseradish aioli.

1 serving: 760 Calories; 52 g Total Fat (26 g Mono, 10 g Poly, 15 g Sat); 100 mg Cholesterol; 24 g Carbohydrate (2 g Fibre, 4 g Sugar); 33 g Protein; 1710 mg Sodium

DAN'S BURGER DOG

MAKES: 4 BURGER DOGS   **DIFFICULTY: ★**

A unique and intriguing twist on the traditional hot dog. Top with your favourite burger or hot dog toppings.

1 1/2 lbs	680 g	lean ground beef
1/2 cup	125 mL	bread crumbs
1 Tbsp	15 mL	Worcestershire sauce
1 Tbsp	15 mL	onion soup mix
2	2	cloves garlic, crushed
1	1	large egg
1 Tbsp	15 mL	2% milk
4	4	drops hot pepper sauce
1/4 tsp	1 mL	salt
		pepper to taste
4	4	hot dog buns, split

In a large bowl, combine first 10 ingredients. Form into rectangles or long tubes, about the size of a hot dog. Grill patties on direct medium heat for about 5 minutes per side, until middle is no longer pink and juices run clear.

Serve patties in buns.

1 burger dog: 600 Calories; 27 g Total Fat (11 g Mono, 1.5 g Poly, 10 g Sat); 135 mg Cholesterol; 36 g Carbohydrates (2 g Fibre, 5 g Sugar); 41 g Protein; 830 mg Sodium

Helpful Tips

The problem with presenting old standbys in the same old way is that you will be compared to all the other men who have done those classic old grilled cheese sandwiches or baseball dogs in doughy buns. But what if they could be made better? Surprise and delight your audience, and eliminate the competition, by putting a twist on the classic. Rev it up, melt cheese on everything and throw on some flavour.

PORTOBELLO PARMESAN BURGERS

MAKES: 4 BURGERS   **DIFFICULTY:** ★ ★

If ordinary veggie burgers have lost their appeal, give these portobello burgers a try. A portobello mushroom cap hides inside a crusty ciabatta bun, complete with Italian-themed burger fixings.

3 Tbsp	45 mL	balsamic vinegar
3 Tbsp	45 mL	olive oil
1/2 tsp	2 mL	granulated sugar
1/4 tsp	1 mL	salt
1/4 tsp	1 mL	pepper
4	4	portobello mushrooms, stems and gills removed
1/2 cup	125 mL	grated Parmesan cheese
1/4 cup	60 mL	mayonnaise
2 Tbsp	30 mL	sundried tomato pesto
1 Tbsp	15 mL	finely chopped pine nuts, toasted
4	4	round ciabatta buns, split
4	4	romaine lettuce leaves

Combine first 5 ingredients in a small cup.

Place mushrooms in a large resealable freezer bag. Pour vinegar mixture over top and seal bag. Turn until coated. Marinate in fridge for 1 hour, turning occasionally. Remove mushrooms and discard remaining marinade. Arrange mushrooms, stem side down, on a greased baking sheet with sides. Cook in a 375°F (190°C) oven for about 10 minutes until tender. Turn mushrooms stem side up.

Sprinkle cheese over mushrooms. Broil on top rack in oven for about 5 minutes until cheese is golden.

Combine next 3 ingredients in small bowl. Spread on bun halves. Serve mushrooms, topped with lettuce, in buns.

1 Burger: 460 Calories; 32 g Total Fat (15 g Mono, 6 g Poly, 6 g Sat); 15 mg Cholesterol; 31 g Carbohydrates (3 g Fibre, 8 g Sugar); 13 g Protein; 730 mg Sodium

Helpful Tips

Because the gills can sometimes be bitter, be sure to remove them from the portobellos before marinating. First remove the stems, then, using a small spoon, scrape out and discard the gills.

Sandwiches are perfect guy grub. They're quick, hearty, portable and versatile. And any food you eat with your hands automatically leaps to the top of the wish list. Plus, there's not much that can't be stuffed between two pieces of bread. Of course, some sandwiches are better than others. To create the perfect sandwich, you need a plan. So here are the basic building blocks of a truly great sandwich.

BREAD: a sandwich is only as good as what holds it together.

Suggestions: Take a spin through a bakery and see what kinds of breads are available beyond just white and sliced. Sourdough, kaiser, ciabatta, baguette, brioche, pita or wraps—the possibilities are endless. Whole grains are healthiest and will keep you fuller for longer.

THE CORE: the star of the show— every other part of the sandwich should complement it.

Suggestions: cold cuts, leftover anything (meatloaf, chicken, the sky's the limit), fish, fried eggs, grilled veggies, or for the truly brave, tofu.

TOPPINGS: time to add a little pizzaz. Go for things that will offer different textures as well as flavour.

Suggestions: bacon, lettuce, tomato slices, bacon, olives, avocado slices, cucumbers, caramelized onions, any kind of cheese, bacon, pickles, anchovies, pineapple slices, bell peppers...what's in your fridge?

FLAVOUR: a good condiment can really pull the sandwich together.

Suggestions: any kind of mustard, hummus, mashed avocado, mayo, barbecue sauce, hot sauce, vinaigrette dressing, salsa, ketchup, fresh herbs.

(NO PHILLY'S) PHILLY CHEESE STEAK

MAKES: 6 SANDWICHES   **DIFFICULTY: ★ ★**

You don't have to go all the way to Philadelphia, PA, to get an authentic Philly cheese steak!

1 1/2 lbs	680 g	beef round steak
1	1	medium green pepper, sliced thinly
1	1	medium onion, sliced thinly
1	1	14 oz (398 mL) can of beef broth
1	1	1 1/4 oz (38 g) envelope of onion soup mix
6	6	submarine buns
6	6	slices provolone cheese

Cut steak into strips and place in a greased slow cooker. Add green pepper, onion, broth and onion soup mix. Cover slow cooker and cook on High for 3 to 4 hours or on Low for 6 to 8 hours.

Spoon meat mixture into buns and top each with a slice of cheese.

1 serving: 510 Calories; 14 g Total Fat (4 g Mono, 2.5 g Poly, 6 g Sat); 70 mg Cholesterol; 55 g Carbohydrates (8 g Fibre, 10 g Sugar); 43 g Protein; 1370 mg Sodium

Helpful Tips

Burgers charred on the outside but undercooked inside? No problem. Scrape off the charred bits and wrap the burger in foil, then toss it back onto the grill at a lower heat until it is cooked through. Slather the burger with barbecue sauce to mask any lingering burnt flavour.

EASY MEATBALL SUB

MAKES: 1 SANDWICH　　　**DIFFICULTY: ★**

The only thing better than meatballs is meatballs served in a bun with all the trimmings. For some added zing, try mixing some game meat in with your meatballs.

1	1	submarine bun, split
1/4 cup	60 mL	shredded mozzarella cheese, *divided*
1/4 cup	60 mL	shredded Cheddar cheese, *divided*
5	5	precooked meatballs, heated
1/2 cup	125 mL	tomato pasta sauce, heated
1 tsp	5 mL	Parmesan cheese
		dried oregano to taste
		dried basil to taste

Put bun on a cookie sheet and place in a 350°F (175°F) oven until lightly toasted. Remove from oven and sprinkle bottom half of bun with 1/8 cup (30 mL) of both mozzarella and Cheddar cheeses. Place heated meatballs in bun and spoon sauce over top. Sprinkle remaining mozzarella, Cheddar and Parmesan cheese over top. Bake for 3 to 5 minutes more, until cheese has melted.

1 serving: 740 Calories; 40 g Total Fat (4 g Mono, 2.5 g Poly, 18 g Sat); 90 mg Cholesterol; 67 g Carbohydrates (11 g Fibre, 15 g Sugar); 32 g Protein; 2000 mg Sodium

Helpful Tips

If you want to reduce the mess factor of this sandwich, pull some of the bread out of the middle of the bun so you have a sort of trench the meatballs can fit in.

GENTLEMEN'S ITALIAN SAUSAGE SUB

MAKES: 4 SUBS   **DIFFICULTY:** ★

Impress your guests with the little-known fact that sausages were NOT actually invented by Italians, but rather by the Greeks. If that doesn't work, at least they'll be impressed by these delicious subs!

4	4	4 oz (113 g) Italian sausage
1	1	small onion, peeled and cut in half crosswise
1	1	bell pepper, halved and seeded
2 tsp	10 mL	olive oil
1/8 tsp	0.5 mL	salt
1/8 tsp	0.5 mL	pepper
1 Tbsp	15 mL	cooking oil
4	4	6 inch (38 cm) submarine buns

Pierce sausages in a few places with a fork and set aside. Slice off bottoms of onion halves so they will sit flat on the grill. Brush bell pepper and onion halves with olive oil. Preheat barbecue or grill for medium heat. Lightly oil grate, and set 4 inches (10 cm) from heat. Place sausages, onions and peppers on preheated grill. Cook sausages, turning often, until well browned and juices run clear. Cook vegetables until tender and peppers are slightly charred. Remove vegetables and sausages from grill. Remove and discard the charred skin from peppers, and slice peppers and onions into strips.

Combine salt, pepper and cooking oil in a medium bowl. Add peppers and onions, and toss until evenly coated.

To serve, place sausages in submarine buns and top with pepper and onion mixture.

1 sub: 600 Calories; 35 g Total Fat (4.5 g Mono, 3 g Poly, 10 g Sat); 65 mg Cholesterol; 52 g Carbohydrates (8 g Fibre, 9 g Sugar); 23 g Protein; 1320 mg Sodium

Pictured on page 36.

CLASSIC REUBEN SANDWICH

MAKES: 1 SANDWICH   **DIFFICULTY: ★**

This mouth-watering favourite can also be made with light rye bread, or you can substitute corned beef for smoked turkey or ham. Two ingredients that should never change are the wine sauerkraut and Swiss cheese. Serve with dill pickles on the side.

1 cup	250 mL	wine sauerkraut, drained and squeezed of excess moisture
3 Tbsp	45 mL	Thousand Island dressing, *divided*
2	2	slices marble rye bread
2	2	slices Swiss cheese
4	4	slices pastrami or corned beef (about 4 oz, 113 g)
1 Tbsp	15 mL	butter, softened

Place drained sauerkraut in a small saucepan and warm on medium heat for 5 minutes. Reduce to low heat.

Spread 1 Tbsp (30 mL) dressing on 1 slice of bread and top with 1 slice of cheese, half of sauerkraut and all of meat. Spread 1 Tbsp (15 mL) dressing over meat and top with remaining sauerkraut and cheese. Spread remaining 1 Tbsp (15 mL) dressing on remaining slice of bread and place it on top of cheese, dressing side down.

Close sandwich, then evenly spread butter on outside of sandwich. Heat a heavy-bottomed frying pan over medium heat. Add sandwich to pan and press down on sandwich with a spatula. Cook until bread is crisp and golden brown, about 4 minutes. Flip and cook until second side is also golden brown, the cheese is melted and the sandwich is warmed through, about 4 minutes.

1 sandwich: 690 Calories; 42 g Total Fat (8 g Mono, 10 g Poly, 17 g Sat); 110 mg Cholesterol; 50 g Carbohydrates (12 g Fibre, 7 g Sugar); 26 g Protein; 2910 mg Sodium

We all need to make time for a burger once in a while.

—Erica Durance

HOMEMADE BEEF DONAIR SANDWICH

MAKES: 12 DONAIRS   **DIFFICULTY: ★ ★**

A donair is a terrific male meal, but thanks to the halitosis-inducing garlic and tzatziki, it may not the best choice for date night.

3 lbs	1.4 kg	lean ground beef
1 Tbsp	15 mL	chopped garlic
1 tsp	5 mL	cayenne pepper
1 tsp	5 mL	white pepper
2 tsp	10 mL	dried oregano
2 tsp	10 mL	chicken soup base
2 tsp	10 mL	paprika
2 tsp	10 mL	onion powder
12	12	pita breads (7 inch, 18 cm, diameter)
1 3/4 cups	425 mL	tzatziki or garlic sauce
1/2 cup	125 mL	diced onions
1/2 cup	125 mL	diced tomato

Combine first 8 ingredients in a large bowl. Knead mixture until well blended, and form into a large loaf. Cook in 350ºF (175ºC) oven for 1 1/2 hours. Remove from oven and let stand for at least 15 minutes. Slice as thin as you can.

Heat pitas in microwave for 15 seconds, or until soft. Place on a piece of foil wrap or heavy waxed paper. Spoon 2 Tbsp (30 mL) tzatziki or garlic sauce on each pita and top with meat. Sprinkle with diced onion and tomato, then add final 1 tsp (5 mL) sauce. Wrap with foil so that sauce does not run out. To serve, unwrap from the top and enjoy.

1 sandwich: 430 Calories; 16 g Total Fat (7 g Mono, 0.5 g Poly, 6 g Sat); 70 mg Cholesterol; 33 g Carbohydrates (2 g Fibre, 5 g Sugar); 29 g Protein; 250 mg Sodium

OUTDOOR GRUB

North American men, for the most part, retain a close connection to the land and outdoor-based recreational activities. Camping, spending time at the cabin and picnicking are outdoor pursuits enjoyed by men and often dominated by men. Perhaps it harkens us back to a time when we relied on living off the land. Whatever the case, most guys we know enjoy time spent in the Great Outdoors; often, that includes other guys in some old-fashioned male bonding. Time spent afield may also include family, friends or that special someone for a romantic weekend at the cottage. This section features some terrific recipes and tips to assist with any outdoor adventure. Most of these outdoor dishes may be prepared on a campfire, or for those more faint at heart, a gas grill or electric stove works. For the ultimate outdoor experience, however, go old school with the campfire. Okay, anyone have matches or a lighter?

HUNT CAMP BREAKFAST QUICHE

MAKES: 6 SERVINGS
DIFFICULTY: ★

This breakfast quiche is meant to be enjoyed by a large group, like at a northern logging camp or a camp full of hunters, but works just as well at home on a Sunday morning.

1/2 lb	225 g	bacon, sliced into small pieces
1	1	medium onion, diced
1/2 lb	225 g	ground pork breakfast sausage
1	1	2 lb (900 g) bag of frozen diced hash browns
12	12	large eggs
1/2 lb	225 g	shredded Cheddar cheese

Prepare campfire or preheat grill to medium, and preheat Dutch oven. Brown bacon and onion in Dutch oven.

Drain fat and add ground sausage and hash browns. Cook for 15 minutes until potatoes begin to brown.

Meanwhile, beat eggs in a small bowl. Pour over bacon mixture and cook until eggs have started to set, about 10 to 15 minutes. Sprinkle with cheese and cook until eggs are set completely and cheese has melted. Slice and serve.

1 serving: 860 Calories; 62 g Total Fat (24 g Mono, 7 g Poly, 24 g Sat); 355 mg Cholesterol; 47 g Carbohydrates (3 g Fibre, 4 g Sugar); 33 g Protein; 1040 mg Sodium

OLD FASHIONED CAMPFIRE BANNOCK

MAKES: 4 SERVINGS
DIFFICULTY: ★ ★

This aboriginal favourite is a terrific outdoor snack for any occasion, and the doughier the better. It can be served with fresh churned butter or homemade jam. This recipe has no set ingredient proportions; the amounts listed below are approximations. The recipe relies more on "feel" than anything.

2 cups	500 mL	all-purpose flour
1 Tbsp	15 mL	baking powder
2 Tbsp	30 mL	oil, butter or lard
1 tsp	5 mL	salt
2/3 cup	150 mL	warm water

Prepare campfire. Place first 4 ingredients in a bowl and mix with your hands until dough clumps. Slowly add water and mix until dough softens. Wrap a handful of dough around end of freshly cut, very green branch. Massage dough so it remains together. Cook over coals for about 10 minutes, rotating to cook evenly.

1 serving: 290 Calories; 7 g Total Fat (4 g Mono, 2 g Poly, 0.5 g Sat); 0 mg Cholesterol; 49 g Carbohydrates (2 g Fibre, 0 g Sugar); 6 g Protein; 680 mg Sodium

CAMPING STEAK

MAKES: 1 SERVING   **DIFFICULTY: ★**

Don't use a fancy cut here, just a simple top sirloin, or even a blade—remember, you are camping. And you can camp in your own backyard.

1	1	**8 oz (225 g) sirloin steak**
1 oz	30 mL	**sriracha sauce**
1 Tbsp	15 mL	**canola oil**
6 oz	170 mL	**beer**

Place steak in a resealable freezer bag and add sriracha sauce. Marinade in fridge for 24 hours. You can even freeze the steak at this point, and the package will act as a "freezer pack" for camping.

To cook, heat a cast iron skillet to smoking hot. Add oil, then add steak and sear for 3 to 5 minutes. Flip steak and sear other side for 3 minutes. Add beer and deglaze pan, basting steak with "sauce" until a nice glaze forms. Let rest 10 minutes, slice on the bias and serve.

1 steak: 550 Calories; 20 g Total Fat (9 g Mono, 1 g Poly, 8 g Sat); 110 mg Cholesterol; 9 g Carbohydrates (0 g Fibre, 3 g Sugar); 44 g Protein; 360 mg Sodium

Pictured on page 54.

The person who controls the axe controls the conversation. Okay, we may not be able to take control of the kitchen, the living room or even the television but at least we can retreat to the wild woods and survive huddled over a campfire. Yes, in this remote and isolated world we can truly be king—as long as no one else is around, in which case the campfire and seating plan become something of a democratic republic with politics blowing with the wind and smoke. Nevertheless, you will be able to assert tremendous influence on this assembly by sheer dint of your skills and fire building prowess.

Foil Chicken and Vegetables, page 55

Grilled New England Lobster Tails, page 29
Camping Steak, page 52

FOIL CHICKEN AND VEGETABLES

MAKES: 4 SERVINGS   **DIFFICULTY: ★**

This dish is a terrific and easy to prepare side for any outdoor adventure. The avid camper may want to cook it over an open campfire, but be prepared to spend extra time building a good fire.

2 cups	500 mL	thinly sliced carrots
2 cups	500 mL	thinly sliced zucchini
4 tsp	20 mL	water
4	4	4 oz (113 g) boneless, skinless chicken breasts
2 cups	500 mL	fruit chutney
4 tsp	20 mL	curry powder
4 tsp	20 mL	butter
2 cups	500 mL	coconut
2 cups	500 mL	chopped nuts

Preheat grill to medium. Tear off 4 pieces of heavy duty (or double layer of regular) foil, about 12 × 14 inch (30 × 36 cm) each, and spray with cooking spray. Divide carrots and zucchini into 4 portions and place in centre of each piece of foil. Sprinkle each with 1 tsp (5 mL) water and place chicken breast on top of vegetables.

Mix chutney, curry powder and butter to make a paste. Spread on chicken.

Sprinkle coconut and chopped nuts over top. Fold each packet until sealed and place on grill for 15 to 20 minutes until chicken is well cooked and no longer pink in centre.

1 serving: 110 Calories; 52 g Total Fat (28 g Mono, 5 g Poly, 15 g Sat); 135 mg Cholesterol; 100 g Carbohydrates (11 g Fibre, 86 g Sugar); 65 g Protein; 2170 mg Sodium

Pictured on page 53.

...Camping is not a date; it's an endurance test. If you can survive camping with someone, you should marry them on the way home.

—Yvonne Prinz

CAMPFIRE TROUT AND BACON

MAKES: 4 SERVINGS   **DIFFICULTY:** ★

Trout cooked on the campfire is about as traditional an outdoor meal as it gets. Bursting with smoky flavour, this recipe has often been used by anglers as a traditional shore lunch.

12	12	**slices bacon**
6	6	**brook trout, cleaned with heads removed**
1 cup	250 mL	**all-purpose flour or cornmeal**

Fry bacon to desired crispiness and transfer to paper towel to drain, reserving bacon fat in skillet.

Clean trout thoroughly and wipe dry with paper towel. Roll in flour or cornmeal, making sure to coat evenly. Fry trout in hot bacon fat until fish flakes easily when tested with a fork, making sure not to overcook. Serve with bacon.

1 serving: 890 Calories; 54 g Total Fat (25 g Mono, 8 g Poly, 15 g Sat); 225 mg Cholesterol; 22 g Carbohydrates (0 g Fibre, 0 g Sugar); 73 g Protein; 790 mg Sodium

Helpful Tips

Want to make sure the fish you are eyeing at the supermarket is fresh? Look for shiny, bulgy eyes, flesh that bounces back when you touch it and shiny scales that are firmly attached to the fish. If the eyes look sunken or the flesh isn't firm, the fish is past its prime.

GREAT OUTDOORS BEEF STROGANOFF

MAKES: 4 SERVINGS   **DIFFICULTY: ★**

There is just something about the great outdoors that builds a healthy appetite. The body's reaction to fresh air and outdoor physical activity probably has something to do with it. Hearty meals like one this fit right in when camping or relaxing outdoors.

3/4 lb	340 g	beef sirloin steak, cut into strips
1	1	large onion, sliced
1 cup	250 mL	sliced mushrooms
2 cups	500 mL	beef broth
1 cup	250 mL	water
1	1	10 oz (284 mL) can of condensed cream of chicken soup
2 1/2 cups	625 mL	egg noodles
1 Tbsp	15 mL	Worcestershire sauce
1/4 tsp	1 mL	pepper
3/4 cup	175 mL	sour cream

Preheat grill to medium. In a skillet, fry beef until browned, stirring often to avoid sticking. Remove to medium bowl and set aside.

Add onion and mushrooms to skillet and cook for 3 minutes. Remove from heat and combine with beef in bowl. Set aside.

Combine broth, water and soup in a skillet. Bring to a boil and add egg noodles. Reduce heat to a gentle boil and cook, stirring often, until noodles are tender. Add Worcestershire sauce and pepper. Simmer for 5 minutes.

Return beef mixture to skillet and heat gently. Stir in sour cream and heat through, but do not boil.

1 serving: 460 Calories; 27 g Total Fat (11g Mono, 2 g Poly, 12 g Sat); 105 mg Cholesterol; 29 g Carbohydrates (1 g Fibre, 4 g Sugar); 26 g Protein; 900 mg Sodium

Camping is nature's way of promoting the motel business.

—Dave Barry

PIE-IRON CROQUE MONSIEUR

MAKES: 4 SERVINGS   **DIFFICULTY:** ★

Just when you thought ham and cheese couldn't get any better together, the French created the pie-iron croque monsieur!

2 Tbsp	30 ml	**butter**
8	8	**slices of sourdough bread**
4	4	**slices Cheddar cheese**
8	8	**slices Black Forest ham**

Prepare campfire. Butter 1 side of 2 slices of bread. Place 1 slice of bread, butter side down, on pie-iron.

Add 1 slice of cheese and 2 slices of ham, and top with the second slice of bread, butter side up. Close iron and trim any excess bread so it does not catch fire. Heat over hot coals until cheese has melted and bread is slightly toasted. Repeat for 3 remaining sandwiches.

1 serving: 380 Calories; 15 g Total Fat (1.5 g Mono, 0 g Poly,9 g Sat); 50 mg Cholesterol; 43 g Carbohydrates (2 g Fibre, trace Sugar); 18 g Protein; 820 mg Sodium

It always rains on tents. Rainstorms will travel thousands of miles, against prevailing winds, for the opportunity to rain on a tent.

—Dave Barry

TOOLBOX
ESSENTIALS

Tools and gadgets offer an area for you to excel. When your wives, girlfriends and mothers, even your children, have given up trying to figure out how something works, you can step in like a hero...having already learned the necessary techniques in secret in the garage late at night. But wait—children are usually much better than we are at figuring out newer gadgets, so it is important to choose dangerous ones so you can restrict their access owing to safety concerns, and thereby gain the upper hand.

Handy gadgets to have in the kitchen are a blender, slow cooker, toaster oven, fondue pot and of course the microwave and dishwasher. Of these, the fondue pot is just like having a campfire on the table, and the dishwasher does more than wash dishes. But there are far too many tools available to us, and if you have to wait for 20 Christmases to get them all you'll be stuck with items that are obsolete.

5 KITCHEN ESSENTIALS

UTENSILS to make your life easier. Think spatula, wooden spoons, pancake flipper, soup ladle, meat mallet, whisk, tongs and an instant-read thermometer.

MEASURING SPOONS AND CUPS. Essential.

CUTTING BOARD. Wood is preferred for many reasons.

GOOD QUALITY POTS AND PANS including a Dutch oven and a cast iron frying pan. A Dutch oven is a heavy, large pot with a lid, and it is very versatile. A cast iron frying pan is equally versatile, plus it is indestructible. Take care of it, and it will take care of you (plus it can be used as a weapon, if you've ever seen the movie *Eating Raoul*). Non-stick pans are also useful, but go good quality if you can.

CHEF'S KNIFE. Keep it sharp, hold it correctly and practise, practise, practise. Other knifes are handy, like a paring knife and a serrated bread knife, but the chef's knife will do the heavy lifting.

Fondue

BBQs and smokers are essential big tools. Principle among some small tools you can sneak indoors is the fondue. It is essentially a mini-campfire and presents danger on the table. A variation is the raclette, which is like a mini-BBQ for adding melted cheese to every food in the world. The French, Germans and Swiss might restrict this list but we have experimented, and everything tastes better with melted cheese.

BEER CHEESE FONDUE

MAKES: 2 1/3 CUPS (575 ML)   **DIFFICULTY:** ★ ★

A nice blend of cheese and beer flavours. Try dipping black Russian bread cubes, French or Italian bread cubes, rye or pumpernickel bread cubes, spoon-size shredded wheat cereal and warm cooked potato chunks.

2 cups	500 mL	grated Swiss cheese
2 cups	500 mL	grated medium Cheddar cheese
3 Tbsp	45 mL	all-purpose flour
1/4 tsp	1 mL	dry mustard
2 tsp	10 mL	chopped chives
1/8 tsp	0.5 mL	garlic powder
1/8 tsp	0.5 mL	pepper
		sprinkle of ground nutmeg
1 cup	250 mL	beer
1 tsp	5 mL	Worcestershire sauce

Combine first 8 ingredients in large bowl. Toss to coat cheese well, to help prevent cheese from clumping.

Heat beer and Worcestershire sauce in a large saucepan until hot. Add cheese mixture, in 3 or 4 additions, stirring after each addition until melted. Carefully pour into fondue pot. Place over low heat.

2 Tbsp (30 mL): 100 Calories; 7 g Total Fat (2 g Mono, 0 g Poly, 4.5 g Sat); 25 mg Cholesterol; 2 g Carbohydrates (0 g Fibre, 0 g Sugar); 6 g Protein; 100 mg Sodium

You won't mind unloading the dishwasher when what you are taking out of it is a perfectly cooked dinner. The dishwasher may seem an unlikely appliance to use for cooking your meal, but it does a great job with many foods, especially fish. The steam keeps the fish nice and moist. Just make sure the container or package you put your food in is airtight.

DEVILISH DISHWASHER SALMON

MAKES: 4 SERVINGS   **DIFFICULTY: ★ ★**

Cooking fish in the dishwasher is one of the easiest and most eco-friendly ways of preparing it, so you'll be saving a little energy as well as effort. And it's delicious!

4	4	6 oz (170 g) salmon fillets
1/4 cup	60 mL	fresh lime juice
1 tsp	5 mL	kosher salt
1/4 tsp	1 mL	pepper
1	1	lemon, cut into wedges

Prepare 2 pieces of heavy duty (or a double layer of regular) foil, about 12 inches (30 cm) in size and spray the shiny side with cooking spray. Place 2 fillets on greased side of each foil. Fold up outer edges (to stop liquid from draining out) and drizzle fish with lime juice. Season with salt and pepper. Fold foil closed to form 2 airtight packets.

Place packets in top rack of dishwasher. Run a normal cycle. Remove fish from foil and insert a meat thermometer into thickest part of fillet. Fish is fully cooked when thermometer reads 145°F (63°C). Serve with lemon wedges.

1 serving: 250 Calories; 11 g Total Fat (3.5 g Mono, 4.5 g Poly, 1.5 g Sat); 95 mg Cholesterol; 1 g Carbohydrates (0 g Fibre, 0 g Sugar); 34 g Protein; 610 mg Sodium

Sure, cooking in the microwave might seem like cheating to some, but there are times when a guy just wants something simpler. With recipes tailor-made for the microwave, no one needs to know how little work was put into achieving such tasty results.

MICROWAVE LASAGNA

MAKES: 6 SERVINGS   **DIFFICULTY: ★**

Who says you can't make good pasta in the microwave? This recipe proves that many great things are just a "start" button away.

1 lb	454 g	lean ground beef
1	1	21 oz (621 mL) jar of spaghetti sauce
12	12	oven-ready lasagna noodles
2 cups	500 mL	ricotta cheese, *divided*
1 1/2 cups	375 mL	shredded mozzarella cheese, *divided*
1 cup	250 mL	grated Parmesan cheese

Crumble ground beef into a microwave-safe glass bowl. Microwave on high (100%) for 5 minutes, stirring once.

Once beef is well browned, drain off grease and mix meat with spaghetti sauce. Spread a third of meat sauce on bottom of a 8 x 12 inch (20 x 30 cm) glass baking dish. Arrange 4 lasagna noodles over sauce to cover bottom of baking dish. Top with 1 cup (250 mL) ricotta and 1/2 cup (125 mL) mozzarella. Add a third of meat sauce. Repeat layers and top with remaining meat sauce. Sprinkle with Parmesan cheese.

Microwave on medium (50%) for 35 minutes, uncovered. Top with remaining 1/2 cup (125 mL) mozzarella and microwave on medium (50%) for 3 minutes or until cheese is melted. Let lasagna stand 5 minutes before slicing.

1 serving: 590 Calories; 23 g Total Fat (6 g Mono, 0 g Poly, 11 g Sat); 80 mg Cholesterol; 45 g Carbohydrates (4 g Fibre, 12 g Sugar); 41 g Protein; 1260 mg Sodium

> Once we sowed wild oats, now we cook them in the microwave.
> —Anonymous

MAGIC MICROWAVE TACOS

MAKES: 8 TACOS   **DIFFICULTY:** ★

Tacos can be made with a variety of fillings including beef, pork, chicken, seafood, vegetables and cheese, and most men have never met a taco they didn't love!

1 lb	454 g	ground beef
1 1/2 tsp	7 mL	chili powder
1/2 tsp	2 mL	salt
1/2 tsp	2 mL	garlic powder
1/8 tsp	1 mL	cayenne pepper
1/4 cup	60 mL	water
8		medium taco shells, warmed
2 cups	500 mL	shredded Cheddar cheese
2 cups	500 mL	shredded lettuce
1/4 cup	60 mL	finely chopped onion
1	1	medium tomato, chopped
1/2 cup	125 mL	salsa

Crumble ground beef into a microwave-safe casserole dish. Cover with a glass lid and microwave on high (100%) for 5 minutes.

Drain grease and combine beef with chili powder, salt, garlic powder, cayenne and water. Cover and microwave for 3 to 4 minutes on high (100%).

Fill each taco shell with about 2 Tbsp (30 mL) ground beef, then top with desired amounts of cheese, lettuce, onion, tomato and salsa.

1 serving: 640 Calories; 39 g Total Fat (12 g Mono, 1 g Poly, 19 g Sat); 125 mg Cholesterol; 24 g Carbohydrates (4 g Fibre, 6 g Sugar); 39 g Protein; 1340 mg Sodium

FUDGE-SAUCED BROWNIES

MAKES: 14 SERVINGS   **DIFFICULTY: ★ ★**

Microwave cheating at its best. No one will believe this rich dish was created in the microwave. The chocolatey brownie has a hint of pecan, and the sauce is smooth and dark.

9 oz	255 g	butter (not margarine), chopped
16	16	semi-sweet chocolate baking squares (1 oz, 28 g, each), chopped, *divided*
2 1/4 cups	550 mL	granulated sugar
5	5	large eggs, fork-beaten
3/4 cup	175 mL	pecans, chopped
1 cup	250 mL	all-purpose flour
1/2 tsp	2 mL	baking powder
1/2 cup	125 mL	cocoa, sifted if lumpy
3/4 cup	175 mL	whipping cream
12		large marshmallows, chopped

For the brownies, combine butter and half of choped chocolate in a large microwave-safe bowl. Microwave, uncovered, on high (100%) for about 2 minutes, stirring twice during cooking, until melted. Cool.

Add sugar, eggs and pecans. Mix well. Add flour, baking powder and cocoa. Mix well. Pour chocolate mixture into greased 8 x 12 inch (20 x 30 cm) microwave-safe dish. Microwave, uncovered, on medium (50%) for about 15 minutes, turning dish at halftime if microwave doesn't have turntable, until almost set in middle. Cool. Cover. Chill for at least 8 hours or overnight. Cut into 28 triangles.

For the sauce, combine whipping cream, remaining chocolate and marshmallows in a medium microwave-safe dish. Microwave, uncovered, on high (100%) for 1 minute. Stir, then microwave, uncovered, on medium (50%) for 1 to 2 minutes until marshmallows are melted. Stir. Drizzle over brownies.

1 serving: 590 Calories; 36 g Total Fat (8 g Mono, 2 g Poly, 20 g Sat); 130 mg Cholesterol; 65 g Carbohydrates (4 g Fibre, 51 g Sugar); 7 g Protein; 150 mg Sodium

If you want quick and easy, dig that old toaster oven out of the basement. Toaster ovens are great—small, convenient and portable little appliances easily totted from house to house, or tailgate to tailgate. They're simple to use and consume a lot less energy than a regular stove. And the meals you can create with them are fantastic.

TOASTER OVEN MUSHROOM CHOPS

MAKES: 4 SERVINGS   **DIFFICULTY: ★**

Toaster ovens aren't just for heating up day-old pizza anymore! These pork chops cook up tender and juicy, just as though they were cooked in the regular oven.

1/2 cup	125 mL	**sliced mushrooms**
1/2	1/2	**large onion, finely chopped**
1	1	**10 oz (284 mL) can of condensed mushroom soup**
4	4	**pork chops**

Combine mushrooms, onion and soup in an 8 x 8 inch (20 x 20 cm) glass baking dish. Add pork chops and turn to coat. Cover with foil and bake in a 375°F (190°C) toaster oven for 20 minutes. Flip chops and cook for 20 minutes more or until pork is cooked through.

1 serving: 290 Calories; 19 g Total Fat (7 g Mono, 2.5 g Poly, 6 g Sat); 60 mg Cholesterol; 7 g Carbohydrates (0 g Fibre; 1 g Sugar); 22 g Protein; 530 mg Sodium

IRIE ISLAND CHICKEN

MAKES: 4 SERVINGS   **DIFFICULTY:** ★

"Yeah mon, everting irie when de island chicken come" is a comment you are likely to hear in Jamaica, and don't be surprised if you speak a little Patois yourself during this meal. Serve with rice and fresh veggies.

1	1	8 oz (227 mL) can of crushed pineapple, with juice
1/4 cup	60 mL	mustard
1/4 cup	60 mL	cider vinegar
2 Tbsp	30 mL	soy sauce
2 Tbsp	30 mL	brown sugar
1/8 tsp	0.5 mL	ground ginger
4	4	4 oz (113 g) boneless, skinless chicken breasts

Combine first 6 ingredients in a small bowl and mix well.

Place chicken breasts in shallow casserole dish or 8 x 8 inch (20 x 20 cm) square baking pan. Pour sauce over chicken and place in a 350ºF (175ºC) toaster oven for 35 to 45 minutes until chicken is no longer pink inside.

1 serving: 340 Calories; 3 g Total Fat (0.5 g Mono, 0.5 g Poly, 1 g Sat); 135 mg Cholesterol; 19 g Carbohydrates (0 g Fibre, 15 g Sugar); 56 g Protein; 810 mg Sodium

The marvellous slow cooker is possibly one of the greatest "guy inventions" in history. With this handy appliance you will never burn a meal, and it can take the toughest cut of meat and turn it into the most delectable meal you've ever tasted. Even the most inexperienced cook can feel like a top chef! And talk about easy! With a little advanced planning, you can prep the ingredients before you head off to work and come home to a piping hot meal. As an added bonus, foods almost never stick in slow cookers, making clean-up a cinch.

SLOW COOKER STEW'RIFFIC

MAKES: 4 SERVINGS   **DIFFICULTY: ★**

The average male can't get enough of this humble, well-balanced meal. Nothing sticks to the ribs quite like warm stew.

1 lb	454 g	cubed stewing beef
1/4 cup	60 mL	all-purpose flour
1 tsp	5 mL	salt
1 tsp	5 mL	pepper
1	1	clove garlic, minced
2 tsp	10 mL	Worcestershire sauce
1	1	medium onion, chopped
1 1/2 cups	375 mL	beef broth
4	4	carrots, sliced
4	4	potatoes, diced
1	1	stalk celery, chopped

Place beef in slow cooker.

Combine flour, salt and pepper in a medium bowl, and sprinkle over beef to coat thoroughly.

Stir in garlic, Worcestershire sauce, onion, beef broth, carrots, potatoes and celery. Place lid on slow cooker, and cook on Low for 8 to 10 hours.

1 serving: 390 Calories; 9 g Total Fat (3 g Mono, 0.5 g Poly, 3 g Sat); 55 mg Cholesterol; 47 g Carbohydrates (5 g Fibre, 7 g Sugar); 31 g Protein; 1020 mg Sodium

TASTY SLOW COOKER MEATLOAF

MAKES: 6 SERVINGS   **DIFFICULTY:** ★

Meatloaf has been a guy staple for centuries, and this moist slow-cooker version adds a bit of flair to an already proven favourite.

2	2	large eggs
3/4 cup	175 mL	milk
3/4 cup	175 mL	bread crumbs
1/2 cup	125 mL	sliced mushrooms
1/2 tsp	2 mL	salt
2 lbs	900 g	ground beef
1/4 cup	60 mL	ketchup
2 Tbsp	30 mL	brown sugar
1	1	1 1/4 oz (38 g) envelope of onion soup mix
1/2 tsp	2 mL	Worcestershire sauce

Combine eggs, milk, bread crumbs, mushrooms and salt in a large bowl. Crumble ground beef into bowl and stir well to combine. Shape into a round loaf and place in slow cooker. Cover and cook on Low for 5 to 6 hours.

Whisk ketchup, brown sugar, onion soup mix and Worcestershire sauce in a small bowl; spoon sauce over meatloaf. Return to slow cooker and cook on Low until heated through, about 15 minutes.

1 serving: 730 Calories; 35 g Total Fat (15 g Mono, 1.5 g Poly, 14 g Sat); 245 mg Cholesterol; 33 g Carbohydrates (2 g Fibre, 16 g Sugar); 54 g Protein; 1500 mg Sodium

Helpful Tips

Be sure to fill your slow cooker between halfway and two-thirds full. Foods won't cook properly in an over-filled slow cooker, and they'll cook to fast if the level is too low. Either way, you won't be happy with the end result.

PULLED PORK

MAKES: 5 SERVINGS   **DIFFICULTY:** ★

Pulled pork was meant to be cooked in a slow cooker, and this recipe is about as easy as it gets. Serve on fresh buns or crusty bread.

1	1	**2 lb (900 g) boneless pork tenderloin**
2 Tbsp	30 mL	**pork spice rub seasoning**
1 cup	250 mL	**water**
20 oz	591 mL	**barbecue sauce**
1/4 cup	60 mL	**firmly packed brown sugar**
2 Tbsp	30 mL	**Worcestershire sauce**
2 Tbsp	30 mL	**hot sauce**
1 tsp	5 mL	**salt**
1 tsp	5 mL	**pepper**

Coat tenderloin with spice rub. Add water and tenderloin to your slow cooker and cook on Low for 6 to 7 hours until meat is tender. Drain any remaining water and fat from slow cooker.

Shred meat with a fork and stir in remaining 6 ingredients. Cook on Low for 1 hour, then serve.

1 serving: 530 Calories; 12 g Total Fat (5 g Mono, 1.5 g Poly, 4.5 g Sat); 150 mg Cholesterol; 54 g Carbohydrates (0 g Fibre, 46 g Sugar); 47 g Protein; 3030 mg Sodium

Pictured on page 71.

Pulled Pork, page 70 • Quick Slaw, page 253 • Home-style Potato Chips, page 203

Elk Chili, page 79

TRADITIONAL SLOW COOKER CHILI

MAKES: 10 SERVINGS   **DIFFICULTY:** ★

This hearty meal hits the spot after a long day at work or after enjoying your favourite recreational activity. Smells amazing, and tastes even better. Serve with fresh bread, bannock or a baguette.

2	2	15 oz (425 mL) cans of red kidney beans, drained and rinsed
2	2	14 oz (398 mL) cans of diced tomatoes
1	1	6 oz (170 mL) can of tomato paste
2 lbs	900 g	lean ground beef, browned and drained
2	2	medium onions, coarsely chopped
2	2	ribs celery, coarsely chopped
1 cup	250 mL	sliced mushrooms
1	1	medium green pepper, coarsely chopped
2	2	cloves garlic, crushed
3 Tbsp	45 mL	chili powder
1 tsp	5 mL	pepper
1 tsp	5 mL	ground cumin
1/2 tsp	2 mL	salt

Combine all ingredients in a slow cooker. Cover and cook on Low for 9 to 12 hours or on High for 4 1/2 to 6 hours, stirring occasionally.

1 serving: 320 Calories; 13 g Total Fat (6 g Mono, 0.5 g Poly, 5 g Sat); 55 mg Cholesterol; 21 g Carbohydrates (9 g Fibre; 6 g Sugar); 23 g Protein; 590 mg Sodium

Pictured on page 269.

GARAGE COOKING

You're going to need some survival food that you can cook in the garage if you get sent to the doghouse. Don't reserve your blowtorch just for welding. It makes a nice crust on a crème brûlée, and you can use it to grill a cheese sandwich, roast some veggies or heat up a bowl of stew or chili.

BAKED ALASKA

MAKES: 8 SERVINGS   **DIFFICULTY:** ★ ★ ★

Baked on the outside, frozen on the inside. Your blowtorch will make short work of turning the meringue golden and crisp. Or, for a more conventional preparation, you could cook the dessert in a 450ºF (230ºC) oven for about 2 minutes.

1	1	**jam-filled jelly roll (about 3 inches, 7.5 cm, in diameter)**
5	5	**egg whites, at room temperature**
1 tsp	5 mL	**vanilla extract**
1/4 tsp	1 mL	**salt**
3/4 cup	175 mL	**granulated sugar**
2 cups	500 mL	**vanilla ice cream**

Cut jelly roll crosswise into eight 1/2 inch (12 mm) thick slices. Arrange slices in a single layer on an ungreased baking sheet.

Beat next 3 ingredients in a medium bowl until soft peaks form. Add sugar, 1 Tbsp (15 mL) at a time, beating constantly until sugar is dissolved.

Place 1 scoop of ice cream in centre of each jelly roll slice. Working quickly, spread egg white mixture over ice cream scoops to edge of jelly roll slice. Freeze until set. When ready to serve, use blowtorch to brown meringue until golden and crisp.

1 serving: 300 Calories; 6 g Total Fat (2 g Mono, 0 g Poly, 3 g Sat); 110 mg Cholesterol; 55 g Carbohydrates (0 g Fibre, 46 g Sugar); 7 g Protein; 230 mg Sodium

CARBECUE

Instead of the usual road-trip snack foods, why not use the heat from your car's engine to cook a hot and tasty meal to eat on the way to your destination? Carbecuing, or engine-block cooking, has apparently been around almost as long as cars themselves. You can cook almost anything, from hot dogs to a pot roast, depending on the time and distance of your trip. The key is to find the hottest part of your engine—usually near the exhaust manifold—and then ensure that your food is securely wrapped in aluminum foil and tightly wedged in place. Cooking times are generally given as distances rather than minutes, but these will vary depending on the make and model of car. Seafood will cook more quickly (in 50–100 kilometres) than chicken wings (225–320 kilometres) or a pork tenderloin (400 kilometres). Because they are less efficient, older engines will cook food faster than modern ones. And if you're stuck in traffic, your 100-kilometre meal may be done in a much shorter distance. Some trial and error is necessary, and you may have to stop periodically to check on your food. As a general rule, dishes with a lot of liquid, such as stews, should be avoided. One final tip— turn off your engine and make sure you have a set of tongs handy before removing your food. Bon appétit!

FAIR GAME

What food is more manly than wild game? It is WILD. Enough said. You don't actually have to bring home the venison for the family everyday. Get to know your local butcher—he can supply a variety of wild meats AND a good story of how it was obtained. No one will know that you didn't have to wrestle a wild animal to the ground with your bare hands so that you could provide food for the family. This section features a variety of dishes perfect for the veteran hunter and gather, those new to these activities, or simply guys who enjoy going "wild" every once in awhile. And whether you catch your own fish or trap your own lobster, or choose to "fish" for the catch of the day at the grocery store, you will find some helpful ways to prepare superb scaled specimens.

MOOSE MEATLOAF

MAKES: 8 SERVINGS   DIFFICULTY: ★ ★

The combination of moose and pork creates a terrific marriage of flavour and texture. Game meats often call for pork to balance out the natural leanness of game.

2 Tbsp	30 mL	butter
1	1	onion, finely chopped
3	3	cloves garlic, finely chopped
2 lbs	900 g	ground moose
1 lb	454 g	ground pork
3/4 cup	175 mL	bread crumbs
3	3	large eggs, beaten
1/4 cup	60 mL	Worcestershire sauce
3 Tbsp	45 mL	soy sauce
3/4 tsp	175 mL	cayenne powder
2 tsp	10 mL	salt
1 Tbsp	15 mL	finely ground pepper

Melt butter in medium skillet on medium heat. Add onion and garlic and cook until tender, about 5 minutes.

Meanwhile, combine remaining ingredients in a large mixing bowl. Stir in onion mixture. Coat a 9 inch (23 cm) loaf pan with cooking spray. Spoon meat mixture into pan, making sure it is level. Cover with foil and bake for about 1 1/2 hours, until loaf is no longer pink in middle. Remove foil and allow meatloaf to stand for 5 minutes before serving.

1 serving: 330 Calories; 18 g Total Fat (7 g Mono, 1.5 g Poly, 7 g Sat); 165 mg Cholesterol; 13 g Carbohydrates (trace Fibre, 3 g Sugar); 38 g Protein; 950 mg Sodium

MARINATED VENISON TENDERLOIN

**MAKES: 4 SERVINGS
DIFFICULTY: ★**

This is a great recipe for any prime game tenderloin, such as venison, elk, moose or caribou.

1	1	venison tenderloin, cut 1 inch (2.5 cm) thick
2 tsp	10 mL	Worcestershire sauce
1 tsp	5 mL	garlic powder
1/2 tsp	2 mL	freshly ground pepper
3 Tbsp	45 mL	extra virgin olive oil, *divided*

Mix first 4 ingredients and 1 Tbsp (15 mL) oil in a large bowl. Add tenderloin, making sure it is completely covered in marinade. Marinate in fridge overnight.

Before grilling, brush 2 Tbsp (30 mL) olive oil over meat. Cook slowly over medium heat, turning every couple of minutes. Venison is done when firm on the outside and slightly pink in centre. Let stand for 5 minutes before serving.

1 serving: 440 Calories; 19 g Total Fat (9 g Mono, 2 g Poly, 3.5 g Sat); 55 mg Cholesterol; 2 g Carbohydrates (trace Fibre; trace Sugar); 67 g Protein; 35 mg Sodium

ELK CHILI

MAKES: 8 SERVINGS   **DIFFICULTY:** ★

When cooking with elk, as with most other game meats, don't use salt during the cooking process. It draws moisture out of the meat and creates a dry final product. With almost zero fat, game meat is about as lean as you can get.

2 Tbsp	30 mL	cooking oil
2 cups	500 mL	chopped onion
1	1	medium red pepper, diced
1 cup	250 mL	celery, diced
2	2	cloves garlic, minced
6 Tbsp	90 mL	chili powder
1 1/2 tsp	7 mL	dried oregano
1/2 tsp	2 mL	ground coriander
1/2 tsp	2 mL	cayenne pepper
2 lbs	900 g	ground elk
2	2	28 oz (796 mL) cans of diced tomatoes
2	2	14 oz (398 mL) cans of tomato sauce
2	2	6 oz (170 g) cans of tomato paste
1	1	28 oz (796 mL) can of red kidney beans, drained and rinsed
1 tsp	5 mL	salt

Heat oil in a large pot on medium-high. Add onion, peppers, celery and garlic and cook until softened.

In a small bowl, combine chilli powder, oregano, ground coriander and cayenne. Add to vegetables and stir well.

Add elk and cook for about 10 minutes or until no longer pink.

Add diced tomatoes, tomato sauce and tomato paste. Bring mixture to a boil, then reduce heat. Simmer for 30 minutes, stirring occasionally.

Add kidney beans and heat for 15 minutes. Add salt and serve.

1 serving: 340 Calories; 11 g Total Fat (4 g Mono, 2 g Poly, 3 g Sat); 45 mg Cholesterol; 42 g Carbohydrates (12 g Fibre, 11 g Sugar); 26 g Protein; 1880 mg Sodium

Pictured on page 72.

RUSTIC ROAST DUCK

MAKES: 4 SERVINGS
DIFFICULTY: ★

Thanks to the efforts of groups like Ducks Unlimited Canada, most species of ducks and geese in this country have stable populations and are kept under a close watchful eye. Serve this dish with potatoes and a salad on the side.

4 Tbsp	60 mL	soy sauce
4	4	cloves garlic, minced
1 Tbsp	15 mL	granulated sugar
4 Tbsp	60 mL	liquid honey
2 Tbsp	30 mL	ground ginger
2 Tbsp	30 mL	orange juice
1/2 tsp	2 mL	pepper
1	1	4 lb (1.8 kg) duck
1/4 cup	60 mL	sliced shallots

Combine soy sauce, garlic, sugar, honey, ginger, orange juice and pepper in a large bowl. Add duck and turn to coat. Marinate duck overnight in fridge.

Place duck in a roasting pan and stuff with shallots. Cook in a 350ºF (175ºC) oven for about 2 hours, basting occasionally. Let stand for 5 minutes before serving.

1 serving: 710 Calories; 11 g Total Fat (7 g Mono, 3.5 g Poly, 11 g Sat); 350 mg Cholesterol; 28 g Carbohydrates (0 g Fibre, 20 g Sugar); 86 g Protein; 1650 mg Sodium

---

GLAZED WILD TURKEY

MAKES: 6 SERVINGS
DIFFICULTY: ★

This simple glaze works just as well on wild goose or duck.

1	1	wild turkey, cleaned, skinned and de-boned
1 cup	250 mL	all-purpose flour
3/4 tsp	4 mL	salt
3/4 tsp	4 mL	pepper
1	1	large egg, fork-beaten
3/4 cup	175 mL	milk
		oil for frying
1/2 cup	125 mL	liquid honey

Cut turkey into strips suitable for frying.

For the batter, combine flour, salt and pepper. Stir in egg and milk and mix until well combined. Dip turkey strips into batter, coating evenly.

Add oil to a large skillet, covering bottom to a depth of 1/2 inch (12 mm). Heat oil to 375ºF (190ºC). Add turkey strips, a few at a time, and fry until brown. Place on towel and allow to drain. Brush turkey with honey and serve. Serves 6

1 serving: 610 Calories; 12 g Total Fat (12.5 g Mono, 3 g Poly, 4 g Sat); 260 mg Cholesterol; 41 g Carbohydrates (trace Fibre, 23 g Sugar); 83 g Protein; 570 mg Sodium

ROASTED GOOSE WITH STUFFING

MAKES: 4 SERVINGS   **DIFFICULTY: ★**

With this stuffed roast goose recipe, you will find your bird is tender and juicy, just as a good roast should be! The stuffing must be prepared the night before to give the flavours a chance to blend.

1 cup	250 mL	water
1/2 cup	125 mL	red wine
1 Tbsp	15 mL	molasses
1 tsp	5 mL	pickling spice
2	2	apples, peeled, cored and diced
1 cup	250 mL	dried apricots
1/2 cup	125 mL	raisins
1	1	3 lb (1.4 kg) goose, cleaned and dressed
1/2 cup	125 mL	lemon juice
		salt and pepper to taste
1/2 cup	125 mL	bread crumbs
1/4 lb	113 g	salt pork, thinly sliced

For the stuffing, combine water, wine, molasses and pickling spice in a small saucepan over medium heat. Mix well and simmer for about 10 minutes.

Add apples, apricots and raisins. Cover and simmer for an additional 5 minutes. Allow to cool and refrigerate overnight.

To prepare the goose, rub inside and outside with lemon juice, salt and pepper. Strain fruit mixture, reserving liquid, and stir in bread crumbs. Stuff goose with stuffing and place in a roasting pan. Lay salt pork over breast. Cook in a 350°F (175°C) oven for about 2 hours, basting occasionally with liquid reserved from stuffing. Let stand for 5 minutes before serving.

1 serving: 850 Calories; 40 g Total Fat (15 g Mono, 4.5 g Poly, 1.5 g Sat); 215 mg Cholesterol; 62 g Carbohydrates (5 g Fibre, 42 g Sugar); 57 g Protein; 780 mg Sodium

Helpful Tips

To pluck a goose, start by pulling out all the feathers by hand and discarding them. Don't worry about removing the tiny pin feathers if you are grilling—they will quickly singe off—but other methods of cooking may call for these tiny feathers to be removed. Next, tear back the skin on the underside of the bird at the stomach cavity. Remove and discard the entrails, then rinse the goose under cool water and place on paper towel to dry.

STUFFED BROOK TROUT

MAKES: 4 SERVINGS   **DIFFICULTY: ★ ★**

This highly sought-after trout along with its cousin the arctic char are often considered to be the most delectable of all freshwater salmonids.

2 Tbsp	30 mL	cooking oil, *divided*
1	1	small onion, sliced
1	1	1 inch (2.5 cm) piece of ginger root, julienned
1/2	1/2	small jalapeño pepper, thinly sliced
2	2	12 oz (340 g) whole brook trout fillets, skin on
1/2 tsp	2 mL	salt
1/2 tsp	2 mL	pepper
6	6	lime leaves
		sprigs of fresh cilantro
1	1	lime, thinly sliced

Preheat grill to medium-high. Heat 1 Tbsp (15 mL) oil in a large skillet and add onion. Cook until soft and golden brown. Add ginger and jalapeño pepper and sauté for 3 minutes more. Remove from heat.

Season fillets with salt and pepper. Lay 1 fillet, flesh side up, on baking sheet. Arrange half of lime leaves and cilantro sprigs on top. Top with half of onion mixture, spreading evenly. Top with lime slices and spread remaining onion mixture on top of limes. Top with remaining lime leaves and cilantro and lay second fillet, skin side up, on top of filling, enclosing stuffing.

Tie fillets securely together with butcher's twine. Brush with remaining 1 Tbsp (15 mL) oil and grill for about 4 to 5 minutes per side until middle of stuffing is hot when tested with a knife.

1 serving: 380 Calories; 22 g Total Fat (3.5 g Mono, 1.5 g Poly, 0 g Sat); 35 mg Cholesterol; 0 g Carbohydrates (trace Fibre, trace Sugar); 43 g Protein; 400 mg Sodium

Helpful Tips

To properly clean a fish, start with a good, sharp fillet knife. Begin at the tail and insert the knife into the fish's vent. With a smooth forward stroke, cut through to the centre of the belly to the middle of the gill plate, making sure not to cut too deep. Remove the gills completely, eviscerate the entire fish and discard the organs. Rinse the fish under cold water, and then remove the kidneys (which run along the inside of the backbone) with the end of your thumbnail. Rinse again under cold water and make sure the body cavity is clean and free of debris. Do not remove the head unless the recipe calls for it.

MACKEREL WITH CREAM SAUCE

MAKES: 4 SERVINGS   **DIFFICULTY:** ★ ★

*In the town of Shediac, New Brunswick, sport fishing for mackerel is taken very
seriously. When the mackerel schools are running, copious fish can be found around
piers and bridges, where they corral bait fish to create a feeding frenzy.*

1/4 cup	60 mL	chopped mushrooms
1	1	tomato, chopped
1/4 cup	60 mL	bread crumbs or cornmeal
4 Tbsp	60 mL	butter, *divided*
1/4 tsp	1 mL	lemon juice
4	4	medium mackerel, backbones removed
2 Tbsp	30 mL	all-purpose flour
1 cup	250 mL	cold milk
		salt and pepper to taste

In a medium bowl, mix mushrooms, tomato, bread crumbs, 2 Tbsp (30 mL) butter and
lemon juice.

Stuff mackerel with mixture and place it in a non-stick baking pan. Cover with foil and
bake in a 400°F (200°C) oven for 15 minutes.

For the sauce, heat remaining 2 Tbsp (30 mL) butter in a small saucepan. Add flour and
cook for 3 to 4 minutes. Lower heat and slowly add milk. Bring to a boil, then lower heat
and stir until slightly reduced. Whisk in salt and pepper. Pour over fish and serve.

1 serving: 400 Calories; 28 g Total Fat (9 g Mono, 4 g Poly, 11 g Sat); 110 mg Cholesterol; 12 g Carbohydrates
(0 g Fibre, 4 g Sugar); 25 g Protein; 310 mg Sodium

FRESH BATTERED NORTHERN PIKE

MAKES: 4 SERVINGS　　　　**DIFFICULTY: ★ ★**

When it comes to table fare, northern pike are the unsung heroes of the freshwater fish world. They have firm, white flesh that practically explodes with excitement.

3 lbs	1.4 kg	boneless pike fillets
3 cups	750 mL	milk
2	2	large eggs, beaten
1/2 tsp	2 mL	garlic powder
1/2 tsp	2 mL	onion salt
1/2 tsp	2 mL	salt
1/2 tsp	2 mL	pepper
2 cups	500 mL	bread crumbs
3 cups	750 mL	cooking oil
1	1	lemon, cut into wedges

Trim all belly meat off fillets. Pat fish dry with paper towel and set aside.

In a medium bowl, combine milk, eggs, garlic powder, onion salt, salt and pepper. Place bread crumbs in a separate bowl.

Heat oil in a large, steep-sided skillet on medium-high. Dip each fillet into milk mixture, allowing excess mixture to run off, then dredge in bread crumbs. Fry fillet in hot oil for about 15 minutes, turning once, until golden brown. Transfer to serving dish, garnish with lemon wedges and serve.

1 serving: 760 Calories; 22 g Total Fat (10 g Mono, 4.5 g Poly, 4 g Sat); 210 mg Cholesterol; 57 g Carbohydrates (2 g Fibre, 13 g Sugar); 84 g Protein; 1230 mg Sodium

CANADIAN MAPLE SALMON

MAKES: 4 SERVINGS   **DIFFICULTY: ★**

What better way to enjoy two distinct Canadian favourites—salmon and real Canadian maple syrup—than together in one symbiotic dish?

1/4 cup	**60 mL**	**pure Canadian maple syrup**
1 tsp	**5 mL**	**Dijon mustard**
2 Tbsp	**30 mL**	**soy sauce**
1 Tbsp	**15 mL**	**lemon juice**
1 1/2 lb	**680 g**	**salmon fillets**
2 Tbsp	**30 mL**	**sliced shallots**

Combine first 4 ingredients in a shallow dish. Remove 1/4 cup (60 mL) marinade and set aside. Lay salmon fillets in a dish and spoon marinade over top. Marinate in fridge for about 30 minutes.

Place fillets in a baking dish and cook in a 400°F (200°C) oven for 15 to 20 minutes, until fish flakes easily. Drizzle reserved marinade over salmon, top with shallots and serve.

1 serving: 290 Calories; 11 g Total Fat (3.5 g Mono, 4.5 g Poly, 1.5 g Sat); 95 mg Cholesterol; 13 g Carbohydrates (0 g Fibre, 10 g Sugar); 35 g Protein; 550 mg Sodium

Fishing is a male-dominated activity boys are often introduced to at a very young age. The image of a little boy with his fishing rod and bait is as stereotypically male as playing catch with Dad. Although not every guy is a seasoned angler who owns 3 fishing boats, 12 rods and 4 tackle boxes, you can bet that most men have at least tried casting a line once in the their life.

SOUTHERN FRIED BULLHEAD

MAKES: 6 SERVINGS   **DIFFICULTY: ★**

Once you've mastered the task of skinning and cleaning bullheads (a type of catfish), you'll find them to be some of the most delicious table fish.

		peanut or sunflower oil for frying
1/4 cup	60 mL	cornmeal or seasoned bread crumbs
1/4 cup	60 mL	all-purpose flour
		salt and pepper to taste
1	1	egg
6	6	bullheads, skinned

Add enough oil to a large, heavy saucepan to create a shallow fry. Heat to 375° F (190° C).

Mix cornmeal, flour, salt and pepper in a shallow bowl.

In a separate shallow bowl, beat egg. Roll fish in flour mixture, then in egg, and back again in flour mixture. Fry for about 5 minutes until golden brown, turning only once. Drain on a plate lined with paper towel before serving.

1 serving: 220 Calories; 13 g Total Fat (6 g Mono, 2.5 g Poly, 2 g Sat); 65 mg Cholesterol; 9 g Carbohydrates (0 g Fibre, 0 g Sugar); 18 g Protein; 170 mg Sodium

Helpful Tips

Skinning catfish is quite simple once you have done it a couple of times. You'll need a wood cutting board or fillet table, a pair of pliers, a dry towel and a sharp fillet knife. Cutting through the fish's skin just below the head, run your knife 360° around the fish. With a dry towel in your right hand, hold onto the head tightly, and then grab the edge of the fish's skin with the pliers. Pull slowly with your left hand and the skin should peel away much like a sausage casing. Stop when you get to the tail and cut the skin away completely with the fillet knife. Rinse the fish off in cold water, and you're all set to go!

DATE BAIT

If ever there was a meal the average male would not want to mess up, it is a date night dinner. Putting together a thoughtful, well-planned meal for someone special can be one of the most stressful activities there is, apart from public speaking or maybe death. Since cooking for that special someone needs also to create that "good first impression," a touch of flair always helps. Not that an intricate and particularly complicated recipe is required, but a good knowledge of the meal and some field-testing may be in order. Once you've decided on the special date night meal, give it a test run on your own. Become familiar with the ingredients and instructions, and only when you have mastered it are you ready for the big time. One of the most impressive things on a romantic dinner date is preparing the meal in front of your date. If you appear to have a handle on things and the meal turns out well, you have hit a homerun. Trust us on this one, gentlemen!

DATE NIGHT GRILLED OYSTERS

MAKES: 2 SERVINGS   **DIFFICULTY:** ★ ★

Oysters are a natural aphrodisiac, so why not serve them on date night and let nature give you a helping hand. These little gems contain the neurotransmitter dopamine, believed to be responsible for the increase in sexual desire.

3 Tbsp	45 mL	extra virgin olive oil
3 Tbsp	45 mL	butter
2	2	cloves garlic, finely minced
1 tsp	5 mL	lemon juice
1/2 tsp	2 mL	chili pepper flakes
1/4 tsp	1 mL	salt
1/4 tsp	1 mL	pepper
1 Tbsp	15 mL	chopped parsley
16	16	whole live oysters in shell

Combine olive oil and butter in a small saucepan over medium heat. Add garlic and cook for about 1 minute. Add lemon juice, chili pepper flakes, salt, pepper and parsley. Remove from heat.

Place oysters, cup side up, on a preheated grill. Cover and cook for 1 minute on high heat. The oysters should open slightly. Quickly remove the oysters. Hold an oyster with an oven mitt and use a shucking knife to pry it open. It should open easily. Spoon sauce into each oyster and return oysters to grill. Cover and cook for 4 to 5 minutes.

1 serving: 580 Calories; 45 g Total Fat (22 g Mono, 4.5 g Poly, 15 g Sat); 195 mg Cholesterol; 16 g Carbohydrates (0 g Fibre, 0 g Sugar); 29 g Protein; 730 mg Sodium

Pictured on page 89.

Helpful Tips

Whether you choose the recipes we've presented here or not, you should still have a few secret recipes that will win their hearts. Make these your signature recipes. You might have to sacrifice your own taste preferences, and instead…this is the tough part…cook for your date's taste preferences. Think about what she (or he) wants. It's not about what you like.

Don't forget to decorate the table (or picnic cloth, or sheet) with something inspiring, like a lit candle or a flower in a wine goblet. Put a tiny bit of garnish on the food and don't mention it. Your date will notice and be impressed. Trust us.

Know something about what you are cooking and include your date in the conversation. You can always make something taste better by adding a story to the seasoning.

Date Night Grilled Oysters, page 88

Private Reserve Barbecue Sauce, page 103 • Peppercorn Sauce with
Red Wine Reduction, page 101 • Tomato Sauce, page 98 • Classic Pesto, page 99
Chicken Stock, page 164

STEAMING STUFFED BELL PEPPERS

MAKES: 4 SERVINGS   **DIFFICULTY:** ★

Regardless whether your date is an omnivore or carnivore, this recipe is sure to please. Served on their own or as a side, stuffed bell peppers are always a hit.

4	4	**medium green peppers**
2/3 lb	300 g	**ground beef**
2 cups	500 mL	**cooked white rice**
1 1/2 cups	375 mL	**marinara sauce,** *divided*
1 tsp	5 mL	**Worcestershire sauce**
1 tsp	5 mL	**salt**
1/4 tsp	1 mL	**pepper**
1 tsp	5 mL	**Italian seasoning**
1/2 cup	125 mL	**Cheddar or mozzarella cheese, shredded**

Cut tops off of peppers and remove seeds and membranes.

Cook ground beef in a skillet over medium heat until no longer pink, about 6 to 8 minutes. Drain off fat. Add rice, 3/4 cup (175 mL) marinara sauce, Worcestershire sauce, salt, pepper and Italian seasoning, and stir to combine.

Stand peppers in a small baking dish, trimming bottoms, if necessary, so they stand upright. Stuff peppers with rice and beef mixture. Top with remaining 3/4 cup (175 mL) sauce. Bake in 350°F (175°C) oven for about 50 minutes. Sprinkle cheese over peppers and cook for another 10 minutes. Peppers are cooked when they are soft but not mushy.

1 serving: 480 Calories; 20 g Total Fat (6 g Mono, 0.5 g Poly, 9 g Sat); 70 mg Cholesterol; 44 g Carbohydrates (3 g Fibre; 14 g Sugar); 25 g Protein; 1190 mg Sodium

BEEF(CAKE) STIR-FRY

MAKES: 4 SERVINGS   **DIFFICULTY: ★**

Stir-fry is always a big hit whether it's for date night, a family dinner or a group of friends. Throughout the year, you can alternate vegetables depending on what's in season. Serve over hot rice.

1/2 lb	225 g	sirloin beef steak
1/3 cup	75 mL	soy sauce, *divided*
2 Tbsp	30 mL	cornstarch, *divided*
1 Tbsp	15 mL	dry sherry
2	2	cloves garlic, crushed
1/4 tsp	1 mL	crushed chili peppers
3/4 cup	175 mL	water
3 Tbsp	45 mL	cooking oil, *divided*
1	1	large onion, cut in chunks
1 cup	250 mL	thinly sliced carrots
12	12	mushrooms, quartered
2	2	tomatoes, cut in chunks

Slice beef into thin strips.

Combine 1 Tbsp (15 mL) soy sauce, 1 Tbsp (15 mL) cornstarch, sherry and garlic in a small bowl. Stir in beef and let stand for 15 minutes.

Meanwhile, combine remaining 1/4 cup (60 mL) soy sauce, remaining 1 Tbsp (15 mL) cornstarch, red chili pepper and water in a small bowl. Set aside.

Heat 1 Tbsp (15 mL) oil in a wok or large skillet over high heat. Add beef mixture and stir-fry for 1 minute. Remove from pan.

Heat remaining 2 Tbsp (30 mL) oil in same wok. Add onion and carrots and stir-fry for 3 minutes. Add mushrooms and stir-fry for 3 more minutes. Add beef mixture and cornstarch mixture and cook, stirring, until mixture boils and thickens. Add tomato and continue cooking until tomato is hot. Remove from heat and serve.

1 serving: 300 Calories; 16 g Total Fat (8 g Mono, 3 g Poly, 3 g Sat); 30 mg Cholesterol; 16 g Carbohydrates (3 g Fibre, 6 g Sugar); 17 g Protein; 1290 mg Sodium

CHARLIE'S CHICKEN CORDON BLEU

MAKES: 2 SERVINGS   **DIFFICULTY:** ★ ★

This wedding favourite is equally suited to a casual Saturday night dinner with your significant other.

2	2	4 oz (113 g) skinless, boneless chicken breasts
2	2	slices Swiss cheese
2	2	thin slices cooked ham
1 Tbsp	15 mL	all-purpose flour
1/4 tsp	1 mL	paprika
2 Tbsp	30 mL	butter
3 Tbsp	45 mL	dry white wine
1/4 tsp	1 mL	chicken bouillon
1 tsp	5 mL	cornstarch
1/3 cup	75 mL	whipping cream

Cut chicken breasts in half lengthwise, almost all the way through, but leaving enough intact so that it can open. Place a slice of cheese and a slice of ham on bottom half of each breast within 1/2 inch (12 mm) of edge. Cover with top half of breast and secure with toothpicks.

Combine flour and paprika in a small bowl, and coat chicken.

Heat butter in a large skillet over medium-high, and cook chicken until browned on all sides. Add wine and bouillon. Reduce heat to low, cover, and simmer for 30 minutes, until chicken is no longer pink and juices run clear.

Remove toothpicks and transfer chicken to a warm platter. Combine cornstarch and cream in a small bowl, and slowly whisk into skillet. Cook, stirring with whisk, until thickened. Pour over chicken and serve.

1 serving: 560 Calories; 28 g Total Fat (6 g Mono, 1.5 g Poly, 16 g Sat); 230 mg Cholesterol; 6 g Carbohydrates (0 g Fibre, 0 g Sugar); 65 g Protein; 520 mg Sodium

PEANUT BUTTER ASIAN CHICKEN

MAKES: 4 SERVINGS   **DIFFICULTY:** ★

This Asian twist on chicken is absolutely amazing and will leave your dinner date gasping at the culinary delight you have so professionally prepared. Serve over hot, cooked white rice.

2 Tbsp	30 mL	cooking oil
1 lb	454 g	skinless, boneless chicken breast halves, cut into 1 inch (2.5 cm) cubes
1	1	medium onion, sliced
7	7	mushrooms, sliced
1/8 tsp	0.5 mL	red pepper flakes
		salt and pepper to taste
1	1	14 oz (398 mL) can of diced tomatoes with juice
3/4 cup	175 mL	chicken stock
3/4 cup	175 mL	smooth peanut butter

Heat oil in a large skillet over medium heat. Add chicken and cook until it starts to turn white. Add onion, mushrooms and red pepper flakes and season with salt and pepper. Cook for about 5 minutes, stirring constantly, until onions are translucent.

Pour tomatoes and chicken stock into skillet and simmer for about 10 minutes, or until chicken is cooked through.

Stir in peanut butter and cook, stirring constantly, for 1 to 2 minutes until sauce thickens. Remove from heat and serve.

1 serving: 510 Calories; 34 g Total Fat (4.5 g Mono, 2 g Poly, 6 g Sat); 65 mg Cholesterol; 19 g Carbohydrates (5 g Fibre, 9 g Sugar); 39 g Protein; 710 mg Sodium

I may not be healthy or wealthy or wise; I may
not have dreamy, mysterious eyes; I may not
wear clothes from a French fashion book; But
I'm never lonely, for boy, I can cook!

—Anonymous

SALT AND PEPPER SHRIMP

MAKES: 2 SERVINGS   **DIFFICULTY: ★**

Prepare this meal on your first date and you'll likely have a second dinner date request just around the corner. This dish can be served on a bed of rice as an entree or alone as an appetizer.

1/2 Tbsp	7 mL	kosher salt
1/2 Tbsp	7 mL	freshly ground pepper
1 Tbsp	15 mL	cooking oil
2	2	large cloves garlic, finely chopped
1 tsp	5 mL	ground ginger
1	1	bunch green onions, chopped
1 lb	454 g	medium shrimp (shell on and deveined)

In a small bowl, combine salt and pepper and set aside.

Heat oil in large skillet on high and add garlic, ginger, green onion and shrimp. Cook until shrimp are no longer opaque, about 3 to 4 minutes. Stir in salt and pepper mixture and serve.

1 serving: 330 Calories; 11 g Total Fat; 4.5 g Mono, 3.5 g Poly, 1.5 g Sat); 345 mg Cholesterol; 8 g Carbohydrates (2 g Fibre, 1 g Sugar); 47 g Protein; 880 mg Sodium

Cooking is like love. It should be entered into with abandon or not at all.

—Harriet Van Horn

EVERY GUY NEEDS A
SECRET
SAUCE

Ssshhhhh. It's a secret.

Sauces and marinades are two of our favourite culinary compliments. There are several thousand sauce recipes from around the world. You don't need all of them. You just need a few tips to make a sauce your own. Learn one, two or three and then name them. It's kind of like having a dog. If you name it, it has to be your dog. Same with a sauce. Then it also becomes a secret sauce.

CHEESY CREAM SAUCE

MAKES: 1 1/4 CUPS (300 ML)   **DIFFICULTY: ★**

It seems topping any vegetable off with this sauce will get even the most reluctant vegetable eater to dig in. It puts broccoli, cauliflower and carrots in a whole new light.

2 Tbsp	30 mL	butter
2 Tbsp	30 mL	all-purpose flour
1 cup	250 mL	milk
2	2	processed cheese slices
1/8 tsp	0.5 mL	salt

Melt butter in a small saucepan over medium heat. Add flour and whisk into a paste. Pour milk, a little at a time, into butter mixture and continue to whisk.

Add cheese slices and whisk until cheese has melted and mixture has thickened, about 3 minutes.

Season with salt and serve over your favourite boiled or steamed vegetables.

1/4 cup (60 mL): 110 Calories; 9 g Total Fat (2 g Mono, 0 g Poly, 5 g Sat); 25 mg Cholesterol; 4 g Carbohydrates (0 g Fibre, 3 g Sugar); 5 g Protein; 125 mg Sodium

TOMATO SAUCE

MAKES: 10 CUPS (2.5 L)   **DIFFICULTY: ★**

Why rely on store-bought tomato sauce when it is so easy to make at home? A simple but tasty homemade tomato sauce recipe is a must-have for everyone's culinary tool box.

1/4 cup	60 mL	olive oil
1	1	onion, finely diced
1 cup	250 mL	red wine
6	6	cloves garlic
2	2	28 oz (796 mL) cans of whole tomatoes
1 cup	250 mL	chicken stock
1 Tbsp	15 mL	dried oregano
1/4 tsp	1 mL	crushed red chili flakes
		sprinkle of granulated sugar
		salt and pepper to taste
		chopped basil to taste

Gently heat oil over medium-low heat. Add onion and cook until softened. Add red wine to deglaze pan, then add garlic and reduce by half.

Meanwhile, drain tomatoes, reserving liquid. Remove seeds from tomatoes, and roughly chop flesh. Add tomatoes, reserved juice, chicken stock, oregano, red chili flakes, salt, pepper and pinch of sugar to pan.

Simmer sauce gently for 1 hour or until it reaches your desired consistency. Add basil and serve.

1 cup (250 mL): 70 Calories; 0 g Total Fat (0 g Mono, 0 g Poly, 0 g Sat); 0 mg Cholesterol; 9 g Carbohydrates (2 g Fibre, 5 g Sugar); 2 g Protein; 490 mg Sodium

Pictured on page 90.

Adding a pinch of sugar to tomatoes helps mellow their acidity and eliminate any bitterness they may add to the dish.

SPEEDY ALFREDO SAUCE

MAKES: 4 CUPS (1 L)
DIFFICULTY: ★

If ever there was a competition to determine what pasta sauce ranks first for men, the prize would surely go to the delicious and versatile Alfredo sauce. Most men cannot get enough of its creamy goodness.

1 cup	250 mL	butter, softened
1 1/2 cups	375 mL	grated Parmesan cheese
2 cups	500 mL	whole cream (30%)

In a medium bowl, beat butter and Parmesan with an electric mixer until fluffy.

Slowly add cream, mixing until sauce is consistency of thick cream. Serve over hot pasta.

1/2 cup (125 mL): 390 Calories; 39 g Total Fat (11 g Mono, 1.5 g Poly, 25 g Sat); 120 mg Cholesterol; 2 g Carbohydrates (0 g Fibre, 0 g Sugar); 8 g Protein; 460 mg Sodium

CLASSIC PESTO

MAKES: ABOUT 1 CUP (250 ML)
DIFFICULTY: ★

Infinite possibilities in a sauce that packs some serious flavour punch. This pesto tastes great on gnocchi or other noodles, but you can also use it on mashed potatoes, steamed vegetables, grilled meats or really any dish that needs a little flavour boost.

2 cups	500 mL	fresh basil leaves, packed
1/4 cup	60 mL	olive oil
1/4 cup	60 mL	pine nuts, toasted
3	3	cloves garlic
1/4 tsp	1 mL	salt
1/2 cup	125 mL	grated Parmesan cheese

Process first 5 ingredients in a blender until smooth. Transfer to a small bowl.

Stir in cheese. Store in fridge in an airtight container for up to 3 days.

2 Tbsp (30 mL): 120 Calories; 11 g Total Fat (6 g Mono, 2.5 g Poly, 2 g Sat); 5 mg Cholesterol; 2 g Carbohydrates (trace Fibre, 0 g Sugar); 3 g Protein; 170 mg Sodium

Pictured on page 90.

REMOULADE SAUCE

MAKES: 3 CUPS (750 ML)   **DIFFICULTY: ★**

This sauce pairs well with any fish or seafood dish, but don't stop there! Try it with fries, on hot dogs, with meatballs, as a sandwich topping, basically anywhere you want a touch of something creamy.

2 cups	500 mL	mayonnaise
1/4 cup	60 mL	finely diced onion
2 Tbsp	30 mL	grainy mustard
2 Tbsp	30 mL	chopped fresh parsley
2 Tbsp	30 mL	hot sauce
1/4 cup	60 mL	chopped gherkins
1 Tbsp	15 mL	roughly chopped capers
1 Tbsp	15 mL	lemon juice
		salt and pepper to taste

Combine all ingredients in a blender and store in airtight container in fridge for 3 to 5 days.

1/4 cup (60 mL): 270 Calories; 27 g Total Fat (16 g Mono, 8 g Poly, 2.5 g Sat); 15 mg Cholesterol; 1 g Carbohydrates (0 g Fibre, 0 g Sugar); 0 g Protein; 320 mg Sodium

A good upbringing means not that you won't spill sauce on the tablecloth, but that you won't notice it when someone else does.

—Anton Chekhov

PEPPERCORN SAUCE WITH RED WINE REDUCTION

MAKES: 1/3 CUPS (75 ML)   **DIFFICULTY: ★ ★**

Every guy should have a nice peppercorn sauce for his favourite cut of beef. This one is especially good on thick sirloin, but can be poured on any cut of beef.

1 Tbsp	15 mL	butter
4	4	mushrooms, sliced
1	1	clove garlic, minced
2 Tbsp	30 mL	whole peppercorns
1/4 cup	60 mL	red wine
1 Tbsp	15 mL	balsamic vinegar
3 Tbsp	45 mL	Worcestershire sauce

Melt butter in a medium saucepan over medium-low heat. Stir in mushrooms, garlic and peppercorns and heat until mushrooms become soft.

Add wine, vinegar and Worcestershire sauce. Increase heat to medium and cook until thickened. Stir regularly and cook until sauce has reduce by a third.

2 Tbsp (30 mL): 60 Calories; 3 g Total Fat (1 g Mono, 0 g Poly, 2 g Sat); 10 mg Cholesterol; 4 g Carbohydrates (0 g Fibre, 3 g Sugar); trace Protein; 4 mg Sodium

Pictured on page 90.

CREAMY BÉARNAISE SAUCE

MAKES: 3/4 CUP (175 ML)   **DIFFICULTY: ★ ★**

A nice, creamy Béarnaise herb sauce is the ultimate sauce to pour over a thick, freshly grilled steak, and if some should spill over onto the vegetables, don't worry— it goes great with them, too.

1/4 cup	60 mL	butter, melted
1 tsp	5 mL	minced onion
1 Tbsp	15 mL	white wine vinegar
2	2	egg yolks, beaten
2 Tbsp	30 mL	whole cream (30%)
1 tsp	5 mL	lemon juice
1 tsp	5 mL	chopped fresh parsley (or tarragon, or a combination)
1/4 tsp	1 mL	salt
1/4 tsp	1 mL	dry mustard

Pour melted butter into a medium, microwave-safe bowl and stir in onion, white wine vinegar, egg yolks, cream and lemon juice.

Season with parsley, salt and dry mustard. Place bowl in microwave and cook until thickened and smooth, 1 to 2 minutes, stirring every 30 seconds. When sauce is thick and consistent throughout, transfer to a gravy boat and serve.

3 Tbsp (45 mL): 140 Calories; 15 g Total Fat (4.5 g Mono, 1 g Poly, 9 g Sat); 140 mg Cholesterol; trace Carbohydrates (0 g Fibre, 0 g Sugar); 2 g Protein; 230 mg Sodium

It's pretty easy to cook pasta, but a good sauce is way more useful.

—Emeril Lagasse

PRIVATE RESERVE BARBECUE SAUCE

MAKES: 1 1/2 CUPS (375 ML)
DIFFICULTY: ★

Every guy needs a quick and dirty recipe for barbecue sauce, one he can call his own private reserve. If you have a barbecue sauce recipe at your fingertips, you can dip anything in it, from chicken fingers to grilled shrimp.

1/4 cup	60 mL	cider vinegar
1/2 cup	125 mL	water
1/2 cup	125 mL	ketchup
3 Tbsp	45 mL	granulated sugar
1 tsp	5 mL	salt
1 tsp	5 mL	chili powder

Combine all ingredients in a small bowl. Mix well and store in fridge for up to 1 month.

1/2 cup (125 mL): 45 Calories; 0 g Total Fat (0 g Mono, 0 g Poly, 0 g Sat); 0 mg Cholesterol; 11 g Carbohydrates (0 g Fibre, 10 g Sugar); 0 g Protein; 630 mg Sodium

Pictured on page 90.

STEAK DRY RUB MIXTURE

MAKES: 3 TBSP (45 ML)
DIFFICULTY: ★ ★

This sweet and savoury rub, which will have your taste buns running a marathon, serves as a great seasoning for a variety of beef dishes. Double or triple the recipe and store in an airtight container to always have a little on hand.

1 Tbsp	15 mL	paprika
1 tsp	5 mL	chili powder
1 tsp	5 mL	dried sage
1 tsp	5 mL	sea salt
1/2 tsp	2 mL	brown sugar

Combine all ingredients in a small bowl. Rub on all surfaces of your steak before grilling.

2 Tbsp (10 mL): 10 Calories; 0 g Total Fat (0 g Mono, 0 g Poly, 0 g Sat); 0 mg Cholesterol; 2 g Carbohydrates (trace Fibre, trace Sugar); 0 g Protein; 540 mg Sodium

BEER MARINADE FOR STEAKS

MAKES: 2 1/4 CUPS (550 ML)   **DIFFICULTY: ★**

This marinade goes great with many cuts of beef but really steps to the forefront when used on sirloin, strip loin or T-bone. You can also use it with wild game meats such as moose and deer.

1	1	12 oz (341 mL) bottle of beer
6 oz	170 mL	Worcestershire sauce
1 tsp	5 mL	minced garlic
1 tsp	5 mL	minced onion
2 Tbsp	30 mL	Montreal steak seasoning

Mix first 4 ingredients in a large resealable freezer bag. When you are ready to marinate your steak, add meat to bag and marinate in fridge for 2 to 24 hours (the longer it marinates, the better.)

Sprinkle steak with Montreal steak seasoning and cook as usual.

1/3 cup (75 mL): 50 Calories; 0 g Total Fat (0 g Mono, 0 g Poly, 0 g Sat); 0 mg Cholesterol; 8 g Carbohydrates (0 g Fibre, 7 g Sugar); 0 g Protein; 1030 mg Sodium

Helpful Tips

Marinades are a necessary evil when it comes to grilling. These concoctions are, of course, not possessed by the devil, yet some old-school diehards would have nothing to do with them. When it comes to grilling, marinades add much-needed moisture and juiciness to many types of meat. Some marinades also break down proteins in some meat. When choosing a good marinade, think of ingredients to complement the dish you are preparing. Marinades are meant to be acidic, which benefits meat in several ways. The acidity usually comes from vinegar, wine or citric juices, which all serve as a good marinade base. The amount of time your meat should marinate is usually dictated by its thickness and density. Thicker more dense red meat like beef will require longer resting periods, while chicken and seafood generally doesn't require more than an hour or so.

WHISKY MARINADE

MAKES: 1 1/4 CUPS (300 ML)
DIFFICULTY: ★

For a bolder, more full-bodied taste, try using a traditional single malt scotch instead of Canadian whisky, or mix half and half.

1/4 cup	60 mL	Canadian whisky (rye)
1/4 cup	60 mL	soy sauce
1/4 cup	60 mL	Dijon mustard
1/4 cup	60 mL	brown sugar
1 tsp	5 mL	salt
1/8 tsp	0.5 mL	Worcestershire sauce
1/4 cup	1 mL	finely chopped green onion or shallot
1/2 tsp	2 mL	pepper

Combine all 8 ingredients in a resealable freezer bag. Marinade chicken, pork or beef overnight in fridge.

1/4 cup (60 mL): 90 Calories; 0 g Total Fat (0 g Mono, 0 g Poly, 0 g Sat); 0 mg Cholesterol; 14 g Carbohydrates (0 g Fibre, 11 g Sugar); 2 g Protein; 1380 mg Sodium

BEEF OR PORK MARINADE

MAKES: 2 1/2 CUPS (625 ML)
DIFFICULTY: ★

Use this marinade with beef or pork. Whether you're grilling a nice pork tenderloin or beef kabobs, this special concoction will make any meat juicier.

1 1/2 cups	375 mL	cooking oil
3/4 cup	175 mL	soy sauce
1/2 cup	125 mL	white wine vinegar
1/3 cup	75 mL	lemon juice
1/4 cup	60 mL	Worcestershire sauce
2 Tbsp	30 mL	ground dry mustard
2 tsp	10 mL	salt
1 Tbsp	15 mL	pepper
1 1/2 Tbsp	22 mL	chopped fresh parsley

Combine oil, soy sauce, vinegar, lemon juice and Worcestershire sauce in a medium bowl. Whisk until well blended.

Add mustard, salt, pepper and parsley and whisk until smooth. Pour marinade into a resealable freezer bag and add meat. Marinate in fridge overnight.

2 Tbsp (30 mL): 160 Calories; 16 g Total Fat (10 g Mono, 4.5 g Poly, 1.5 g Sat); 0 mg Cholesterol; 1 g Carbohydrates (0 g Fibre, trace Sugar); 1 g Protein; 830 mg Sodium

JALAPEÑO SAUCE

MAKES: 2 CUPS (500 ML)
DIFFICULTY: ★

If you like hot and spicy, this sauce is for you. You can plunge everything from mozzarella sticks to zucchini in this wonderful hot sauce. Warning – keep your hands away from your eyes after handling those jalapeño peppers –they can make a man cry!

1/2 tsp	2 mL	cooking oil
10	10	fresh jalapeño peppers, sliced
1	1	clove garlic, minced
1/4 cup	60 mL	finely diced onion
1/2 tsp	2 mL	salt
1 cup	250 mL	water
1/2 cup	125 mL	white vinegar

In a medium saucepan over medium-high heat, combine oil, peppers, garlic, onion and salt. Cook for 3 or 4 minutes.

Add water and cook for 20 minutes, stirring often. Remove from heat and allow mixture to cool to room temperature.

Transfer mixture to a food processor and purée until smooth. Add vinegar and blend for 1 minute. Pour mixture into a bottle and refrigerate for up to 1 week.

1/2 cup (125 mL): 10 Calories; 0 g Total Fat (0 g Mono, 0 g Poly, 0 g Sat); 0 mg Cholesterol; 2 g Carbohydrates (trace Fibre, trace Sugar); 0 g Protein; 150 mg Sodium

CHINESE-STYLE MUSTARD

MAKES: 2/3 CUP (150 ML)
DIFFICULTY: ★

Use this mustard with anything you'd normally put mustard on. Especially good in sandwiches.

1/4 cup	60 mL	granulated sugar
2 Tbsp	30 mL	dry mustard
1/4 cup	60 mL	red wine vinegar
1	1	egg yolk
6 Tbsp	90 mL	sour cream

In a medium bowl whisk together sugar, dry mustard and vinegar. Whisk well to ensure there are no lumps.

Add egg yolk and cook over simmering water until thick ribbons form, about 10 minutes.

Chill, then fold in sour cream. Keep refrigerated for up to 2 weeks.

1 Tbsp (15 mL): 45 Calories; 2.5 g Total Fat (0.5 g Mono, 0 g Poly, 1 g Sat); 25 mg Cholesterol; 5 g Carbohydrates (0 g Fibre, 4 g Sugar); trace Protein; 5 mg Sodium

Tomato, Asparagus and Egg Sandwiches, page 112

Ultimate Breakfast Sandwich, page 111

CRÈME FRAÎCHE

MAKES: 2 CUPS (500 ML)
DIFFICULTY: ★

Rich, creamy and slightly tangy, crème fraîche makes an excellent dip or topping for fresh fruit, or use it to make decadent desserts, like tarts or crepes. Or add a little horseradish or mustard, and it can be stirred into sauces, too.

1 cup	250 mL	buttermilk
1 cup	250 mL	whipping cream

Combine buttermilk and cream in a jar with a tight-fitting lid and leave in a warm spot for 24 hours. Refrigerate for up to 2 weeks.

1/4 cup (60 mL): 100 Calories; 10 g Total Fat (3 g Mono, 0 g Poly, 6 g Sat); 40 mg Cholesterol; 2 g Carbohydrates (0 g Fibre, 0 g Sugar); trace Protein; 35 mg Sodium

HOT FUDGE SAUCE

MAKES: 1 3/4 CUPS (425 ML)
DIFFICULTY: ★

Warm and gooey, this sauce can be used to top any number of decadent treats— ice cream, brownies...or just eat it with a spoon.

1	1	11 oz (300 mL) can of condensed milk
12 oz	340 g	chocolate
2 tsp	10 mL	vanilla extract
1/2 cup	125 mL	half-and-half cream

Melt ingredients over low, stirring until well combined. If sauce is too thick, add a little extra cream. Chill. To serve, reheat until warm and pour over ice cream.

3 Tbsp (45 mL): 300 Calories; 14 g Total Fat (5 g Mono, 0 g Poly, 7 g Sat); 25 mg Cholesterol; 38 g Carbohydrates (1 g Fibre, 35 g Sugar); 5 g Protein; 80 mg Sodium

BREAKFAST SPECIALS

Real men eat egg pies. Some might call it quiche, frittata or even tortilla. But breakfast is a great place to shine and gain lots of points that could be used as bartering points against all your multitude of sins from the night before (and don't forget the possibilities of breakfast in bed). You can impress your girlfriend, wife, children, in-laws, hung-over guests—even your sister, the one who makes bacon onion marmalade!—with these versatile selections from what's left in the fridge. Eggs. Stale baguette. Sausage. Two kinds of mustard. Bacon onion marmalade. Thanks, Sis.

ULTIMATE BREAKFAST SANDWICH

MAKES: 4 SANDWICHES   **DIFFICULTY:** ★

This hearty dish uses the warm yolk of a soft poached egg to sauce the sandwich. A freshly made sandwich can be a healthier, more nutritious alternative to your typical fast food breakfast. It may seem like a big job, but if you are organized, this sandwich can be easily be made in 15 minutes.

2 cups	500 mL	water
1 Tbsp	15 mL	vinegar
4	4	large eggs
4	4	bacon strips
1 Tbsp	15 mL	butter
1	1	Yukon Gold potato, shredded into cold water
1/4 tsp	1 mL	dried oregano
1/4 tsp	1 mL	salt
1/4 tsp	1 mL	pepper
2 oz	57 g	grated Cheddar cheese
1/2 tsp	2 mL	paprika
4	4	English muffins
2 Tbsp	30 mL	ketchup
1	1	head butter leaf lettuce

Add water and vinegar to a shallow pot and set on high heat to boil. Once pot of water has reached a boil, lower heat to just below a simmer. Gently crack eggs into water one at time and cook until white is firm but yolk is still soft, about 4 to 5 minutes.

Heat a medium pan over medium. Cook bacon until crispy. Transfer cooked strips to paper towel and set aside.

Pour out remaining bacon fat and return pan to high heat. Add butter. Drain potatoes and add to hot pan, tossing continuously as they brown. Once potatoes begin to crisp, season with oregano, salt and pepper. Lower heat to medium-high and cover with cheese. Remove from heat and sprinkle with paprika. Allow to rest for 2 minutes so cheese can melt.

Lightly toast English muffins. Do not add butter. Layer sandwich in following sequence: 1/2 English muffin, ketchup, lettuce, potatoes, egg, bacon, 1/2 English muffin

Give sandwich a quick little punch down to crack egg yolk, and serve.

1 serving: 520 Calories; 31 g Total Fat (10 g Mono, 3 g Poly, 13 g Sat); 260 mg Cholesterol; 434 g Carbohydrates (5 g Fibre, 6 g Sugar); 19 g Protein; 1230 mg Sodium

Pictured on page 108.

TOMATO, ASPARAGUS AND EGG SANDWICHES

MAKES: 2 SANDWICHES   **DIFFICULTY: ★**

Asparagus, tomato pesto and prosciutto transform the popular breakfast sandwich into something divine! To save time in the morning, you could prepare the asparagus, eggs and prosciutto the night before, then toast the bread and assemble the sandwich before you head out the door.

14	14	asparagus spears
2 Tbsp	30 mL	sundried tomato pesto
1 tsp	5 mL	lime juice
1 Tbsp	15 mL	cooking oil
2	2	large eggs
1/4 tsp	1 mL	black pepper
4	4	prosciutto slices
4	4	whole wheat bread slices
2 Tbsp	30 mL	light mayonnaise

In a shallow pan bring water to a boil. Add asparagus and cook for 4 minutes. Drain and finely chop. In bowl, combine pesto, lime juice and asparagus. Set aside.

Heat oil in a medium frying pan over medium. Add eggs and cook over easy to desired doneness. Sprinkle with pepper. Remove to plate. Add prosciutto to same frying pan and cook until crisp.

Toast bread slices. To assemble, spread tomato mixture on 2 bread slices and mayonnaise on other 2 slices. Layer asparagus, prosciutto and eggs on tomato mixture and top with remaining bread slices.

1 sandwich: 460 Calories; 28 g Total Fat (8 g Mono, 6 g Poly, 6 g Sat); 24 mg Cholesterol; 34 g Carbohydrates (7 g Fibre, 7 g Sugar); 24 g Protein; 1102 mg Sodium

Pictured on page 107.

EGG AND SAUSAGE CUPCAKE

MAKES: 12 CUPCAKES   **DIFFICULTY:** ★

This non-traditional method of cooking two complementary foods will be sure to get people talking. You don't need a knife and fork for this breakfast. Besides that, they are just plain delicious! Feel free to play around with the ingredients, subbing bacon for the sausage and adding in your favourite veggies.

12	12	**breakfast sausage patties**
1	1	**onion, finely chopped**
8	8	**large eggs**
1/2 cup	125 mL	**half-and-half cream**
1 cup	250 mL	**Cheddar cheese**
1/4 tsp	1 mL	**salt**
1/4 tsp	1 mL	**pepper**

Line a 12 cup muffin pan with cupcake liners. In a medium skillet, cook sausage patties according to package directions. Place one cooked patty into each muffin cup.

In same skillet, cook onion for 5 minutes or until soft.

In a separate bowl, mix eggs, cream, cheese, salt and pepper. Stir in onion and divide mixture evenly into prepared muffin cups. Bake in a 350°F (175°C) oven for 30 minutes or until egg has set.

1 cupcake: 130 Calories; 9 g Total Fat (2.5 g Mono, 0.5 g Poly, 4 g Sat); 165 mg Cholesterol; 3 g Carbohydrates (0 g Fibre, 1 g Sugar); 10 g Protein; 320 mg Sodium

> I have a carpe diem mug and, truthfully, at six in the morning the words do not make me want to seize the day. They make me want to slap a dead poet.
>
> —Joanne Sherman

TASTY BREAKFAST BURRITOS

MAKES: 8 BURRITOS   **DIFFICULTY: ★**

Perfect for breakfast on the go. It sure beats stopping by the fast-food window.

8	8	flour tortillas (12 inch, 30 cm, diameter)
8	8	large eggs
1	1	16 oz (454 g) can of baked beans
1 lb	454 g	bacon, cooked but not crispy
8 oz	225 g	shredded Cheddar cheese

Wrap tortilla shells in foil and place on a cookie sheet in a 250°F (120°C) oven until warm.

Crack eggs into a medium bowl and whisk until well blended. Pour into a medium skillet and fry until eggs are cooked and fluffy. Remove from heat and set aside.

Heat beans in a separate medium skillet until hot and sticky. Remove from heat and set aside.

Remove tortillas from oven and add 2 strips of bacon. Divide beans and egg among tortillas and sprinkle with cheese. Roll tortillas into a burrito shape and serve.

1 burrito: 710 Calories; 45 g Total Fat (16 g Mono, 4 g Poly, 17 g Sat); 280 mg Cholesterol; 45 g Carbohydrates (7 g Fibre, 3 g Sugar); 29 g Protein; 1400 mg Sodium

One should not attend even the end of the world without a good breakfast.

—Robert A. Heinlein

COUNTRY-STYLE BREAKFAST CASSEROLE

MAKES: 4 SERVINGS   **DIFFICULTY: ★**

If you're looking for something hearty first thing in the morning, this dish is for you. Feel free to substitute bacon or sausage for the ham.

1/4 cup	60 mL	butter, melted
1/2 cup	125 mL	croutons
1/2 cup	125 mL	shredded Cheddar cheese
4	4	large eggs
3/4 cup	175 mL	milk
1 tsp	5 mL	dry mustard
1 cup	250 mL	cubed cooked ham

Place butter in an 8 x 8 inch (20 x 20 cm) glass baking dish or small casserole dish.

Add croutons and toss to coat. Sprinkle cheese over croutons.

In a large bowl, beat together eggs, milk and dry mustard. Pour mixture over croutons and cheese. Sprinkle cubed ham over top. Bake, uncovered, in a 350°F (175°C) oven for 40 minutes, until eggs are set and top is golden brown. Let stand for 5 minutes before serving.

1 serving: 330 Calories; 25 g Total Fat (8 g Mono, 2 g Poly, 13 g Sat); 280 mg Cholesterol; 6 g Carbohydrates (0 g Fibre, 3 g Sugar); 20 g Protein; 820 mg Sodium

ASPARAGUS OMELETTE

MAKES: 1 OMELETTE   **DIFFICULTY: ★ ★**

The appealing omelette is bursting with asparagus, roasted red peppers, ham and cheese. Hearty and delicious. We've used Swiss cheese, but feel free to switch it up with whatever cheese you like best.

1/3 cup	75 mL	fresh asparagus, trimmed of tough ends and cut into 1 inch (2.5 cm) pieces
1 tsp	5 mL	butter
1	1	clove garlic, minced
3 Tbsp	45 mL	thin strips of Black Forest ham (about 1 oz, 28 g)
2 Tbsp	30 mL	roasted red peppers, drained, blotted dry and cut into thin strips
3/4 tsp	4 mL	chopped fresh parsley
1 tsp	5 mL	lemon juice
		pepper to taste
3	3	large eggs
1/4 tsp	1 mL	salt
1 tsp	5 mL	cooking oil
1/3 cup	75 mL	grated Swiss cheese

Cook asparagus in water in a small saucepan for 3 to 5 minutes until bright green and tender-crisp. Drain, then quickly cool asparagus under cold running water. Drain well and transfer to a small bowl. Set aside.

Melt butter in same saucepan on medium-low. Add garlic and cook for about 1 minute, stirring often, until fragrant.

Stir in next 5 ingredients. Add asparagus and cook, stirring, until heated though, about 2 minutes. Cover to keep warm.

Beat eggs and salt with whisk in a small bowl until smooth.

Heat oil in a small non-stick frying pan on medium. Pour egg mixture into frying pan and cook, stirring gently, for about 1 minute, until starting to set. Spread evenly in pan and cook for about 1 minute, until bottom starts to turn golden. Reduce heat to medium-low. Scatter asparagus mixture over half of omelette. Sprinkle cheese over asparagus, then fold other half of omelette over filling. Cover and cook for about 2 minutes until cheese is melted.

1 serving: 310 Calories; 19 g Total Fat (5 g Mono, 1.5 g Poly, 9 g Sat); 60 mg Cholesterol; 8 g Carbohydrates (1 g Fibre, 4 g Sugar); 27 g Protein; 1030 mg Sodium

MEXICAN FRITTATA

MAKES: 8 WEDGES   **DIFFICULTY: ★**

A versatile dish perfect for any time of day. Cut into smaller wedges if you want to serve it as an appetizer.

2	2	whole medium potatoes, peeled
3/4 tsp	4 mL	salt, *divided*
2 Tbsp	30 mL	olive oil
2	2	cloves garlic, halved
5	5	large eggs
1 Tbsp	15 mL	chopped fresh chives
1/4 tsp	1 mL	pepper
1/4 cup	60 mL	salsa
1/4 cup	60 mL	finely grated medium Cheddar cheese

Cook potatoes in water and 1/2 tsp (2 mL) salt and in medium saucepan until tender but firm. Drain and set aside to cool. Cut into thin slices.

Heat oil in medium frying pan on medium. Add garlic and cook for 2 to 3 minutes until fragrant. Remove and discard garlic. Layer potato slices in pan. Reduce heat to low.

In a medium bowl, whisk next 3 ingredients and remaining 1/4 tsp (1 mL) salt until well combined. Pour over potato slices. Cover and cook for 20 to 25 minutes until egg is set. Remove from heat.

Spread salsa over top of frittata, then sprinkle with cheese. Place frying pan on top rack in over and broil for 1 to 2 minutes until cheese is melted. Remove from oven. Let stand for 10 minutes before cutting into wedges and serving.

1 serving: 90 Calories; 4.5 g Total Fat (3 g Mono, 0 g Poly, 1 g Sat); trace Cholesterol; 9 g Carbohydrates (trace Fibre, 1 g Sugar); 4 g Protein; 230 mg Sodium

SMOKED SALMON EGGS BENEDICT

MAKES: 2 SERVINGS   **DIFFICULTY: ★ ★ ★**

Smoked salmon elevates a breakfast classic, taking it to a whole new level. This recipe is a bit of work, so it's best left to a relaxed weekend morning rather than a busy workday. So good even the biggest sluggard will be drawn out of their warm, comfortable bed.

1 cup	250 mL	butter, unsalted
3	3	egg yolks
1 1/2 tsp	7 mL	white wine vinegar
1 Tbsp	15 mL	lemon juice
1/2 tsp	2 mL	hot sauce
1/2 tsp	2 mL	salt
1/4 tsp	1 mL	pepper
4 cups	2 L	water
1 Tbsp	15 mL	white vinegar
4	4	eggs
2	2	English muffins
1 Tbsp	15 mL	butter
6 oz	170 g	smoked salmon
2 Tbsp	30 mL	chives, chopped

For the Hollandaise sauce, melt butter in a small sauce pan until bubbling. Set aside, keeping warm. In top of a double boiler combine egg yolks, vinegar and lemon juice. Set top pan over, but not touching, barely simmering water. Whisk yolk mixture constantly until light and fluffy, about 4 minutes. Remove top from heat and continue to whisk until slightly cool, about 1 minute. Gradually pour butter into yolk mixture, whisking continuously until all butter is absorbed. Whisk in hot sauce, salt and pepper. Cover pan and set aside. The sauce can be kept warm for up to 30 minutes by replacing pan over hot, but not simmering, water in bottom of double boiler, away from heat.

Bring water to a gentle simmer in a small sauce pan. Add vinegar. Break 1 egg into a small bowl and gently slide it into simmering water, just below surface. Repeat with remaining eggs. Let them cook in for 3 minutes for a runny yolk and 5 for a set yolk. Remove with a slotted spoon.

While eggs are cooking, toast English muffins and spread muffins with butter. Divide smoked salmon onto each half and top with a poached egg. Spoon 1 Tbsp (15 mL) Hollandaise sauce over each egg, and sprinkle with chives.

1 serving: 560 Calories; 37 g Total Fat (10 g Mono, 2.5 g Poly, 21 g Sat); 185 mg Cholesterol; 26 g Carbohydrates (1 g Fibre, 2 g Sugar); 29 g Protein; 1290 mg Sodium

WILD BLUEBERRY MAPLE PANCAKES

MAKES: 8 PANCAKES   **DIFFICULTY: ★**

Nothing says "comfort" like a stack of steaming pancakes, and if they are loaded with wild blueberries, all the better! Top with maple or blueberry syrup.

4 Tbsp	60 mL	maple syrup, *divided,* plus more for serving
2 cups	500 mL	wild blueberries, *divided*
1 cup	250 mL	flour
1 tsp	5 mL	baking powder
1/2 tsp	2 mL	baking soda
1 cup	250 mL	milk
1	1	egg, beaten
2 Tbsp	30 mL	melted butter

In a small pot, heat 2 Tbsp (30 mL) maple syrup until just warm. Add 1 cup (250 mL) blueberries to syrup and mash. Heat syrup and blueberries until mixture just starts to boil. Remove from heat and set aside.

In a medium bowl, combine flour, baking powder and baking soda and mix well.

In a separate bowl, combine milk, egg, butter, 2 Tbsp (30 mL) maple syrup and 1 cup (250 mL) blueberries. Pour wet batter into dry ingredients and mix well.

Preheat grill to medium. In a pan or greased skillet, pour about 1/4 cup (60 mL) batter. When deep holes or bubbles appear in pancake, flip over and cook other side. Repeat for each pancake.

2 pancakes: 190 Calories; 5 g Total Fat (1.5 g Mono, 0 g Poly, 3 g Sat); 45 mg Cholesterol; 32 g Carbohydrates (2 g Fibre, 14 g Sugar); 5 g Protein; 220 mg Sodium

Helpful Tips

Pancakes flip easily when they are made to match the size of your flipper.

HOME-STYLE FLAPJACKS

MAKES: 8 FLAPJACKS   **DIFFICULTY: ★**

Yes, it is simple to pull out a box of prepared pancake mix, but it is almost as easy to whip up a batch of homemade pancakes, and they taste much better.

3/4 cup	175 mL	milk
2 Tbsp	30 mL	vinegar
1 cup	250 mL	all-purpose flour
2 Tbsp	30 mL	granulated sugar
1 tsp	5 mL	baking powder
1/2 tsp	2 mL	baking soda
1/2 tsp	2 mL	salt
1	1	large egg
2 Tbsp	30 mL	butter, melted

Combine milk with vinegar in a medium bowl and set aside for 5 minutes.

In a large bowl, combine flour, sugar, baking powder, baking soda and salt, and mix well.

Whisk egg and butter into milk. Pour flour mixture into wet ingredients and whisk until lumps are gone. Heat a large skillet over medium heat, and coat with cooking spray. Pour 1/4 cup (60 mL) batter onto skillet and cook until bubbles appear on surface. Flip with a spatula, and cook until browned on other side. Top with maple syrup or fruit topping.

2 flapjacks: 230 Calories; 8 g Total Fat (2 g Mono, 0.5 g Poly, 4.5 g Sat); 70 mg Cholesterol; 33 g Carbohydrates (trace Fibre, 9 g Sugar); 8 g Protein; 610 mg Sodium

Helpful Tips

If you run out of maple syrup, try sprinkling brown sugar and a few drops of lemon juice on top of your pancakes. Simple but delicious.

QUEBEC-STYLE CREPES WITH CHOCOLATE FILLING

MAKES: 4 SERVINGS   **DIFFICULTY: ★ ★**

Make getting out of bed worth it with these delicious crepes. With their sinfully decadent chocolate filling, they taste more like dessert than breakfast. Of course, if you want to make your first meal of the day a little healthier, you could always skip the chocolate and substitute a fresh fruit or cream cheese filling. Serve with maple syrup or your choice of toppings.

1 cup	250 mL	all-purpose flour
2	2	large eggs
1/2 cup	125 mL	milk
1/2 cup	125 mL	water
1/4 tsp	1 mL	salt
2 Tbsp	30 mL	butter, melted
1/2 cup	125 mL	chocolate chips

In a large mixing bowl, whisk together flour and eggs. Add milk, water, salt and melted butter and beat until smooth. Spray a medium crepe pan or frying pan with cooking spray and preheat over medium-high. Pour or scoop batter onto griddle, using approximately 1/4 cup (60 mL) for each crepe. Tilt pan with a circular motion so batter coats surface evenly. Cook crepe for about 2 minutes, until bottom is light brown. Flip crepe and cook about 2 minutes more.

On cooked side, add about 15 chocolate chips in a line down centre of crepe. When the bottom is lightly browned, flip each side over to create your crepe shape.

1 serving: 360 Calories; 17 g Total Fat (2.5 g Mono, 0.5 g Poly, 10 g Sat); 120 mg Cholesterol; 46 g Carbohydrates (3 g Fibre, 18 g Sugar); 10 g Protein; 240 mg Sodium

CINNAMON FRENCH TOAST

MAKES: 8 FRENCH TOASTS   **DIFFICULTY:** ★

French toast is one of those creature comforts and always makes for a nice break-fast. It's also an efficient way to use your stale bread. Try switching white bread out for cinnamon raisin bread. Serve with maple syrup or your favourite fruit topping.

4	4	large eggs
2/3 cup	150 mL	milk
1 tsp	5 mL	ground cinnamon
1 tsp	5 mL	vanilla
8	8	slices bread
1 tsp	5 mL	butter

Beat eggs in a small bowl. Whisk in milk, cinnamon and vanilla.

Dip each slice of bread into egg mixture, allowing bread to soak up some of mixture.

Melt butter in a large skillet on medium-high. Add as many slices of bread as will fit in skillet at one time. Fry until brown on both sides, flipping bread when necessary.

1 serving: 340 Calories; 10 g Total Fat (3 g Mono, 3 g Poly, 3 g Sat); 215 mg Cholesterol; 45 g Carbohydrates (2 g Fibre, 3 g Sugar); 15 g Protein; 400 mg Sodium

> I went to a restaurant that serves breakfast at any time so I ordered French toast during the Renaissance.
>
> —Steven Wright

MEALS YOUR KIDS WILL ACTUALLY EAT

Kids are the fussiest eaters in the world. Some will separate out all the individual ingredients in a casserole and only eat the parts they like. Some cannot distinguish between broccoli and celery. Oh wait, some adults are like that too! So cook what you like and they'll like it too. Grilled cheese, BLT, sloppy joes, gooey mac 'n' cheese. Get them involved as well, and you might contribute to the next generation of foodies.

ROCKET RED BURGERS

MAKES: 12 MINI BURGERS   **DIFFICULTY: ★ ★**

No kid is going to resist these burgers.

1 3/4 lbs	790 g	extra lean ground beef
1/2 cup	125 mL	diced red onion
4	4	cloves garlic, finely diced
2	2	large eggs
1/2 cup	125 mL	bread crumbs
1/4 cup	60 mL	chopped Italian parsley
1/4 tsp	1 mL	salt
1/2 tsp	2 mL	pepper
1 Tbsp	15 mL	paprika
1 Tbsp	15 mL	low-sodium soy sauce
1/4 tsp	1 mL	chopped fresh thyme
1/2 cup	125 mL	roasted red pepper
1	1	clove garlic
1 tsp	5 mL	lemon juice
1/8 tsp	0.5 mL	chipotle chili powder
1/4 tsp	1 mL	paprika
1/2 cup	125 mL	light mayonnaise
1 Tbsp	15 mL	mustard
6 oz	170 g	mozzarella cheese, sliced into 12 pieces
2 cups	500 mL	arugula, lightly packed
3	3	Roma (plum) tomatoes, thinly sliced
1	1	red onion, halved vertically and thinly sliced
12	12	mini ciabatta buns

Mix first 11 ingredients together in a medium bowl then press into 3 oz (85 g) balls—slightly larger than the size of a golf ball. Allow to rest in fridge for 20 minutes.

Blend roasted red peppers and mix with next 6 ingredients. Set aside.

Preheat oven to 400°F (200°C). Flatten each burger with your palm until it is 3/4 inch (2 cm) thick and 3 inches (7.5 cm) in diameter. Cook for 10 minutes, then flip each burger and return to oven. Increase heat to 475°F (240°C) and cook for an additional 10 minutes. Remove from oven, place 1 slice of mozzarella over top and allow to rest for 5 minutes. Meanwhile, lightly toast ciabatta buns. Assemble burgers with sauce, tomato, arugula and onion, and serve.

1 serving (2 burgers): 560 Calories; 24 g Total Fat (8 g Mono, 5 g Poly, 9 g Sat); 185 mg Cholesterol; 41 g Carbohydrates (3 g Fibre, 5 g Sugar); 43 g Protein; 750 mg Sodium

Pictured on page 125.

Rocket Red Burgers, page 124

Creamy Artichoke Dip, page 204 • Stuffed Game Day Potato Skins, page 200
Pulled Pork Quesadillas, page 196

SIMPLE SLOPPY JOES

MAKES: 4 SLOPPY JOES   **DIFFICULTY:** ★

Every kid knows food tastes best when it's messy. This sloppy but hearty meal has been a family favourite for generations and appeals to children of all ages.

1 Tbsp	15 mL	olive oil
1	1	medium onion, chopped
1/2 cup	125 mL	chopped celery
1/2 cup	125 mL	chopped bell pepper
2	2	cloves garlic, minced
1 1/4 lb	560 g	ground beef
		salt to taste
1/2 cup	125 mL	ketchup
2 cups	500 mL	tomato sauce
1 Tbsp	15 mL	Worcestershire sauce
1 Tbsp	15 mL	red wine vinegar
2 Tbsp	30 mL	brown sugar
1/4 tsp	1 mL	pepper
		sprinkle of cayenne pepper
4	4	hamburger buns, split

In a large frying pan, heat olive oil and cook onion, celery and peppers until vegetables have softened and onions are translucent. Add garlic and cook for 30 more seconds. Remove from heat, transfer vegetables to a medium bowl and set aside.

Crumble ground beef into a pan and add salt. Cook on high heat until no longer pink inside. Drain off excess fat.

Combine beef and vegetables in pan. Add ketchup, tomato sauce, Worcestershire sauce, vinegar, brown sugar, pepper and cayenne. Stir to mix well.

Lower heat to medium-low and simmer for 10 minutes. Adjust seasonings to taste. Serve on hamburger buns.

1 serving: 560 Calories; 25 g Total Fat (12 g Mono, 2 g Poly, 9 g Sat); 85 mg Cholesterol; 40 g Carbohydrates (3 g Fibre, 17 g Sugar); 33 g Protein; 1460 mg Sodium

PORCUPINE BALLS

MAKES: 4 SERVINGS **DIFFICULTY:** ★

This prickly childhood favourite harkens back to a simpler time when rice was queen and beef its king! Easy to make but oh so tasty.

1 lb	454 g	lean ground beef
1/2 cup	125 L	uncooked white rice
1 1/2 cups	375 mL	cups water, *divided*
1/3 cup	75 mL	chopped onion
1 tsp	5 mL	salt
1/2 tsp	2 mL	celery salt
1/8 tsp	0.5 mL	garlic powder
1/8 tsp	0.5 mL	pepper
1	1	15 oz (425 mL) can of tomato sauce
2 tsp	10 mL	Worcestershire sauce

In a large bowl, combine ground beef, rice, 1/2 cup (125 mL) water, onion, salt, celery salt, garlic powder, and pepper. Mix with your hands until ingredients are well combined; roll mixture into 12 meatballs. Cook meatballs in a large skillet over medium-high heat, turning occasionally, until evenly browned. Drain and discard any excess fat.

Add tomato sauce, remaining 1 cup (250 mL) water and Worcestershire sauce. Reduce heat to medium-low. Cover and simmer until meatballs are no longer pink in centre and rice is tender, about 45 minutes. Add extra water if sauce becomes too dry.

1 serving: 390 Calories; 16 g Total Fat (7 g Mono, 0 g Poly, 6 g Sat); 70 mg Cholesterol; 27 g Carbohydrates (2 g Fibre, 5 g Sugar); 25 g Protein; 1320 mg Sodium

CHICKEN BREAST STRIPS A LA DAD

MAKES: 6 SERVINGS
DIFFICULTY: ★

Frozen chicken strips are okay in a pinch, but nothing beats homemade. It takes bit more effort, but there's no comparison in flavour. Serve with your favourite dipping sauce; honey barbecue is a good choice. Round out the meal with carrot and celery sticks with ranch dip.

6	6	**4 oz (113 g) skinless boneless chicken breast**
2 1/2 cups	625 mL	**bread crumbs**
1/4 cup	60 mL	**Parmesan cheese**
1/2 cup	125 mL	**butter, melted**

Cut chicken into strips.

Combine bread crumbs and Parmesan in a small bowl. Pour melted butter into a separate bowl. Dip chicken strips in melted butter, then roll in bread crumb mixture. Bake in a 350°F (175°C) oven for 40 minutes, turning once.

1 serving: 440 Calories; 16 g Total Fat (4 g Mono, 1.5 g Poly, 9 g Sat); 135 mg Cholesterol; 24 g Carbohydrates (2 g Fibre, 2 g Sugar); 47 g Protein; 490 mg Sodium

GARLIC GRILLED CHEESE SANDWICHES

MAKES: 4 SANDWICHES
DIFFICULTY: ★

Short on time but need to get dinner on the table? This garlicky spin on old-school grilled cheese will be sure to win over a crowd of hungry young people. It is also a perfect guy lunch on Sunday after a night out.

4 Tbsp	60 mL	**butter, softened**
1	1	**clove garlic, finely chopped**
2 Tbsp	30 mL	**finely chopped parsley**
8	8	**slices bread**
4	4	**slices Cheddar cheese (or Swiss, mozzarella or any other favourite)**

In a small bowl, mix butter, garlic and parsley. Allow to rest for 10 minutes so that butter can absorb garlic flavour. Spread butter on top of bread slices. Flip bread over and sprinkle 4 pieces with cheese. Top with remaining bread slices, butter side up. Fry sandwiches in a large frying pan over high heat 2 to 3 minutes on each side, until golden brown and the cheese has melted.

1 sandwich: 420 Calories; 22 g Total Fat (4 g Mono, 3 g Poly ,12 g Sat); 55 mg Cholesterol; 42 g Carbohydrates (2 g Fibre, 2 g Sugar); 0 g Protein; 520 mg Sodium

CHICKEN AND CHILI PIZZA

MAKES: 8 WEDGES   **DIFFICULTY:** ★

Two favourite kid foods in one colourful, tasty package. No one will be able to stop at just one slice.

1	1	4 oz (113 g) boneless, skinless chicken breast, slivered
1 tsp	5 mL	cooking oil
1	1	14 oz (398 mL) can of red kidney beans, drained and rinsed
1	1	small tomato, diced
2 tsp	10 mL	chili powder
1/4 tsp	1 mL	onion powder
1/8 tsp	0.5 mL	garlic powder (optional)
1	1	purchased baked pizza shell (12 inch, 30 cm, size)
1 1/2 cups	375 mL	grated sharp Cheddar cheese
2	2	green onions, sliced
1/2 cup	125 mL	diced green pepper

Cook chicken in oil in a medium frying pan over medium-high heat until no pink remains.

Add next 5 ingredients and garlic powder, if using. Heat for about 5 minutes, stirring and slightly mashing beans, until mixture is fairly dry.

Spread chili over pizza shell. Cover with cheese, green onion and green pepper. Place on greased 12 inch (30 cm) pizza pan. Bake in 425°F (220°C) oven for 10 minutes until crust is brown. Let stand for 5 minutes before cutting into wedges.

1 wedge: 220 Calories; 8.9 g Total Fat (2.5 g Mono, 0 g Poly, 5 g Sat); 30 mg Cholesterol; 24 g Carbohydrates (5 g Fibre, 2 g Sugar); 14 g Protein; 360 mg Sodium

Helpful Tips

The Napolitano oven in the traditional style can be 900°F (480°C). Many thin crust pizzas are cooked for just 90 seconds, and in the last 10 seconds the pizza is raised to the ceiling of the oven for an even higher temperature. We can't achieve that in most ovens or barbecues, but we can boost the temperature with pizza stones. Preheat the stones so they are red hot when the pizza dough hits them.

BEEF AND CHEESE ENCHILADAS

This meal will make a hero out of fathers everywhere, and the best part is no one has to know how easy it is to prepare. Garnish with lettuce and a sprinkle of cheese.

1 lb lean	454 g	ground beef
1	1	medium onion, chopped
1 tsp	5 mL	salt
1/4 tsp	1 mL	pepper
2	2	10 oz (284 mL) can of enchilada sauce, *divided*
1/2 cup	125 mL	sour cream
1 cup	250 mL	grated Cheddar cheese
8	8	flour tortillas (12 inch, 30 cm, diameter)

Combine beef, onion, salt and pepper in a large skillet over medium heat. Cook until beef is no longer pink inside. Drain off fat and discard, and set mixture aside.

Spread about a quarter of enchilada sauce into an ungreased 9 x 13 inch (23 x 33 cm) baking dish.

Add sour cream and cheese to ground beef mixture. Spoon 2 Tbsp (30 mL) enchilada sauce on each tortilla and then about 1/4 cup (60 mL) beef mixture. Roll up tortilla to enclose filling, and place seam side down in pan. Pour remaining sauce over top. Bake in a 350°F (175°C) oven for 20 minutes.

1 serving: 420 Calories; 20 g Total Fat (8 g Mono, 1 g Poly, 9 g Sat); 55 mg Cholesterol; 33 g Carbohydrates (2 g Fibre, 2 g Sugar); 20 g Protein; 980 mg Sodium

BOURBON STREET CHICKEN

MAKES: 4 SERVINGS   **DIFFICULTY: ★**

This New Orleans favourite has garnered a lot of attention across North America in recent years and for good reason—it's a beauty! Serve over a bed of white rice.

2 lbs	900 g	boneless chicken breasts
2 Tbsp	30 mL	olive oil
1	1	clove garlic, crushed
1/4 tsp	1 mL	ground ginger
3/4 tsp	4 mL	crushed red pepper flakes
1/4 cup	60 mL	apple juice
1/3 cup	75 mL	brown sugar
2 Tbsp	30 mL	ketchup
1 Tbsp	15 mL	cider vinegar
1/2 cup	125 mL	water
1/3 cup	75 mL	soy sauce

Cut chicken into small pieces. Heat oil in a large skillet over medium-high. Add chicken and cook until lightly browned. Transfer to a bowl and set aside.

Combine remaining ingredients and mix well until all ingredients are dissolved. Add to same skillet and place over medium heat. Once mixture is hot, return chicken to skillet and bring to a hard boil. Reduce heat and simmer for 20 minutes.

1 serving: 400 Calories; 10 g Total Fat (6 g Mono, 1.5 g Poly, 1.5 g Sat); 130 mg Cholesterol; 20 g Carbohydrates (0 g Fibre, 20 g Sugar); 55 g Protein; 1480 mg Sodium

Don't want to argue,
I don't want to debate
Don't want to hear about what
kind of food you hate
You won't get no dessert
'till you clean off your plate
So eat it!

—"Weird Al" Yankovic

SUPER STUFFED PORK CHOPS

MAKES: 2 SERVINGS　　　**DIFFICULTY: ★ ★**

You haven't lived until you've stuffed a pork chop using this recipe. Go easy when cutting into the chop—you want to create a small pocket opening without cutting through completely.

2 Tbsp	30 mL	butter, *divided*
2 Tbsp	30 mL	chopped celery leaves
1 Tbsp	15 mL	chopped onion
3/4 cup	175 mL	dry bread crumbs
2/3 cup	250 mL	chicken broth, *divided*
1 Tbsp	15 mL	minced fresh parsley
1/2 tsp	2 mL	salt
1/2 tsp	2 mL	paprika
1/4 tsp	1 mL	pepper
1/4 tsp	1 mL	dried thyme
2	2	pork chops (1 1/2 inches, 3.8 cm, thick)

For the stuffing, add 1 Tbsp (15 mL) butter to a frying pan or skillet over medium heat. Add celery leaves and onion and cook until soft. Once soft, remove from heat and stir in bread crumbs, 1/3 cup (75 mL) broth and seasonings. Mix well.

Cut a pocket in each pork chop by slicing from the fat side almost to the bone. Spoon about 1/2 cup (125 mL) stuffing into each pocket and secure with string or toothpicks. Melt remaining butter in skillet and brown chops on both sides. Place in a greased 7 x 11 inch (18 x 28 cm) baking dish and pour remaining broth over top. Cover and bake in a 350°F (175°C) oven for 40 to 50 minutes or until juices run clear. Remove string or toothpicks before serving.

1 chop: 490 Calories; 28 g Total Fat (10 g Mono, 3 g Poly, 13 g Sat); 90 mg Cholesterol; 31 g Carbohydrates (2 g Fibre, 3 g Sugar); 27 g Protein; 1230 mg Sodium

PORK POTSICKERS

MAKES: ABOUT 36 POTSTICKERS   **DIFFICULTY: ★ ★ ★**

These potstickers are a little fussy but well worth the effort. If you like, you can use wonton wrappers instead of making the dough. Try dipping the potstickers in Thai dipping sauce on page 211.

4 cups	1 L	finely chopped cabbage
1 Tbsp	15 mL	salt, *divided*
1/2 lb	225 g	ground pork
2 Tbsp	30 mL	finely chopped ginger root
2 tsp	10 mL	soy sauce
3 Tbsp	45 mL	sesame oil
1	1	large egg, fork-beaten
4 cups	1 L	all-purpose flour
2 cups	500 mL	boiling water, *divided*

For the filling, combine cabbage with 1/2 Tbsp (7 mL) salt in a large bowl and let stand for 30 minutes. Wring through a clean dishtowel to get rid of any extra liquid.

Add next 5 ingredients and 1/2 Tbsp (7 mL) salt. Set aside in fridge.

For the dough, mix flour and remaining 1/2 tsp (2 mL) salt. Slowly add water to flour mixture, mixing into a dough. Once a ball is formed, remove from bowl and knead for 5 minutes or so, until smooth. You may not need to use all of the water. Let dough relax for 1 hour.

Divide dough in half. Roll each half into logs about 1 inch (2.5 cm) in diameter, then cut in 1/2 inch (12 mm) disks. Roll each disk into a 3 inch (7.5 cm) circle. Place 1/2 Tbsp (7 mL) filling in centre. Fold over, and pinch in middle of half moon. Starting in middle, pinch dough forming pleats and making sure that dough is properly sealed. It sounds fussy, but keep at it.

Fry dough in a large non-stick skillet until crisp. Add 1/2 cup (125 mL) water, cover and steam for 10 minutes, ensuring there is water in pan at all times. Remove lid and fry until crispy and all water has evaporated.

1 potsticker: 80 Calories; 2.5 g Total Fat (1 g Mono, 0.3 g Poly, 0.5 g Sat); 10 mg Cholesterol; 11 g Carbohydrates (trace Fibre, 0 g Sugar); 3 g Protein; 250 mg Sodium

BACON RULES

Everything is better with bacon. Brad Smoliak even has a bestselling bacon jam. And a maple-bacon ice cream sundae. Be creative. Spread the word. Spread the bacon. Add it to anything. But really, where can you go wrong with bacon? Maybe bacon toothpaste is too much. But have you tried it?

BACON BUTTER

MAKES: ABOUT 2 CUPS (500 ML)   **DIFFICULTY: ★**

Try this butter melted on steaks, burger or even popcorn.

1 lb	454 g	bacon
1/2 cup	125 mL	diced onions
1 Tbsp	15 mL	minced garlic
1 lb	454 g	butter, at room temperature
1 Tbsp	15 mL	liquid honey
1/4 cup	60 mL	chopped green onions
1/2 tsp	2 mL	cracked black pepper

Cut bacon into 1/2 inch (12 mm) pieces and cook in a medium skillet over medium-high heat until crisp. Remove to paper towels, and drain all but 2 Tbsp (30 mL) fat from pan. Reserve drained fat for another use. Add onion to pan and cook until soft, about 5 minutes. Add garlic and cook another 5 minutes until soft. Remove from heat and set aside to cool to room temperature.

Meanwhile, whip butter until soft and pale, 5 to 7 minutes. Slowly add onions, garlic and bacon, and mix until well combined. Stir in honey, green onions, pepper and then roll mixture into a tube or place in a plastic container. Store in fridge for up to 2 weeks.

1 Tbsp (15mL): 170 Calories; 18 g Total Fat (6 g Mono, 1 g Poly, 9 g Sat); 40 mg Cholesterol; trace Carbohydrates (0 g Fibre, trace Sugar); 2 g Protein; 200 mg Sodium

> You're thinking I'm one of those wise-ass California vegetarians who is going to tell you that eating a few strips of bacon is bad for your health. I'm not. I say it's a free country and you should be able to kill yourself at any rate you choose, as long as your cold dead body is not blocking my driveway.
>
> —Scott Adams

CHEESY BACON FRITTATA

MAKES: 6 WEDGES   **DIFFICULTY: ★**

Jeff says he first saw a frittata being prepared on one his favourite cooking shows and thought he'd give it a try. Having now fallen in love with them, he also proved that watching TV eventually pays off.

5	5	slices bacon
6	6	large eggs
1 cup	250 mL	milk
2 Tbsp	30 mL	butter
1/2 tsp	2 mL	salt
1/4 tsp	1 mL	pepper
1/4 cup	60 mL	chopped green onions or shallots
1 1/3 cup	325 mL	Cheddar cheese

Cook bacon in a large skillet over medium-high heat, turning occasionally, until evenly browned, about 10 minutes. Transfer to paper towels to drain, then crumble and set aside.

Beat eggs, milk, butter, salt and pepper in a medium bowl. Pour into a lightly greased 7 x 11 inch (18 x 28 cm) baking dish. Sprinkle with onions, bacon and Cheddar cheese. Bake in 350°F (175°C) oven for 25 to 30 minutes or until a knife inserted near the centre comes out clean. Cut into 6 wedges and serve.

1 serving: 340 Calories; 28 g Total Fat (11 g Mono, 2.5 g Poly, 12 g Sat); 260 mg Cholesterol; 4 g Carbohydrates (0 g Fibre, 3 g Sugar); 18 g Protein; 710 mg Sodium

BACON ON A BUN

Does anything say "Canadian" or "man" quite the way bacon on a bun does? This recipe will have every guy within earshot over at your house faster than you can say "Bacon's on!"

1	1	**large bell pepper, quartered**
1	1	**large onion, sliced**
1 Tbsp	15 mL	**olive oil**
1/8 tsp	1 mL	**salt**
1/8 tsp	1 mL	**pepper**
1/4 cup	60 mL	**Dijon mustard**
2 Tbsp	30 mL	**liquid honey**
1 lb	454 g	**sliced back bacon or peameal bacon**
4	4	**fresh bread rolls**

Preheat grill to medium-high and grease grates. Brush pepper and onion with oil and sprinkle with salt and pepper. Place on grill and close lid. Grill, turning once, until tender and grill marks appear, about 6 minutes.

Meanwhile, combine mustard and honey in a small bowl. Add bacon to grill and brush with half of mustard mixture. Grill, covered, for 3 minutes. Turn and brush with remaining mustard mixture. Grill until grill marks appear, about 3 minutes.

Place bacon, onion and red pepper in sliced buns and serve.

1 serving: 410 Calories; 10 g Total Fat (3 g Mono, 0 g Poly, 2 g Sat); 65 mg Cholesterol; 49 g Carbohydrates (4 g Fibre, 12 g Sugar); 32 g Protein; 1980 mg Sodium

BACON-WRAPPED JALAPEÑO SHRIMP

MAKES: 32 SHRIMP   **DIFFICULTY:** ★ ★

These tasty mouth-watering morsels are a real hit on game day so be sure to stock up on shrimp. Remember, when buying shrimp, bigger is always better!

		cooking oil, for frying
32	32	**large tiger shrimp (peeled and deveined), tails on**
3	3	**jalapeño peppers, sliced thinly**
1 lb	454 g	**bacon**
32	32	**toothpicks**

Heat cooking oil in a pan or deep-fryer until temperature reaches 350°F (175°C).

Butterfly shrimp by cutting almost but not quite all the way through the back. Stuff a slice of jalapeño into each shrimp.

Cut bacon slices in half. Wrap each shrimp with a bacon half, and secure with a toothpick. Deep fry shrimp in batches until bacon is golden brown and crispy, 3 to 4 minutes. Drain on a plate lined with paper towel and serve.

1 shrimp: 110 Calories; 9 g Total Fat (4.5 g Mono, 1.5 g Poly, 2.5 g Sat); 40 mg Cholesterol; 0 g Carbohydrates (0 g Fibre, 0 g Sugar); 6 g Protein; 150 mg Sodium

Helpful Tips

Use your thumbs to peel back the sides of the shrimp shell. Slowly pull away any fibres of legs that remain once the shell has been removed. Hold the body of the shrimp and gently tug on the tail. The shell will come off with the tail. To devein shrimp, use a small, sharp knife to make a shallow cut down the back, exposing the vein. Pull the vein out gently with your fingers.

SMOKY BACON DRUMSTICKS

MAKES: 12 DRUMSTICKS **DIFFICULTY:** ★

Everything's better wrapped in bacon! Especially these juicy drumsticks, enhanced by smoky paprika.

1 Tbsp	15 mL	smoked sweet paprika
1 tsp	5 mL	garlic powder
1 tsp	5 mL	salt
1/2 tsp	2 mL	pepper
12	12	3 oz (85 g) chicken drumsticks, skin removed
12	12	bacon slices

Combine first 4 ingredients in a small cup.

Rub paprika mixture over drumsticks. Wrap 1 bacon slice around each drumstick and secure with wooden picks. Preheat barbecue to medium. Place chicken on greased grill and close lid. Cook for about 35 minutes, turning occasionally, until internal temperature reaches 170°F (77°C). Remove and discard wooden picks and serve.

1 drumstick: 240 Calories; 20 g Total Fat (8 g Mono, 2.5 g Poly, 6 g Sat); 65 mg Cholesterol; trace Carbohydrates (0 g Fibre, 0 g Sugar); 15 g Protein; 560 mg Sodium

> I'd be a vegetarian if bacon grew on trees.
> —Homer Simpson

BACON AND EGG TOSSED SALAD

MAKES: 8 CUPS (2 L)   **DIFFICULTY: ★ ★**

Bacon and eggs aren't just for breakfast anymore. This recipe features them as sensational salad toppings. Also a great option for brunch or lunch.

3 cups	750 mL	cut or torn iceberg lettuce, lightly packed
3 cups	750 mL	cut or torn romaine lettuce, lightly packed
1 cup	250 mL	chopped Roma (plum) tomato
1/2 cup	125 mL	grated sharp Cheddar cheese
1/2 cup	125 mL	unseasoned croutons
6	6	bacon slices, cooked crisp and crumbled
2	2	large hard-cooked eggs, chopped
3 Tbsp	45 mL	sliced green onion
3 Tbsp	45 mL	white vinegar
2 Tbsp	30 mL	cooking oil
1 tsp	5 mL	Dijon mustard
1 tsp	5 mL	granulated sugar
1/4 tsp	1 mL	salt
1/8 tsp	0.5 mL	pepper

Toss first 8 ingredients in a large bowl.

Whisk remaining 6 ingredients in a small bowl. Drizzle over lettuce mixture and toss to coat.

1 serving: 460 Calories; 40 g Total Fat (18 g Mono, 5 g Poly, 13 g Sat); 160 mg Cholesterol; 10 g Carbohydrates (2 g Fibre, 3 g Sugar); 15 g Protein; 800 mg Sodium

Bacon is the candy of meat.

—Kevin Taggart

BEEF AND BISON MEATLOAF

MAKES: 48 PIECES   **DIFFICULTY:** ★ ★

If the guys are coming over for a game, this is what to make for them. They'll gobble it up. Serve it with roasted or mashed potatoes, seasonal veggies and plenty of beer.

1/3 cup	75 mL	canola oil
3 lbs	1.4 kg	onion, cut in 1/4 inch dice
2 lbs	900 g	celery, cut in 1/4 inch dice
1/4 cup	60 mL	salt
1/4 cup	60 mL	pepper
1/4 cup	60 mL	crushed garlic
1/4 cup	60 mL	thyme
6 lbs	2.8 kg	ground bison
6 lbs	2.8 kg	extra lean ground beef
8	8	large eggs
60	60	pieces bacon (approximately)

Heat canola oil in a large frying pan over medium heat. Add next 6 ingredients, and cook until soft, about 10 to 12 minutes. Drain, then set aside to cool.

Transfer celery mixture to the bowl of a stand mixer and add bison, beef and eggs. Mix with a paddle on low speed until well combined.

Line 2 large baking pans with bacon, reserving 4 strips. Divide bison mixture between pans and spread over bacon, shaping bison mixture into a tight loaf shape. Fold bacon lining pan over loaves to cover. Lay 2 pieces of reserved bacon in a straight line on top of each loaf. Cover tightly with foil and bake in a 350°F (175°C) oven for 1 1/2 hours or until the internal temperature reaches 150°F (65°C).

Let loaves stand for 10 minutes before cutting into slices.

1 slice: 480 Calories; 37 g Total Fat (16 g Mono, 3.5 g Poly, 13 g Sat); 140 mg Cholesterol; 4 g Carbohydrates (trace Fibre, 2 g Sugar); 29 g Protein; 1080 mg Sodium

Pictured on page 143.

> Even apocalypse looks less dire when viewed over a plate of bacon.
>
> —Stephanie Stamm

Beef and Bison Meatloaf, page 142 • Roasted Brussels Sprouts, page 272

Terrific Turkey Pot Pie,
page 160

MAPLE BACON ICE CREAM

MAKES: 6 SERVINGS   **DIFFICULTY: ★**

This recipe was inspired by a friend of Brad's. The sweet familiarity of the maple syrup combines so well with the saltiness of the bacon, the crunchiness of the nuts and the cold ice cream. Your family is going to love this. Bourbon Vanilla or Rye Vanilla ice cream work well, if you can find them.

1 cup	250 mL	maple syrup
1/2 cup	125 mL	cooked, crispy double-smoked bacon (not burnt), crumbled
1/2 cup	125 mL	chopped pecans
		vanilla ice cream

Put syrup in a saucepan and bring to a boil; let cook to reduce a little. Add bacon crumbles and give it a good stir. Add nuts and remove from heat. Let sauce stand for a while.

Spoon a couple of scoops of ice cream into each dish and top with sauce. Yum yum.

1 sundae: 340 Calories; 17 g Total Fat (7 g Mono, 2.5 g Poly, 6 g Sat); 40 mg Cholesterol; 44 g Carbohydrates (1 g Fibre, 41 g Sugar); 6 g Protein; 125 mg Sodium

Life expectancy would grow by leaps and bounds if green vegetables smelled as good as bacon.

—Doug Larson

CLASSIC COMFORT FOOD

Let's face it: Mom's cooking is the best. Hands down, bar none. The best. Sunday roasts, shepherd's pie, apple pie, peanut butter cookies with the little cross-hatches done with a fork, it's all food cooked with love. Thanks, Mom.

On the other hand, comfort food, by definition, is any food item that brings with it a sense of emotional well-being and that one turns to for temporary relief or reward. It can mean different things to different people; however, it tends to share two common elements: fat and carbohydrates. From our experience, male comfort foods are various and wide-ranging yet all share that common sense of satisfaction once eaten. Just as we got attached to our security blankets as children, male comfort foods are a hard habit to kick and, really, why would we want to? In this section, the guys in need of a short-term fix to fill that void will be right at home. The recipes were put together by a self-proclaimed comfort food addict with the idea of creating items you would commonly serve at an all-male support group.

ITALIAN-STYLE POT ROAST

MAKES: 10 SERVINGS   **DIFFICULTY: ★**

This dish smells amazing as it cooks. When it's done, it's fork tender and delicious.
Serve with mashed potatoes or plenty of crusty bread.

1	1	chuck roast (about 2 lb, 900 g)
		salt and pepper to taste
1/4 cup	60 mL	all-purpose flour
2 Tbsp	30 mL	canola oil
1	1	medium onion, sliced
1/2 cup	125 mL	chicken stock
1/2 cup	125 mL	red wine
2 cups	500 mL	chopped grape or cherry tomatoes
2 Tbsp	30 mL	balsamic vinegar
3	3	sprigs of thyme
3	3	cloves garlic
3 Tbsp	45 mL	chopped parsley
1/2 cup	125 mL	roughly chopped olives, optional

Heat a heavy Dutch oven over medium-high heat. Season beef generously with salt and pepper, then dust with flour to evenly coat. Pour oil into pan and brown roast on all sides.

Remove meat from pot, reduce heat, remove any excess fat, and then add onions and cook until soft.

Add stock, wine, tomatoes, vinegar, thyme and garlic. Bring to a boil, then gently place roast in pot, cover with tight-fitting lid or wrap with foil. Braise in a 300°F (150°C) oven for 2 to 3 hours or until fork tender.

Remove meat from pot and keep warm. Strain liquid, reserving solids, and reduce to de-grease liquid. Season if needed, add solids back to liquid, and process with an immersion blender until smooth. Slice roast and sprinkle with parsley and olives. Serve with sauce.

1 serving: 380 Calories; 27 g Total Fat (13 g Mono, 1.5 g Poly, 10 g Sat); 95 mg Cholesterol; 6 g Carbohydrates (trace Fibre, 2 g Sugar); 24 g Protein; 380 mg Sodium

CUBAN PORK ROAST

MAKES: 8 SERVINGS   **DIFFICULTY: ★ ★**

The mojo sauce is what sets this dish apart from its brethren.

1 cup	250 mL	Italian dressing
1 Tbsp	15 mL	hot sauce
1 Tbsp	15 mL	seasoning salt
1 tsp	5 mL	pepper
1 tsp	5 mL	cumin
2 Tbsp	30 mL	lime juice
1/4 cup	60 mL	orange juice
2 Tbsp	30 mL	olive oil
2 Tbsp	30 mL	vinegar
2 lbs	900 g	pork loin
1 Tbsp	15 mL	chopped garlic
1 tsp	5 mL	salt
1/2 cup	125 mL	olive oil
1/2 tsp	2 mL	cumin
1/4 cup	60 mL	white vinegar
1/4 cup	60 mL	orange juice
1/4 tsp	1 mL	dried oregano
1/8 tsp	0.5 mL	pepper

Combine first 9 ingredients in a large resealable freezer bag. Add pork and marinate overnight in fridge. Roast in a 325°F (160°C) oven for about 45 minutes to 1 hour or until the meat reaches an internal temperature of 155°F (68°C). Let stand for 10 to 15 minutes before slicing.

For the mojo sauce, combine remaining 8 ingredients in a small bowl. Let come to room temperature before serving with pork.

1 serving: 460 Calories; 37 g Total Fat (17 g Mono, 3.5 g Poly, 7 g Sat); 75 mg Cholesterol; 7 g Carbohydrates (0 g Fibre, 4 g Sugar); 24 g Protein; 930 mg Sodium

EASY SHEPHERD'S PIE

MAKES: 6 SERVINGS   **DIFFICULTY:** ★

Mothers across the land all cook a slightly different shepherd's pie, sometimes with leftover roast beef. Below is a simple version using ground beef, so you can have it anytime.

4	4	medium potatoes, peeled and cut up
1 Tbsp	15 mL	butter (or hard margarine)
1/2 tsp	2 mL	seasoned salt
8 Tbsp	120 mL	milk, *divided*
2 tsp	10 mL	cooking oil
1 1/2 lbs.	680 g	lean ground beef
1 cup	250 mL	chopped onion
1 Tbsp	15 mL	all-purpose flour
1 1/2 tsp	7 mL	salt
1/4 tsp	1 mL	pepper
1 cup	250 mL	cooked peas
1 cup	250 mL	cooked sliced carrot
1 Tbsp	15 mL	ketchup
1 tsp	5 mL	Worcestershire sauce
1 tsp	5 mL	prepared horseradish
2 Tbsp	30 mL	butter, melted
		sprinkle of paprika

Cook potato in boiling salted water in a large saucepan until tender. Drain and add next 2 ingredients and 3 Tbsp (45 mL) milk. Mash, then cover and set aside.

Heat cooking oil in a large frying pan on medium. Add beef and onion. Scramble-fry for about 10 minutes until beef is no longer pink. Drain.

Stir in next 3 ingredients. Slowly add remaining 1/3 cup (75 mL) milk, stirring constantly. Heat and stir for about 2 minutes until boiling and thickened.

Stir in next 5 ingredients. Spread in a greased 2 quart (2 L) shallow baking dish. Spread mashed potatoes on beef mixture.

Brush with melted butter and sprinkle with paprika. Bake, uncovered, in a 350°F (175°C) oven for about 30 minutes until heated through and potatoes are golden.

1 serving: 500 Calories; 23 g Total Fat (9 g Mono, 1 g Poly, 10 g Sat); 85 mg Cholesterol; 36 g Carbohydrates (4 g Fibre, 7 g Sugar); 28 g Protein; 930 mg Sodium

QUICK TUNA CASSEROLE

MAKES: 4 SERVINGS **DIFFICULTY:** ★

Nothing says yummy in the tummy like good old-fashioned tuna casserole—single-handedly responsible for sustaining thousands of starving students through their college years. And still a big hit today!

12 oz	340 g	broad egg noodles, cooked
2	2	10 oz (284 mL) cans of condensed cream of chicken soup
1/2 cup	125 mL	milk
1 1/2 cups	375 mL	Cheddar cheese
2	2	6 oz (170 g) cans of tuna, drained
1/2 tsp	2 mL	salt
1/2 tsp	2 mL	pepper
3/4 cup	175 mL	bread crumbs
1 Tbsp	15 mL	melted butter

Combine noodles, soup, milk, cheese and tuna in a greased 3 quart (3 L) casserole dish. Season with salt and pepper.

In a small bowl, mix bread crumbs with melted butter and sprinkle over pasta. Bake in a 350°F (175°C) oven for 30 minutes, until casserole is hot and bubbly and crumbs have browned.

1 serving: 850 Calories; 32 g Total Fat (8 g Mono, 3 g Poly, 15 g Sat); 175 mg Cholesterol; 90 g Carbohydrates (4 g Fibre, 10 g Sugar); 52 g Protein; 2130 mg Sodium

Ask not what you can do for your country.
Ask what's for lunch.

—Orson Welles

DOWNHOME TURKEY CASSEROLE

MAKES: 4 SERVINGS   **DIFFICULTY:** ★

Every guy loves a good casserole, and this one, featuring leftover turkey, has a homey and traditional feel—qualities most men can appreciate.

1/4 cup	60 mL	butter
1	1	onion, chopped
1/2	1/2	green pepper, chopped
6 Tbsp	90 mL	all-purpose flour
1	1	10 oz (284 mL) can of cream of chicken soup
1 cup	250 mL	milk
1 cup	250 mL	diced mushrooms
1/4 tsp	1 mL	salt
4 cups	1 L	diced cooked turkey
1 cup	250 mL	soft bread crumbs
1 cup	250 mL	shredded Cheddar cheese

Melt butter in a large skillet on medium-high. Add onion and green pepper and cook for 5 minutes until softened.

Whisk flour into mixture and stir until pasty. Add cream of chicken soup, milk, diced mushrooms and salt and stir until smooth.

Add turkey and cook for another 5 minutes. Pour mixture into a 2 quart (2 L) casserole dish and sprinkle with bread crumbs and cheese. Bake in a 350°F (175°C) for about 50 minutes until casserole is bubbling and cheese is melted. Let stand 5 minutes before serving.

1 serving: 590 Calories; 20 g Total Fat (6 g Mono, 2 g Poly, 9 g Sat); 140 mg Cholesterol; 4.5 g Carbohydrates (2 g Fibre, 7 g Sugar); 58 g Protein; 1250 mg Sodium

We like to experiment with recipes and always add more of what we like. That's okay. But be sure to make up something in advance to explain your overabundant presentation. Like…you need enough for leftovers…more people might show up the last minute…people love your cooking so much they have three helpings. As long as you get to carry a giant platter to the table, all will be forgiven.

SPICY BAKED POTATOES WITH SAUSAGE

MAKES: 4 SERVINGS
DIFFICULTY: ★

Potatoes don't need to be relegated to a side; they are equally at home as the centre of attention. For some added panache, look for Desiree or King Edward baking potatoes.

4	4	**Russet potatoes**
1 lb	454 g	**ground Italian sausage**
1 cup	25 mL	**grated Cheddar cheese**
8	8	**drops hot sauce**

Pierce potatoes a few times with a fork. Bake in a 400°F (200°C) oven for 1 hour, or until tender.

While potatoes are baking, cook ground sausage in a large preheated skillet over medium-high for 6 to 8 minutes or until no longer pink in middle. Drain on paper towels. Split potatoes open and serve each topped with cooked sausage, 1/4 cup (60 mL) grated cheese, and 2 drops of hot sauce, or to taste.

1 serving: 790 Calories; 45 g Total Fat (19 g Mono, 4.5 g Poly, 19 g Sat); 115 mg Cholesterol; 66 g Carbohydrates (6 g Fibre, 3 g Sugar); 31 g Protein; 1030 mg Sodium

CHILI-TOPPED BAKED POTATOES

MAKES: 4 SERVINGS
DIFFICULTY: ★

If you are short on time, whip up this quick dinner in your microwave, and add other toppings such as sour cream, salsa and green onion.

4	4	**large baking potatoes**
1/2 tsp	2 mL	**salt**
1/2 tsp	2 mL	**pepper**
1	1	**19 oz (540 mL) can of prepared chili**
3/4 cup	175 mL	**shredded Cheddar cheese**

Pierce each potato several times using a fork. Place on a microwave-safe plate and cook uncovered for 5 minutes on high (100%). Turn potatoes over and cook for an additional 5 minutes, until easily pierced by a fork (cook for 1 minute increments until done).

Cut each potato in half lengthwise. Mash insides a bit with a fork, season with salt and pepper and top with 1/4 can of chili per potato. Return the potatoes to the microwave and cook for about 1 minute more until the chili is hot.

Garnish with shredded cheese.

1 serving: 520 Calories; 15 g Total Fat (5 g Mono, 1 g Poly, 8 g Sat); 45 mg Cholesterol; 81 g Carbohydrates (11 g Fibre, 5 g Sugar); 20 g Protein; 1150 mg Sodium

MEATLOAF

MAKES: 6 SERVINGS   **DIFFICULTY: ★**

Leftovers are great cold for sandwiches, or sliced thick and grilled like a burger!

2 Tbsp	30 mL	canola oil
2 cups	500 mL	chopped onion
1 Tbsp	15 mL	chopped garlic
3 lbs	1.4 kg	ground beef
1 cup	250 mL	chili sauce, *divided*
1 Tbsp	15 mL	Dijon mustard
1 tsp	5 mL	Worcestershire sauce
1	1	large egg
1 tsp	5 mL	salt
1/2 tsp	2 mL	pepper
2 Tbsp	30 mL	sriracha or hot sauce, *divided*
1/4 cup	60 mL	brown sugar

Heat canola oil over medium heat and add onion. Cook until soft and translucent, about 10 minutes. Add garlic and cook another 5 minutes. Remove from heat and allow to cool to room temperature.

Place beef in a large bowl and add cooked onions and garlic, 1/2 cup (125 mL) chili sauce, mustard, Worcestershire sauce, egg, salt, pepper and hot sauce. Mix until well combined.

Place in a loaf pan, pressing down to get rid of any air bubbles. Place on a rimmed baking sheet (to catch splatters; makes for easier clean-up) and bake in a 350°F (175°C) oven for 40 minutes or until internal temperature reaches 150°F (65°C).

For the topping, combine brown sugar, remaining 1/2 cup (125 mL) chili sauce and 1 Tbsp (15 mL) hot sauce. Pour over loaf and turn oven up to 400°F (200°C). Bake another 10 minutes, then allow to stand for 10 minutes before slicing.

1 slice: 350 Calories; 18 g Total Fat (8 g Mono, 1 g Poly, 7 g Sat); 85 mg Cholesterol; 14 g Carbohydrates (12 g Fibre, 0 g Sugar); 23 g Protein; 540 mg Sodium

SWEET AND SOUR MEATBALLS

MAKES: 6 SERVINGS   **DIFFICULTY: ★**

If you want a change from beef, switch things up a little by substituting ground pork or veal. Serve over a bed of rice.

1 lb	454 g	ground beef
1/2 cup	125 mL	water
1	1	large egg
1 Tbsp	15 mL	brown sugar
1 Tbsp	15 mL	vinegar
1 cup	250 mL	grated carrot
1 cup	250 mL	bread crumbs
		salt and pepper to taste
2 Tbsp	30 mL	cooking oil
1/2 cup	125 mL	chopped celery
1/2 cup	125 mL	chopped onions
1/2 cup	125 mL	chopped carrots
1	1	10 oz (284 mL) can of tomato soup
1	1	10 oz (284 mL) can of cold water
2 Tbsp	30 mL	vinegar
1/4 cup	60 mL	brown sugar

Mix together first 9 ingredients until well incorporated. Shape into 30 balls and set aside.

Heat a heavy saucepan over medium-high and add oil. Brown meatballs on all sides. Drain fat from pan.

Add celery, onions and carrots, and cook until soft, about 5 minutes.

Add soup, water, vinegar and brown sugar and mix well. Return meatballs to saucepan or place in a casserole dish and bake in a 300°F (150°C) oven until meatballs are cooked.

1 serving: 290 Calories; 8 g Total Fat (3 g Mono, 1 g Poly, 3 g Sat); 75 mg Cholesterol; 35 g Carbohydrates (2 g Fibre, 18 g Sugar); 20 g Protein; 530 mg Sodium

CLASSIC SALISBURY STEAK

MAKES: 6 SERVINGS　　　　**DIFFICULTY:** ★

Some comfort foods just never go out of style. Serve with hot buttery noodles or mashed potatoes.

1	1	10 oz (284 mL) can of condensed French onion soup, *divided*
1 1/2 lbs	680 g	ground beef
1/2 cup	125 mL	dry bread crumbs
1	1	large egg
1/4 tsp	1 mL	salt
		pepper to taste
1 Tbsp	15 mL	all-purpose flour
1/4 cup	60 mL	ketchup
1/4 cup	60 mL	water
2 tsp	10 mL	Worcestershire sauce
1/2 tsp	2 mL	dry mustard

In a large bowl, combine 1/3 can soup with ground beef, bread crumbs, egg, salt and pepper. Mix well then shape into 6 patties. Place patties in a large skillet on medium-high heat and brown both sides. Pour off excess fat.

In a small bowl, combine flour and remaining soup and mix until smooth. Stir in ketchup, water, Worcestershire sauce and dry mustard. Pour over patties in skillet. Cover and cook for 20 minutes, stirring occasionally.

1 serving: 350 Calories; 17 g Total Fat (7g Mono, 0.5 g Poly, 7 g Sat); 105 mg Cholesterol; 14 g Carbohydrates (trace Fibre, 5 g Sugar); 26 g Protein; 810 mg Sodium

CHEESY CHICKEN PARM

MAKES: 4 SERVINGS   **DIFFICULTY:** ★ ★

Chicken parm is an old Italian favourite that can be prepared, at any time, on any day of the week. It is one of those meals that everyone will enjoy. Serve with spaghetti or other pasta.

4	4	4 oz (113 g) skinless, boneless chicken breasts
1/2 tsp	2 mL	salt
1/2 tsp	2 mL	pepper
2	2	large eggs
4 cups	1 L	dry bread crumbs
1/2 cup	125 mL	grated Parmesan cheese
2 Tbsp	30 mL	all-purpose flour
1 1/8 cups	280 mL	olive oil, *divided*
1 1/4 cups	300 mL	tomato sauce
1/4 cup	60 mL	shredded mozzarella
1/4 cup	60 mL	chopped fresh basil
1/2 cup	125 mL	grated provolone cheese
1/4 cup	60 mL	grated Parmesan cheese

Place chicken breasts between 2 sheets of plastic wrap on a solid, level surface. Firmly pound chicken with smooth side of a meat mallet to a thickness of 1/2 inch (12 mm). Season chicken thoroughly with salt and pepper.

Beat eggs in a shallow bowl and set aside.

In a separate bowl, mix bread crumbs and Parmesan. Set aside.

Sprinkle flour over chicken breasts, evenly coating both sides. Dip in beaten eggs, then in bread crumb mixture, pressing crumbs into both sides. Let stand for about 15 minutes.

Heat 1 cup (250 mL) olive oil in a large skillet on medium-high. Add chicken and cook until golden, about 2 minutes per side. Transfer to a baking dish.

Top each breast with about 1/3 cup (75 mL) tomato sauce. Layer each chicken breast with equal amounts of mozzarella cheese, fresh basil, and provolone cheese. Sprinkle with Parmesan cheese on top and drizzle with 1 Tbsp (7 mL) olive oil. Bake in a 450°F (230°C) oven until cheese is browned and bubbly and chicken breasts are no longer pink in centre, 15 to 20 minutes.

1 serving: 960 Calories; 30 g Total Fat (13 g Mono, 4.5 g Poly, 10 g Sat); 235 mg Cholesterol; 84 g Carbohydrates (5 g Fibre, 8 g Sugar); 83 g Protein; 1700 mg Sodium

CRISPY FRIED CHICKEN

MAKES: 8 SERVINGS   **DIFFICULTY: ★**

Nothing says down-home cooking quite like fried chicken. I don't think there's a guy in the country that doesn't enjoy it. To really live life on the edge, why not whip up a batch of homemade French fries to go along with it! Delicious fried meals like this are a treat and should be eaten in moderation.

2 cups	500 mL	all-purpose flour
1 tsp	5 mL	paprika
1/8 tsp	0.5 mL	salt
1/8 tsp	0.5 mL	pepper
1 cup	250 mL	buttermilk
4 lbs	1.8 kg	chicken pieces
2 quarts	2 L	cooking oil for frying

Place flour in a large resealable freezer bag and add paprika, salt and pepper. Shake dry ingredients until blended.

Place buttermilk in a medium bowl. Dip each piece of chicken in buttermilk and add to flour. Seal bag and shake to coat well. Place coated chicken on a cookie sheet or tray, and cover with waxed paper. Allow chicken to sit until the flour is a paste-like consistency.

Heat a large, steep-sided skillet (or deep-fryer) over high. Fill about 1/3 to 1/2 full with cooking oil and heat until very hot, about 375°F (190°C). Place as many chicken pieces into skillet as it can hold and brown both sides. When browned, reduce heat and cover skillet. Cook for 30 minutes until chicken is cooked through. Remove cover, raise heat again and continue to fry until crispy. Drain chicken on paper towels and repeat process with remaining chicken pieces. Keep finished chicken in a slightly warm oven while preparing the rest.

1 serving: 480 Calories; 17 g Total Fat (8 g Mono, 4 g Poly, 2.5 g Sat); 165 mg Cholesterol; 26 g Carbohydrates (trace Fibre, 0 g Sugar); 52 g Protein; 270 mg Sodium

Helpful Tips

To test the temperature of your oil, drop in a single popping corn kernel. If the kernel pops within a few seconds, your temperature is at least 350°F (175°C). You can also dip the end of a wooden spoon into your oil—it begins bubbling around the wooden end when it is 350°F to 375°F (175°C to 190°C).

"BUZZED" TURKEY WITH COFFEE AND CHOCOLATE

MAKES: 6 SERVINGS　　　　**DIFFICULTY:** ★ ★

Coffee and chocolate? With turkey? Mmmmmmm....

1 cup	250 mL	strong brewed coffee, chilled
2 lbs	900 g	turkey thighs, cut in pieces
2 Tbsp	30 mL	cooking oil
1	1	onion, diced
1 Tbsp	15 mL	crushed garlic
1	1	red pepper, diced
1	1	whole wheat tortilla (12 inch, 30 cm, diameter)
1/2 tsp	2 mL	ground cinnamon
1/2 tsp	2 mL	dried coriander
1/2 tsp	2 mL	thyme
1 tsp	5 mL	chipotle chili powder
1 tsp	5 mL	cumin
1 Tbsp	15 mL	corn syrup
2 cups	500 mL	chicken stock
2 oz	55 g	semi-sweet chocolate
		salt and pepper to taste

In resealable freezer bag, pour coffee over turkey and marinate in fridge for 3 to 6 hours. Drain and pat dry.

Heat oil in a heavy pot over medium-high. Add turkey and cook until browned. Remove and set aside.

Drain all but 1 Tbsp (15 mL) fat from pan, then add onions, garlic and red pepper and cook until just soft.

Tear tortilla into pieces and add to pan. Add next 7 ingredients and bring to a boil. Reduce heat to a simmer and add turkey. Simmer for about 1 hour until turkey is done.

Remove turkey and strain liquid. Remove fat from liquid, then blend solids and liquid together until smooth. Add chocolate and whisk in until melted. Adjust seasoning, add the turkey, stirring until well coated, and serve.

1 serving: 350 Calories; 17 g Total Fat (7 g Mono, 3 g Poly, 4.5 g Sat); 125 mg Cholesterol; 16 g Carbohydrates (2 g Fibre, 9 g Sugar); 31 g Protein; 710 mg Sodium

NASI GORENG

DIFFICULTY: ★ ★ ★

Nasi goreng is an Indonesian fried rice dish. Ketjap manis, basically a thick, sweet soy sauce, can be found in Asian supermarkets. Serve with an assortment of condiments such as diced pineapple, crushed peanuts and mango chutney.

1 cup	250 mL	rice
2 cups	500 mL	water
2 tsp	10 mL	sambal olek
1/4 cup	60 mL	mango chutney
1 cup	250 mL	shredded cabbage
1 lb	454 g	thinly sliced chicken, pork or shrimp, or a combination
1/2	1/2	medium onion, sliced
1/2	1/2	medium red pepper
1/2	1/2	medium yellow pepper
1	1	stalk of celery, angle cut
1	1	carrot, angle cut
1	1	small head of broccoli
1/2	1/2	bunch of green onion, cut into 1 inch (2.5 cm) pieces
1/4 cup	60 mL	ketjap manis
1/4 cup	60 mL	mirin
1/4 cup	60 mL	warm water
1 Tbsp	15 mL	sesame oil
1 Tbsp	15 mL	freshly grated ginger root
1 Tbsp	15 mL	curry paste
1 Tbsp	15 mL	chopped garlic
1 Tbsp	15 mL	cornstarch
1/4 cup	60 mL	cold water

Combine rice, water, sambal olek and chutney in a large pot over high heat and bring to a rolling boil. Add cabbage and cook over low heat for 30 minutes. Remove from heat and let stand 10 minutes, or until needed.

Stir-fry meat in a hot wok until just done, then set aside in warm bowl .

In a hot wok or large frying pan, add next 7 ingredients, one at a time, starting with onion. When all ingredients have been added, cover wok and cook for 3 minutes. Add meat and stir-fry until all of the ingredients are well incorporated.

Combine next 7 ingredients in a small bowl, then add to wok. Bring to a boil. Stir cornstarch into cold water until dissolved, then add to wok. Cook until thickened. Add rice and stir-fry until heated through. Garnish with fresh cilantro and serve.

1 serving: 600 Calories; 12 g Total Fat (4 g Mono, 4 g Poly, 2.5 g Sat); 95 mg Cholesterol; 84 g Carbohydrates (5 g Fibre, 28 g Sugar); 29 g Protein; 920 mg Sodium

TERRIFIC TURKEY POT PIE

MAKES: 4 SERVINGS   **DIFFICULTY: ★ ★**

Nothing says "Momma's home cooking" quite like turkey pot pie! It's also the perfect meal for a cool fall or winter's evening. Pour a tall glass of pilsner and dig in.

2	2	purchased pie crusts
4 Tbsp	60 mL	butter, *divided*
1	1	onion, finely chopped
2	2	stalks celery, chopped
2	2	carrots, diced
3 Tbsp	45 mL	dried parsley
1/4 tsp	1 mL	salt
1/4 tsp	1 mL	pepper
2	2	chicken bouillon cubes
2 cups	500 mL	water
3	3	potatoes, peeled and cubed
3 Tbsp	45 mL	all-purpose flour
1/2 cup	125 mL	milk
1 1/2 cups	375 mL	cooked turkey, chopped

Place one of the pie crusts in a 10 inch (25 cm) pie pan and set aside.

In a large skillet over medium heat, melt 2 Tbsp (30 mL) butter. Add onion, celery, carrots, parsley, salt and pepper. Cook, stirring, until vegetables are soft.

Stir in bouillon and water and bring mixture to a boil. Stir in potatoes, and cook until tender but still firm.

In a medium saucepan, melt remaining 2 Tbsp (30 mL) butter. Add flour and stir into a paste. Add milk and whisk mixture until it thickens.

Add turkey and heat through. Stir turkey mixture into vegetable mixture and cook until thickened.

Cool slightly, then pour mixture into the unbaked pie shell. Roll out the top crust, and place on top of filling. Flute edges, and make 4 slits in the top crust to let out steam.

Bake in a 425°F (220°C) oven for 15 minutes. Reduce oven temperature to 350°F (175°C) and continue baking for 20 minutes or until crust is golden brown.

1 serving: 820 Calories; 44 g Total Fat (17 g Mono, 9 g Poly, 16 g Sat); 70 mg Cholesterol; 79 g Carbohydrates (7 g Fibre, 8 g Sugar); 27 g Protein; 1270 mg Sodium

Pictured on page 144.

Root Beer Ribs, page 199 • Cajun Cornbread, page 276

Crab Cakes with Creole Sauce, page 210 • Shrimp Lollipops, page 211

SAVOURY CHICKEN AND DUMPLINGS

MAKES: 6 SERVINGS   **DIFFICULTY: ★**

Nothing fills the void quite like chicken and dumplings and, we believe, most men could actually live on it.

3	3	celery ribs, chopped
1 cup	250 mL	sliced carrots
3	3	10 oz (284 mL) cans of chicken broth
3 cups	725 mL	cubed cooked chicken breast
1/2 tsp	2 mL	poultry seasoning
1/8 tsp	0.5 mL	pepper
1 2/3 cups	400 mL	biscuit mix
2/3 cup	150 mL	milk

In a greased Dutch oven on medium-high heat, cook celery and carrots for 5 minutes. Stir in broth, chicken, poultry seasoning and pepper. Bring to a boil, then reduce heat to a gentle simmer.

For dumplings, combine biscuit mix and milk. Drop by tablespoon full onto simmering broth. Cover and simmer for 10 to 15 minutes or until a toothpick inserted in a dumpling comes out clean.

1 serving: 330 Calories; 10 g Total Fat (2 g Mono, 1 g Poly, 2.5 g Sat); 55 mg Cholesterol; 34 g Carbohydrates (2 g Fibre, 3 g Sugar); 24 g Protein; 1410 mg Sodium

I don't know what it is about food your mother makes for you, especially when it's something that anyone can make - pancakes, meat loaf, tuna salad - but it carries a certain taste of memory.

—Mitch Albom

COMFORT CHICKEN NOODLE SOUP

MAKES: ABOUT 7 CUPS (1.75 L) **DIFFICULTY: ★**

This long-simmered, made-from-scratch soup is well worth the effort. Freeze home-made stock in different sizes of containers to flavour soups, gravies, sauces and risottos.

CHICKEN STOCK

4 lbs	1.8 kg	bone-in chicken parts
10 cups	2.5 L	water
2	2	celery ribs, with leaves, halved
1	1	large onion, quartered
1	1	large carrot, halved
3	3	sprigs of fresh thyme
1	1	sprig of fresh parsley
2	2	bay leaves
1	1	clove garlic
12	12	whole black peppercorns
2 tsp	10 mL	cooking oil
1/2 cup	125 mL	chopped onion
1/2 cup	125 mL	chopped carrot
1/2 cup	125 mL	chopped celery
3 oz	85 g	spaghetti, broken into about 3 inch (7.5 cm) pieces
1/4 cup	60 mL	chopped fresh parsley
3/4 tsp	4 mL	salt
1/4 tsp	1 mL	pepper

For the chicken stock, put chicken and water into a large pot. Bring to a boil and cook, uncovered, for 5 minutes without stirring. Skim and discard foam.

Stir in next 8 ingredients and bring to a boil. Reduce heat to medium-low and simmer, uncovered, for about 3 hours, stirring occasionally, until chicken starts to fall off bones. Remove from heat. Transfer chicken to cutting board. Remove chicken from bones. Chop enough chicken to make 2 cups (500 mL). Reserve remaining chicken for another use. Strain stock through a sieve into a large bowl and discard solids. Skim fat from stock.

For the soup, heat cooking oil in a large saucepan on medium. Add next 3 ingredients. Cook for 5 to 10 minutes, stirring often, until onion is softened. Add stock. Bring to a boil.

Add spaghetti. Cook, uncovered, for about 10 minutes, stirring occasionally, until spaghetti and vegetables are tender.

Add chicken and remaining 3 ingredients. Heat and stir until chicken is heated through.

1 cup (250 mL): 120 Calories; 3 g Total Fat (1 g Mono, 0.5 g Poly, 1 g Sat); 30 mg Cholesterol; 11 g Carbohydrates (trace Fibre, trace Sugar); 12 g Protein; 310 mg Sodium

Pictured on page 90.

GUMBO

MAKES: 6 SERVINGS **DIFFICULTY: ★ ★**

For this recipe you need to make a roux, which is a dark paste of flour and butter or oil and is used to thicken sauces and soups. For something a little different, try substituting chicken or duck for the pork, and crab for the shrimp. Tastes great sprinkled with a few drops of hot sauce.

1 cup	250 mL	butter
1 cup	250 mL	all-purpose flour
2 Tbsp	30 mL	cooking oil
2 lbs	900 g	pork loin, cut into 1 inch (2.5 cm) pieces
2 cups	500 mL	diced onion
2 cups	500 mL	diced celery
2 cups	500 mL	diced sweet peppers
6	6	cloves garlic, diced or crushed
1/4 tsp	1 mL	cayenne pepper
2 Tbsp	30 mL	barbecue rub
1 tsp	5 mL	dried oregano
1 tsp	5 mL	thyme
2 cups	500 mL	canned tomatoes
8 cups	2 L	chicken stock
1/4 cup	60 mL	hot sauce
		salt and pepper to taste
2 lbs	900 g	raw shrimp (peeled and deveined)
6 cups	2.5 mL	cooked rice

Heat butter in a medium frying pan over medium. Add flour and cook for 3 to 5 minutes, until you have a rich, dark brown roux. Set aside.

Heat oil in a medium frying pan over medium-high and brown pork until golden brown. Remove from pan and set aside.

Add onions, celery and peppers, and cook until soft. Add roux and cook for 2 to 3 minutes.

Add next 10 ingredients and pork, and simmer over low heat for 1 to 2 hours.

Adjust seasoning, then add shrimp and cook another 5 minutes or until shrimp are just done. Ladle over rice and serve.

1 serving: 500 Calories; 20 g Total Fat (6 g Mono, 2 g Poly, 10 g Sat); 200 mg Cholesterol; 39 g Carbohydrates (2 g Fibre, 2 g Sugar); 37 g Protein; 730 mg Sodium

NOVA SCOTIA CLAM CHOWDER

MAKES: 4 SERVINGS
DIFFICULTY: ★ ★

In Nova Scotia, clams are often called steamers and may be served deep-fried, baked or steamed. Serve with oyster crackers.

3	3	5 oz (140 g) cans of clams, drained with juice reserved
2 cups	500 mL	cubed potatoes
1 cup	250 mL	diced celery
1/2 cup	125 mL	water
3/4 cup	175 mL	butter
3/4 cup	175 mL	all-purpose flour
1 cup	250 mL	whole cream (30%)
2 cups	500 mL	milk
2 tsp	10 mL	salt
1 tsp	5 mL	pepper

Add juice from clams, potato cubes, celery and water to a large skillet over medium heat. Cook until potatoes soften.

In a medium saucepan over medium, mix butter, flour, cream and milk. Cook until smooth, stirring constantly to prevent sticking.

Add potato mixture and clams, and season with salt and pepper. Cover and simmer for 10 minutes until chowder is smooth and creamy.

1 serving: 620 Calories; 47 g Total Fat (12 g Mono, 2 g Poly, 30 g Sat); 140 mg Cholesterol; 40 g Carbohydrates (2 g Fibre, 8 g Sugar); 11 g Protein; 1760 mg Sodium

---

BAKING POWDER BISCUITS

MAKES: 24 BISCUITS
DIFFICULTY: ★ ★

There is no better accompaniment for a steaming bowl of soup than hot, home-made biscuits. They also taste great slathered with butter or jam.

3 1/2 cups	975 mL	all-purpose flour
1 Tbsp	15 mL	baking powder
2 tsp	10 mL	salt
6 oz	170 g	cold butter, cut in cubes
1 1/4 cup	300 mL	buttermilk

Combine first 3 ingredients in bowl of a mixer. Add butter cubes and work with your fingers until mixture resembles coarse meal.

Slowly add buttermilk and mix only until incorporated. Portion with an ice cream scoop onto a baking sheet and bake in a 350°F (175°C) oven for 15 minutes or until golden brown.

1 biscuit: 120 Calories; 6 g Total Fat (1.5 g Mono, 0 g Poly, 3.5 g Sat); 15 mg Cholesterol; 13 g Carbohydrates (0 g Fibre, 0 g Sugar); 2 g Protein; 280 mg Sodium

PHILIPPINE CHICKEN STEW

MAKES: 6 SERVINGS   **DIFFICULTY:** ★

Be sure to brown the chicken well as it helps develop the flavour of the stew. Serve over steamed basmati rice.

2 Tbsp	30 mL	cooking oil
1	1	roasting chicken, cut into 8 pieces
1 cup	250 mL	finely diced onion
1 cup	250 mL	red wine vinegar
1/2 cup	125 mL	soy sauce
2	2	bay leaves
6	6	cloves garlic, crushed
1 tsp	5 mL	pepper
1 cup	250 mL	chicken stock
1 cup	250 mL	coconut milk
2 Tbsp	30mL	liquid honey
1 cup	250 mL	diced dates

Add oil to a heavy bottomed pot and brown chicken over medium-high until light golden brown. Remove chicken and set aside.

Drain fat from pan and add onions, then deglaze with red wine vinegar.

Add next 5 ingredients and mix well. Add chicken to pot and cover. Reduce heat and simmer for 1 to 1 1/2 hours.

Remove chicken and set aside, keeping it warm. Add remaining 3 ingredients and adjust seasoning. Simmer until sauce has reduce to your desired consistency, approximately 20 to 30 minutes. Add chicken and stir to coat with sauce, then serve.

1 serving: 330 Calories; 11 g Total Fat (4 g Mono, 2 g Poly, 3 g Sat); 75 mg Cholesterol; 32 g Carbohydrates (2 g Fibre, 24 g Sugar); 27 g Protein; 1430 mg Sodium

Pictured on page 269.

BLACK BEAN SOUP

MAKES: 12 SERVINGS   **DIFFICULTY:** ★ ★

Black beans are also called turtle beans. If you buy dried beans, they must be pre-cooked to soften them up. It has been suggested that a longer cooking time reduces how much gas the beans cause when eaten. You can use canned black beans instead in this recipe.

4 cups	1 L	dried black beans
16 cups	4 L	chicken stock
1 cup	250 mL	diced bacon
1 cup	250 mL	diced onion
1 cup	250 mL	diced celery
1 cup	250 mL	diced carrots
1 Tbsp	15 mL	cumin
1 Tbsp	15 mL	chili powder
1 Tbsp	15 mL	hot sauce
1 tsp	5 mL	thyme
1 Tbsp	15 mL	garlic
		salt and freshly cracked pepper to taste

sour cream or yogurt for garnish
freshly chopped cilantro or parsley for garnish

Helpful Tips

VEGAN OPTION: Replace the chicken stock with water or vegetable stock and omit the bacon. The seasonings will have to be adjusted. Fresh chopped herbs may be added if more flavour is required because the bacon has been omitted.

Bring beans and stock to a boil in a large stock pot, then reduce heat to a simmer and cook for 2 hours, loosely covered with a lid.

In a large frying pan, fry bacon until it is crisp and has rendered most of its fat. Remove bacon from pan and set aside.

Add next 3 ingredients to pan and cook in bacon fat until tender.

Add next 7 ingredients and set aside.

Once beans are cooked, top up liquid level with water or stock (there will be some evaporation during the cooking process). Transfer half of beans to a food processor or blender and purée to your desired consistency. Add puréed beans back to pot and stir in vegetable mixture and bacon. Bring to a simmer and adjust seasonings.

Serve with a dollop of sour cream or yogurt, and fresh chopped cilantro or parsley.

1 serving: 350 Calories; 4.5 g Total Fat (1.5 g Mono, 1 g Poly, 1.5 g Sat); 10 mg Cholesterol; 57 g Carbohydrates (12 g Fibre, 6 g Sugar); 21 g Protein; 1130 mg Sodium

Pictured on page 269.

RISOTTO

MAKES: 6 SERVINGS   **DIFFICULTY: ★ ★**

You can use this plain risotto as a base for your own creations. Try adding fresh herbs and roasted garlic. Toss a few sautéed mushroom on top. For something really different, substitute 2 cups (500 mL) pumpkin soup for the stock.

1 Tbsp	30 mL	butter
2 Tbsp	30 mL	olive oil
1/2 cup	125 mL	finely chopped onion
2 cups	500 mL	arborio rice
1 cup	250 mL	white wine, optional
6 cups	1.5 L	warm chicken stock, *divided*
1/2 cup	125 mL	grated Parmesan cheese
		salt and pepper to taste

In a heavy saucepan melt butter and olive oil together and add onions. Cook over medium-low heat until just soft.

Add the rice and stir to coat all grains evenly, then add white wine. Cook, stirring, until only about one-third of the wine is remaining.

Add 1 cup (250 mL) chicken stock and cook until liquid is just absorbed. Repeat until all of the chicken stock is used.

Remove from heat and stir in cheese. Season with salt and pepper and serve.

1 serving: 260 Calories; 11 g Total Fat (4.5 g Mono, 0.5 g Poly, 4.5 g Sat); 15 mg Cholesterol; 27 g Carbohydrates (2 g Fibre, 2 g Sugar); 5 g Protein; 720 mg Sodium

Risotto must be cooked over low heat and stirred frequently to achieve the "creamy" texture. The stock should be warm but not boiling hot. To make the risotto ahead, prepare the dish as indicated above but hold back on the last cup (250 mL) chicken stock. Transfer risotto to a bowl and chill immediately. To reheat, warm it over low heat and add the remaining stock, then add the cheese and seasonings.

The Wide World of Guy
PASTAS

If BBQ is the ultimate man's meal, then pasta must be the penultimate man's meal. Many factors leads us to this conclusion. We often first explored these dishes in our childhood when we first learned to boil water. Pasta dishes are relatively easy to make, with common ingredients in the sauces; the results are filling for all your family and friends; and they can be scaled up at the last moment to include last-minute drop-ins. They are one-dish wonders where a little garlic toast or a side salad adds enough flair to accompany the onslaught of the full course of pasta. The leftover sauces and even pasta can be chilled or frozen for a perfect snack or salad.

MACARONI AND CHEESE

MAKES: 12 SERVINGS   **DIFFICULTY:** ★ ★

The hot sauce and crushed potato chips are what sets this mac 'n' cheese apart from the blue box. Make this dish for your family instead—they'll love you for it. Leftovers, if there are any, taste great sliced about 1 inch (2.5 cm) thick and pan-fried for breakfast with bacon and eggs. Don't limit yourself to good ol' Cheddar for this recipe—throw in a little Parmesan, Asiago, pecorino, Swiss or Monterey jack, too.

1 lb	454 g	macaroni
4	4	large eggs
2 cups	500 mL	evaporated milk
1 tsp	5 mL	grainy mustard
1/4 cup	60 mL	butter
		salt and pepper to taste
4 1/2 cups	1.1 L	grated cheese
1/4 cup	60 mL	sour cream
1 tsp	5 mL	hot sauce, optional
1 cup	250 mL	crushed potato chips

Cook pasta according to package directions and drain.

Mix together next 6 ingredients and cook over low heat until the mixture begins to thicken. Add macaroni, stirring to coat evenly, then add cheese and sour cream and cook until melted and creamy.

The macaroni can be served at this point, or you can pour it into an ovenproof dish, top it with last 2 ingredients, then bake it in a 400°F (200°C) oven for 10 to 20 minutes or until golden brown on top.

1 serving: 410 Calories; 20 g Total Fat (4 g Mono, 1 g Poly, 11 g Sat); 120 mg Cholesterol; 37 g Carbohydrates (1 g Fibre, 4 g Sugar); 21 g Protein; 450 mg Sodium

Helpful Tips

But here's the real beauty of pastas. The slow-release carbohydrates of pasta are perfect for long workout support and even marathon running. Pastas are filling but don't have as high a glycemic index as many other filling staples. Whole wheat pasta is a great way to get insoluble fiber, the B vitamins, vitamin E, magnesium, zinc and potassium. THERE! We've almost convinced ourselves that pasta is the perfect health food.

That kind of delusion is very much a man's trait and therefore pasta is a great man dish.

SLOW-ROASTED SALMON WITH PESTO, PASTA AND PEAS

MAKES: 4 SERVINGS   **DIFFICULTY: ★**

Cooking salmon slowly at low heat ensures that you will have a tender, succulent fillet. This elegant meal is simple to prepare but sophisticated enough to serve to company. Perfect for date night!

1 Tbsp	15 mL	canola oil
2	2	6 oz (170 g) red spring salmon fillets
		salt and pepper to taste
2 tsp	10 mL	butter, *divided*
8 oz	225 g	tagliatelle or other wide noodle
1/2 cup	125 mL	pesto sauce
1/4 cup	60 mL	diced red pepper or grape tomatoes
1/4 cup	60 mL	peas
2 Tbsp	30 mL	whipping cream, optional

Pour oil in a non-stick skillet and spread around, then place salmon fillets in, skin side down. Season with salt and pepper and crown each fillet with 1 tsp (5 mL) butter.

Place in a 250°F (120°C) oven and cook for 18 to 20 minutes for medium rare, and 25 to 30 minutes for medium well.

As fish is cooking, add pasta to rapidly boiling salted water in a large pot and cook until al dente. Meanwhile, heat pesto in a non-stick skillet over medium-high, then add red pepper and peas. Cook until heated through, then stir in whipping cream and cook another 2 minutes. Add drained pasta and toss well to coat each pasta strand. Plate in a hot bowl, and top with slow-roasted salmon.

1 serving: 550 Calories; 30 g Total Fat (4.5 g Mono, 3 g Poly, 6 g Sat); 65 mg Cholesterol; 41 g Carbohydrates (10 g Fibre, 6 g Sugar); 30 g Protein; 350 mg Sodium

> Part of the secret of success in life is to eat what you like and let the food fight it out inside.
>
> —Mark Twain

SHRIMP ALFREDO

MAKES: 6 SERVINGS　　　　**DIFFICULTY: ★ ★**

Pasta lovers will adore this traditional dish—the savoury Alfredo sauce will draw them in, and the shrimp will serve as the perfect exclamation point. If you have any leftovers, toss them in the fridge for lunch the next day. It's like a gift that keeps on giving.

12 oz	340 g	fettuccini
1/4 cup	60 mL	butter
2 Tbsp	30 mL	extra virgin olive oil
1	1	onion, diced
2	2	cloves garlic, minced
1	1	medium red pepper, diced
1/2 lb	225 g	diced white mushrooms
1 lb	454 g	medium shrimp (peeled and deveined)
1	1	15 oz (425 mL) jar of Alfredo sauce
1/2 cup	125 mL	grated Romano cheese
1/2 cup	125 mL	cream
1 tsp	5 mL	cayenne pepper
1/4 tsp	1 mL	salt
1/4 tsp	1 mL	pepper
1/4 cup	60 mL	chopped parsley

Bring a large pot of lightly salted water to a boil. Add pasta and cook for 8 to 10 minutes or until al dente. Drain and set aside.

Meanwhile, in a saucepan over medium heat, melt butter and add olive oil. Stir in onion and cook until softened and translucent, about 2 minutes.

Stir in garlic, red pepper and mushrooms and cook over medium-high heat until soft, about 2 minutes more.

Stir in shrimp and cook until firm and pink. Add Alfredo sauce, Romano cheese and cream, and bring to a simmer. Cook, stirring constantly until thickened, about 5 minutes.

Season with cayenne, salt and pepper. Stir drained pasta into sauce, sprinkle with chopped parsley and serve.

1 serving: 590 Calories; 29 g Total Fat (8 g Mono, 1.5 g Poly, 15 g Sat); 185 mg Cholesterol; 54 g Carbohydrates (2 g Fibre, 7 g Sugar); 31 g Protein; 690 mg Sodium

CHILI VODKA LINGUINE WITH SHRIMP

MAKES: 4 SERVINGS   **DIFFICULTY: ★ ★**

Not your average cream sauce! We've spiked this seafood-laden pasta with vodka and jalapeños for a spicy bite you won't soon forget.

12 oz	340 g	linguine
1 tsp	5 mL	olive oil
1/3 cup	75 mL	finely chopped prosciutto (or deli) ham
2	2	cloves garlic, minced
2 cups	500 mL	half-and-half cream
1/2 cup	125 mL	vodka
2 Tbsp	30 mL	butter
1 Tbsp	15 mL	finely chopped canned sliced jalapeño pepper, drained
1/2 tsp	2 mL	salt
1/4 tsp	1 mL	pepper
1/2 lb	225 g	small bay scallops
1/2 lb	225 g	uncooked medium shrimp (peeled and deveined)
1 Tbsp	15 mL	lemon juice
1 Tbsp	15 mL	chopped fresh parsley

Bring a large pot of salted water to a boil over high heat. Add pasta and cook, uncovered, for 10 to 12 minutes, stirring occasionally, until tender but firm. Drain and return to same pot, covering to keep warm.

Heat olive oil in a large frying pan over medium. Add ham and garlic and cook, stirring, for about 2 minutes until fragrant.

Stir in next 6 ingredients. Simmer, uncovered, for 8 to 10 minutes, stirring occasionally, until slightly thickened.

Stir in scallops and shrimp. Cook for 3 to 5 minutes until shrimp turn pink and scallops are opaque. Remove from heat.

Stir in lemon juice. Add to pasta and toss until coated. Transfer to a large serving platter. and sprinkle with parsley.

1 serving: 490 Calories; 25 g Total Fat (2.5 g Mono, 1 g Poly, 13 g Sat); 195 mg Cholesterol; 39 g Carbohydrates (3 g Fibre, 7 g Sugar); 49 g Protein; 1450 mg Sodium

SPAGHETTI WITH SHRIMP AND GREENS

MAKES: 4 SERVINGS   **DIFFICULTY:** ★ ★ ★

Shrimp, pasta and salad…all in the same bowl! For the greens, try a spring mix, baby spinach, kale or arugula. For the tomato sauce, skip the store-bought variety this time and use the recipe on page 98. It really does make a difference. If you make the sauce in advance, you can just throw the rest of the dish together when you get home from work.

1 lb	454 g	spaghetti or linguine
1 Tbsp	15 mL	olive oil
4	4	cloves garlic
1/2 tsp	2 mL	red chili flakes
2 cups	500 mL	tomato sauce
1 lb	454 g	raw shrimp (peeled and deveined)
2	2	handfuls of greens
		salt and pepper to taste

Cook pasta according to package directions in heavily salted, rapidly boiling water

Meanwhile, in a heavy skillet gently warm olive oil, garlic and red chilies. Cook for 5 minutes or until garlic just turns golden brown.

Add tomato sauce and bring to a simmer.

Add shrimp and cook until almost done, then add greens—don't worry, they will cook down. Drain pasta and add to pan. Toss pasta in sauce until evenly coated and serve.

1 serving: 610 Calories; 7 g Total Fat (3 g Mono, 2 g Poly, 1 g Sat); 170 mg Cholesterol; 94 g Carbohydrates (5 g Fibre, 7 g Sugar); 40 g Protein; 900 mg Sodium

FETTUCCINI WITH BROCCOLI AND CHERRY TOMATOES

MAKES: 4 SERVINGS   **DIFFICULTY: ★**

As most pasta aficionados will tell you, the key to great-tasting pasta is to cook it in generously salted boiling water. The salted water flavours the pasta and reduces how much salt you'll need to add to the finished dish.

1 lb	454 g	fettuccini
2 Tbsp	30 mL	olive oil
4	4	cloves garlic, finely chopped
1/2 tsp	2 mL	hot pepper flakes
4 cups	1 L	fresh or frozen broccoli florets
2 cups	500 mL	halved cherry tomatoes
1/4 cup	60 mL	chopped fresh Italian parsley
1/4 tsp	1 mL	salt
1/4 tsp	1 mL	pepper
1/4 cup	60 mL	shredded Parmesan cheese

Bring a large pot of salted water to a boil over high heat. Add pasta and cook, uncovered, until tender but firm, about 8 to 10 minutes. Drain and return to pot, reserving 3/4 cup (175 mL) of cooking water.

Meanwhile, heat oil in a large skillet over medium heat. Add garlic and hot pepper flakes, stirring often, until garlic is slightly golden, about 2 minutes.

Add broccoli. Cover and cook for 4 minutes

Add tomatoes and cook, stirring, until broccoli is tender-crisp, about 3 minutes.

Add parsley, salt and pepper and toss to combine. Add broccoli and tomato mixture to pasta and toss to coat, adding enough of the reserved cooking water to moisten. Sprinkle with Parmesan cheese and serve.

1 serving: 170 Calories; 11 g Total Fat (6 g Mono, 1 g Poly, 2 g Sat); 5 mg Cholesterol; 51 g Carbohydrates (5 g Fibre, 6 g Sugar); 20 g Protein; 270 mg Sodium

PASTA GRILLATO

MAKES: 4 SERVINGS   **DIFFICULTY: ★**

Here's a quick pasta dish that tastes great. Make sure you use fresh herbs, not dried. Long noodles, such as linguini, fettuccini or pappardelle work well. Serve sprinkled with grated cheese.

24 oz	680 g	pasta
1 Tbsp	15 mL	olive oil
1	1	sliced onion
6	6	cloves garlic, thinly sliced
1/4 cup	60 mL	sundried tomatoes
1 cup	250 mL	chopped fresh tomatoes
2 Tbsp	30 mL	capers
2 Tbsp	30 mL	lemon juice
1/4 cup	60 mL	brandy
2 cups	500 mL	whipping cream
1/4 cup	60 mL	freshly shaved herbs (basil, oregano or a combination)

Bring a large pot of salted water to a boil over high heat. Add pasta and cook, uncovered, until tender but firm, about 8 to 10 minutes. Drain and return to same pot, reserving 3/4 cup (175 mL) cooking water.

Heat oil in a medium frying pan over medium. Add onion and cook until just soft, about 5 minutes.

Add garlic, sundried tomatoes and fresh tomatoes and cook for about 5 minutes or until the tomatoes are losing their liquid.

Add remaining ingredients and continue to cook for 5 minutes. Add some reserved cooking water to sauce and stir until sauce is nice and thick. Add pasta and toss to coat.

1 serving: 910 Calories; 26 g Total Fat (6 g Mono, 1 g Poly, 14 g Sat); 80 mg Cholesterol; 134 g Carbohydrates (5 g Fibre, 9 g Sugar); 24 g Protein; 230 mg Sodium

SPEEDY CHICKEN CARBONARA

MAKES: ABOUT 2 CUPS   **DIFFICULTY: ★**

So you won't have to rely on commercially produced high-salt sauces, here's a recipe with the true method for making a carbonara sauce from scratch—and a touch of chili heat adds a dash of adventure.

12 oz	340 g	spaghetti
4	4	egg yolks
1/2 cup	125 mL	grated Parmesan cheese
1/4 cup	60 mL	finely chopped fresh parsley
1/2 tsp	2 mL	chili paste (sambal olek)
6	6	bacon slices, chopped
1 1/2 cups	375 mL	chopped cooked chicken
1 cup	250 mL	chicken broth, heated

Cook pasta according to package directions. Drain and return to same pot. Cover to keep warm.

Combine next 4 ingredients in a small bowl. Set aside.

Cook bacon in large frying pan on medium until crisp. Remove with slotted spoon to paper towels to drain. Drain and discard all but 1 Tbsp (15 mL) drippings from pan.

Add chicken and pasta to same frying pan. Reduce heat to medium-low and cook, stirring, for about 2 minutes until heated through.

Whisk hot broth into egg mixture. Add to pasta mixture. Add bacon. Toss until coated. Serve immediately.

1 cup (250 mL): 330 Calories; 24 g Total Fat (10 g Mono, 2.5 g Poly, 8 g Sat); 205 mg Cholesterol; 23 g Carbohydrates (2 g Fibre, 2 g Sugar); 29 g Protein; 580 mg Sodium

Pictured on page 179.

Speedy Chicken Carbonara, 178

Wild Salmon en Papillote, page 191

WHEN QUICK COUNTS

Ya, ya, everyone is in a rush these days, everyone juggles schedules to survive. There's just not enough time in the day for all the things we have to do. Sometimes the day you have to stay late at work is the same day one kid has a ballet recital and the other has a soccer practice. At the same time. Here are some recipes to help in that less-than-an-hour of need.

QUICK AND DIRTY RICE

MAKES: 4 SERVINGS   **DIFFICULTY: ★**

Learn this recipe well. It is quick and easy to prepare, can be called upon at any moment and most ingredients are readily available in the average guy's kitchen.

1 lb	454 g	lean ground beef
1/4 cup	60 mL	minced onion
1 3/4 cup	425 mL	chicken broth
1/2 cup	125 mL	long-grain rice
1 tsp	5 mL	dried parsley flakes
1/2 tsp	2 mL	salt
1/2 tsp	2 mL	pepper

Brown ground beef in a medium skillet until no longer pink, breaking up with a fork. Add minced onion and cook 2 minutes longer. Pour off most of the excess fat.

Stir in broth and rice. Simmer gently, covered, for 18 to 20 minutes or until rice is tender and most of broth is absorbed.

Add parsley, salt and pepper. Toss and serve.

1 serving: 360 Calories; 16 g Total Fat (7 g Mono, 0 g Poly, 6 g Sat); 70 mg Cholesterol; 21 g Carbohydrates (0 g Fibre, trace Sugar); 24 g Protein; 610 mg Sodium

I wish my stove came with a Save As button like Word has. That way I could experiment with my cooking and not fear ruining my dinner.

—Jarod Kintz

BEEF AND BROCCOLI STIR-FRY

MAKES: 6 SERVINGS   **DIFFICULTY: ★ ★**

This tasty stir-fry places beef as the star of the dish, and though the broccoli and egg noodles play second fiddle, they are still crucial elements. Try it with broad egg noodles if you want to mix it up a little.

1 lb	454 g	fresh thin egg noodles
2 tsp	10 mL	sesame oil
1/4 cup	60 mL	peanut oil, *divided*
1 lb	454 g	beef fillet, thinly sliced
1 Tbsp	15 mL	ground ginger
2	2	cloves garlic, crushed
1/2 cup	125 mL	snow peas, trimmed, halved
1/2 cup	125 mL	chicken stock, *divided*
2 Tbsp	30 mL	soy sauce
2 Tbsp	30 mL	oyster sauce
2 cups	500 mL	broccoli florets
1/4 tsp	1 mL	pepper

Place noodles in a heatproof bowl and cover with boiling water. Let stand for 5 minutes or until heated through. Drain noodles and add sesame oil. Toss to combine.

Heat a wok over high heat and add 2 Tbsp (30 mL) peanut oil. Add beef and stir-fry for 3 to 5 minutes or until seared. Remove from wok and set aside.

Heat remaining 2 Tbsp (30 mL) peanut oil in wok. Add ginger and garlic and stir-fry for 1 minute. Add snow peas and 1/4 cup (60 mL) stock and stir-fry for 2 minutes or until liquid is reduced by half. Return beef and any juices to wok.

Add noodles, soy sauce, oyster sauce, remaining 1/4 cup (60 mL) stock, broccoli and pepper. Stir-fry for 2 to 3 minutes or until heated throughout, then serve.

1 serving: 410 Calories; 11 g Total Fat (4 g Mono, 1.5 g Poly, 3 g Sat); 45 mg Cholesterol; 52 g Carbohydrates (5 g Fibre, 4 g Sugar); 26 g Protein; 1320 mg Sodium

"Broccoli and beef" sounds so much better and healthier than "beef and broccoli." They taste exactly the same, but the calories are obviously lower in the first dish. But if you're serving it to your guy friends, remember to call it beef and broccoli.

CHICKEN CUTLETS WITH PESTO

MAKES: 4 SERVINGS   **DIFFICULTY: ★ ★**

Pesto is so fast to make at home. All you need is some basil, pine nuts, olive oil and some good Parmesan. If you prefer not to make it, farmers' markets are great places to find fresh pesto.

4	4	4 oz (113 g) skinless, boneless chicken breasts
		salt and pepper to taste
2 Tbsp	30 mL	olive oil
1 cup	250 mL	chicken stock
1/2 cup	125 mL	grape tomatoes
1/2 cup	125 mL	pesto

Pound chicken breasts until even in thickness, and season with salt and pepper. Heat a large frying pan over medium-high. Once hot, add oil and brown chicken on both sides, 2 to 3 minutes, per side. Remove and keep warm.

Drain all but 1 Tbsp (15 mL) fat. Add chicken stock to deglaze pan, then add chicken and tomatoes. Turn heat down to a gentle simmer and cover loosely with a lid or with foil. Cook for 5 minutes or until chicken is just cooked. Remove and set aside where it will keep warm.

Add pesto to pan and cook for 2 to 3 minutes, or until well incorporated. Adjust seasonings and transfer chicken back to pan. Toss to coat, then serve.

1 serving: 480 Calories; 24 g Total Fat (6 g Mono, 1.5 g Poly, 4 g Sat); 145 mg Cholesterol; 4 g Carbohydrates (1 g Fibre, 3 g Sugar); 58 g Protein; 560 mg Sodium

GREEK SHRIMP

This elegant yet super fast dish can be served with bread as an appetizer or with rice and salad as main course.

1/4 cup	60 mL	olive oil
1/2	1/2	finely diced onion
3	3	cloves garlic, crushed
3	3	tomatoes, diced
1 tsp	5 mL	dried oregano
2 lbs	900 g	shrimp (peeled and deveined)
2 oz	60 mL	ouzo or metaxa
		salt and pepper to taste
2 Tbsp	30 mL	capers
3 Tbsp	45 mL	chopped parsley

Heat oil in a large pan over medium, then add onion and cook until soft. Add garlic and tomatoes and continue to cook until tomatoes start to break down and extract their liquid.

Add oregano and shrimp, tossing to coat, and cook until shrimp turn pink.

Remove from heat and add ouzo to pan, being careful as it may flare up. Return pan to heat, stir in remaining 4 ingredients and serve.

1 serving: 210 Calories; 9 g Total Fat (5 g Mono, 1.5 g Poly, 1.5 g Sat); 170 mg Cholesterol; 4 g Carbohydrates (trace Fibre, 2 g Sugar); 24 g Protein; 200 mg Sodium

Let God worry about your modesty;
I want to see your enthusiasm.

—Robert Farrar Capon

PAN-SEARED JUMBO SHRIMP

MAKES: 2 SERVINGS   **DIFFICULTY: ★**

Quick and easy, but unbelievably good. Use a blood orange if they are available.

1 Tbsp	15 mL	olive oil
1 lb	454 g	jumbo shrimp (peeled and deveined), patted very dry
2 oz	60 mL	sambuca
1	1	orange, zested and juiced
1 Tbsp	15 mL	shaved fresh basil
		salt and pepper to taste

In a large pan, heat oil to just below smoking point, then add shrimp. Pan-fry until they just turn pink, about 1 minute. Remove from heat and add sambuca to deglaze pan.

Add orange juice and basil, then season with salt and pepper.

1 serving: 320 Calories; 7 g Total Fat (4.5 g Mono, 0.5 g Poly, 1 g Sat); 170 mg Cholesterol; 11 g Carbohydrates (2 g Fibre, 9 g Sugar); 37 g Protein; 950 mg Sodium

Shrimp are sold according to size, but keep in mind that the perception of size varies from region to region, as well as between fish markets. As a general guideline, these are the number of shrimp you can expect to get from a 1 lb (454 g) measure:

- Jumbo   11 – 15
- Extra-large   16 – 20
- Large   21 – 30
- Medium   31 – 35
- Small   36 – 45
- Baby   about 100

PAD THAI

MAKES: 4 SERVINGS   **DIFFICULTY: ★ ★**

Forget take-out. Try this quick dish next time you have a yen for this spicy cuisine.

1/2 lb	225 g	shrimp (peeled and deveined)
2 Tbsp	30 mL	cooking oil
2	2	cloves garlic, crushed
2 Tbsp	30 mL	fish sauce
1 Tbsp	15 mL	rice vinegar
1 tsp	5 mL	chili powder
2 cups	500 mL	rice noodles
2	2	large eggs
2 Tbsp	30 mL	granulated sugar
1 cup	250 mL	bean sprouts
1/4 cup	60 mL	chopped green onions

Heat wok over medium-high. Add shrimp and cook until they just turn pink, about 1 minute. Transfer to a plate, and wipe out wok.

Add oil and garlic, and quickly stir-fry until garlic is fragrant, about 1 minute.

Add fish sauce, vinegar and chili powder, thinning sauce out with water if it is too thick. Stir in noodles, then push them aside. Add eggs and quickly stir-fry.

Add remaining 3 ingredients and give it a quick toss. Thin out with a little water, if necessary and serve.

1 serving: 510 Calories; 11 g Total Fat (5 g Mono, 2.5 g Poly, 1.5 g Sat); 155 mg Cholesterol; 83 g Carbohydrates (2 g Fibre, 7 g Sugar); 18 g Protein; 870 mg Sodium

LESS MESS IS BETTER

Go ahead, confess. Hello, my name is XXX...and I "hate cleaning dishes."
We are not alone. For reasons that have much to do with our Paleolithic
ancestors and the male chromosome, male humans have an aversion to
washing up after meals. Yes, we do it, even gracefully if we have to, but
that's because someone else cooked the dinner and we are trying to make
up for lost ground. If we cook, we often steer away from dishes that
require a lot of clean up. And if we cook, we can reverse the shame we
have always felt, and coerce others to wash up after us. Search out
one-pot wonders, recipes using throwaway foil, and even edible dishes.

KOREAN CHILI

MAKES: 6 SERVINGS   **DIFFICULTY:** ★

If you are unfamiliar with sambal olek, taste it before you add a whole lot to this dish. It is quite spicy. Serve this chili over rice or noodles.

2 tsp	10 mL	canola oil
1 cup	250 mL	diced onion
1 cup	250 mL	diced bell peppers
1/4 cup	60 mL	crushed garlic
1/4 cup	60 mL	crushed ginger root
2 lbs	1 kg	ground turkey
1 cup	250 mL	sliced white mushrooms
1/3 cup	75 mL	soy sauce
1/3 cup	75 mL	granulated sugar
1/4 cup	60 mL	sesame oil
1 tsp	5 mL	pepper
1/2 tsp	2 mL	red chili powder or cayenne pepper
1	1	28 oz (796 mL) can of diced tomatoes
2 Tbsp	30 mL	sambal olek
1/4 cup	60 mL	cornstarch
1 cup	250 mL	water
1 cup	250 mL	bean sprouts

Heat oil in a Dutch oven over medium-high. Add onions and peppers and cook for 5 minutes.

Add garlic and ginger and cook another 5 minutes.

Add ground turkey and cook until no longer pink.

Add next 8 ingredients. Dissolve cornstarch in water and add to pot. Bring to a simmer, then turn to low and cook for 1 hour over low heat.

Remove pot from heat and adjust seasoning. Add bean sprouts, cover with lid and allow to "steep" for 30 minutes.

1 serving: 450 Calories; 23 g Total Fat (9 g Mono, 7 g Poly, 5 g Sat); 120 mg Cholesterol; 30 g Carbohydrates (2 g Fibre, 18 g Sugar); 31 g Protein; 1460 mg Sodium

BUTTER CHICKEN

MAKES: 7 SERVINGS   **DIFFICULTY:** ★

The ingredient list may be long, but this dish is actually simple to prepare. Cook some rice as you prepare the chicken, and serve everything alongside a salad.

1/4 cup	60 mL	unsalted butter
1/4 cup	60 mL	diced white onions
1 tsp	5 mL	ground ginger
2 tsp	10 mL	crushed garlic
1 1/2 Tbsp	22 mL	paprika
1/4 tsp	1 mL	turmeric
1 tsp	5 mL	salt
1/2 tsp	2 mL	dried coriander
1/2 tsp	2 mL	cumin
1/4 tsp	1 mL	pepper
1/3 cup	75 mL	tomato paste
1 1/2 cups	375 mL	half-and-half cream
1 1/2 cups	375 mL	chicken stock
1/4 cup	60 mL	diced tomatoes
1 Tbsp	15 mL	cornstarch
2 lbs	900 g	chicken breast, cut in 1/2 inch (12 mm) pieces

Melt butter in a medium frying pan over medium heat. Add onions and cook until softened, about 2 minutes.

Add next 9 ingredients and cook until butter starts to bubble through tomato paste mixture.

Whisk in next 4 ingredients and bring to a simmer. Cook over low heat for 15 minutes, then adjust seasoning.

Add chicken and cook until meat is no longer pink inside, about 15 to 20 minutes. Plate and serve.

1 serving: 550 Calories; 43 g Total Fat (12 g Mono, 2 g Poly, 26 g Sat); 220 mg Cholesterol; 8 g Carbohydrates (trace Fibre, 2 g Sugar); 32 g Protein; 980 mg Sodium

WILD SALMON EN PAPILLOTE

MAKES: 4 SERVINGS   **DIFFICULTY: ★ ★ ★**

Salmon fillets smothered with butter and dill are wrapped in parchment paper and baked in the oven. The end result is fork tender fish in a neat little package. No plates necessary! Watch out for steam when you open the packets.

4	4	**4 oz (115 g) wild salmon fillets**
4	4	**leeks, white part only, sliced thin and well washed**
1/4 cup	60 mL	**dry white wine**
		sea salt and pepper to taste
1	1	**bunch dill or other fresh herb, chopped**
1/4 cup	60 mL	**unsalted butter, cut into 4 pieces**
1	1	**egg white, lightly beaten**
1	1	**lemon, sliced**
		a variety of sautéed vegetables

Heat oven to 350°F (175°C). Fold a 24 inch (60 cm) sheet of parchment paper in half, and cut out a heart shape about 4 inches (10 cm) larger than a fish fillet. Place fillet near fold, and place a handful of leeks next to it; sprinkle with wine, salt, pepper and dill and top with a piece of butter. Brush edges of parchment paper with egg white, fold paper to enclose fish, and make small overlapping folds to seal edges, starting at the curve of the heart. Be sure each fold overlaps previous one to create an airtight seal.

Repeat with rest of fillets. Put packages on a baking sheet, and bake until paper is puffed and brown, about 10 to 15 minutes. Serve salmon in packets with lemon slices and sautéed vegetables.

1 serving: 380 Calories; 22 g Total Fat (6 g Mono, 4.5 g Poly, 9 g Sat); 160 mg Cholesterol; 13 g Carbohydrates (2 g Fibre, 4 g Sugar); 30 g Protein; 240 mg Sodium

Pictured on page 180.

TASTY CRAB BISQUE

MAKES: 4 SERVINGS   **DIFFICULTY: ★ ★**

Seafood soup lovers will go crazy for this crab bisque and will quickly discover that one bowl is never enough.

4	4	corncobs
1/4 cup	60 mL	butter
3/4 cup	175 mL	chopped chives or shallots
3	3	cloves garlic, minced
3 1/2 cups	825 mL	chicken broth
1/2 tsp	2 mL	cayenne pepper
1/4 tsp	60 mL	salt
1/4 tsp	60 mL	pepper
3 Tbsp	45 mL	all-purpose flour
2/3 cup	150 mL	half-and-half cream
3	3	6 oz (170 g) cans of crabmeat

Cut kernels from corn and set aside.

In a large, steep-sided skillet over medium heat, cook butter, chives and garlic until chives soften.

Slowly add corn, chicken broth, cayenne pepper, salt and pepper. Lower heat, cover and let simmer.

Stir flour and cream together in a small bowl and slowly pour into soup. Add crabmeat and let simmer for 10 minutes until slightly thick.

1 serving: 400 Calories; 21 g Total Fat (6 g Mono, 1.5 g Poly, 12 g Sat); 170 mg Cholesterol; 23 g Carbohydrates (2 g Fibre, 3 g Sugar); 31 g Protein; 1170 mg Sodium

Pictured on page 197.

ALBERTA CHOWDER

MAKES: 8 SERVINGS   **DIFFICULTY: ★**

A mushroomy chowder is a soothing, tasty way to end a stressful day. There's a lot of guts to this mixture, so it's really filling.

1/2 cup	125 mL	dried mushrooms
1 cup	250 mL	hot water
1/4 cup	60 mL	butter
1/2 cup	125 mL	finely chopped onion
2	2	cloves garlic
1 cup	250 mL	chopped shitake mushrooms
1 cup	250 mL	chopped oyster mushrooms
1 cup	250 mL	chopped button mushrooms
1/4 cup	60 mL	white wine
6 cups	1.5 mL	chicken stock
1/2 cup	125 mL	barley
1 1/2 cups	375 mL	diced potatoes
1 cup	250 mL	white beans, cooked or canned (drain and rinse)
1/3 cup	75 mL	liquid honey
2 cups	500 mL	whipping cream
1 Tbsp	15 mL	rosemary, chopped
		salt and pepper to taste

Rehydrate dried mushrooms with hot water.

Meanwhile, melt butter in a medium frying pan, and cook onion and garlic until soft. Add mushrooms and cook for 2 to 3 minutes.

Deglaze pan with a splash of white wine, then add remaining wine, chicken stock and barley. Simmer over low heat for 45 minutes.

Add potatoes and cook another 30 minutes until potatoes are tender.

Add beans, honey, cream and seasonings and cook for another 15 minutes, until soup has reduced and is thickened. Adjust seasoning. Serve with crusty bread.

1 serving: 340 Calories; 17 g Total Fat (4.5 g Mono, 0.5 g Poly, 11 g Sat); 55 mg Cholesterol; 40 g Carbohydrates (6 g Fibre, 14 g Sugar); 8 g Protein; 600 mg Sodium

GAME DAY

You have to master multi-tasking, such as how to use your remote control and your stove at the same time, all the while keenly aware of the timing of the commercials. You must develop an acute perception of the average time between commercials during different sporting events. Develop a few make-ahead appetizers and some classics and you may become the new go-to game day couch arena. Check out the pointers sprinkled through this section.

For most men, game day gatherings, whether hosted in the living room or in the back of your pickup truck, are the closest thing there is to heaven and are events we will look forward to all year long. Great competitive action, fabulous food and copious alcoholic beverages lay a solid foundation for the perfect tail-gating party! For that foundation to remain solid year after year, what you as a party hosting game day male must do is ensure the quality of those game day foods. Sure, several cocktails into the average tailgating party, importance placed on food quality will diminish exponentially. Up until that point where your party guests are slumped over in a pitcher of draught, you must insure that tasty nibblies are scattered liberally between periods in a hockey game, or during halftime in that big football game. It's game day for goodness sake, this is serious business!

NACHOS

MAKES: 6 SERVINGS   **DIFFICULTY: ★**

Chips...cheese...bacon...mmmmm, the perfect game day snack. This version is made on the barbecue, freeing up the oven for other dishes, but you could also cook it in a 375°F (190°C) oven.

1	1	**9 oz (240 g) bag of corn (or tortilla) chips**
1 1/4 cups	300 mL	**grated Monterey Jack cheese**
1 1/4 cups	300 mL	**grated medium Cheddar cheese**
6	6	**bacon slices, cooked crisp and crumbled**
1	1	**4 oz (113 g) can of diced green chilies**
3	3	**green onions, sliced**

Cut six 12 inch (30 cm) squares of heavy duty (or double layer of regular) foil. Grease each square with cooking spray. Arrange chips in 6 inch (15 cm) circle on each square. Crowd chips together so little or no foil is visible through them.

Divide and layer remaining 5 ingredients, in order given, on top of chips. Preheat barbecue to medium-low. Place squares on an ungreased grill. Close lid and cook for 5 to 10 minutes until cheese is melted. Check often, as they burn easily.

1 serving: 580 Calories; 47 g Total Fat (10 g Mono, 2 g Poly, 17 g Sat); 70 mg Cholesterol; 25 g Carbohydrates (2 g Fibre, 0 g Sugar); 19 g Protein; 910 mg Sodium

A Key to Sports Eating

HOCKEY: Learn how to slow it down and warm it up with a slow cooker. You can get to the kitchen and back to fill up your plate if you hurry.

FOOTBALL: 50 recipes with beer. With football you try to mimic the raw fun of a tailgate party at the big games. Except the Superbowl, which has quick and unpredictable commercials. You have to be in shape to run to the kitchen and get back in time. That said, Superbowl commercials are the best, so stock up as though you are a survivalist so you never have to leave the couch.

BASEBALL: The link between statistics and food largely has to do with chemical formulas, so you won't have to memorize any important recipes for this sport.

CURLING: an Olympic sport in slow motion. Learn how to speed it up and warm it up with spices.

PULLED PORK QUESADILLAS

MAKES: 6 SERVINGS   **DIFFICULTY: ★ ★**

All the flavour of a pulled pork sandwich with the crispy, cheesy goodness of a quesadilla. Finger food at its finest. Serve with salsa and sour cream.

2 Tbsp	30 mL	butter, *divided*
1	1	bone-in pork shoulder, trimmed of fat and cut into 2 inch (5 cm) cubes
1	1	12 oz (355 mL) can or Dr. Pepper soda
1	1	orange, quartered
1/4 tsp	1 mL	ground cinnamon
1/2 cup	125 mL	tomato paste
1/4 tsp	1 mL	ground cloves
2	2	bay leaves
3 cups	750 mL	water
1/2 tsp	2 mL	salt
1/4 tsp	1 mL	cracked pepper
1/2 cup	125 mL	diced red onion
1/2 cup	125 mL	diced red peppers
1/4 cup	60 mL	finely chopped fresh jalapeño pepper
1/4 cup	60 mL	chopped pineapple
1 cup	250 mL	arugula, chopped
6	6	whole grain tortillas (12 inch, 30 cm, diameter)
6 oz	170 g	grated Cheddar cheese

Melt 1 Tbsp (15 mL) butter in a large heavy bottomed pan over medium-high and sear pork until golden brown on all sides. Transfer to a large pot with next 9 ingredients. Bring to a boil, then reduce heat to a simmer. Allow to simmer until pork will tear with a fork, about 3 hours. Once pork is cooked, allow it to cool in cooking liquid for 30 minutes.

Remove pork from liquid and shred by hand. Pour some cooking liquid over top and set aside. Melt remaining 1 Tbsp (15 mL) butter over medium-high heat. Add onion and cook for 1 minute, then add red peppers, jalapeños and pineapple, cooking for an additional 3 minutes or until onions begin to soften. Fold in pork and 1/2 cup (125 mL) cooking liquid. Cook until liquid has evaporated. Set pan aside to rest for 4 minutes.

Arrange 3 tortillas flat on a work surface and spoon pork mixture equally over top. Sprinkle each with cheese and cover with 1 of remaining tortillas. Place under hot grill press for 1 1/2 minutes on each side, or until toasted and crispy. Allow to rest for 2 minutes, then cut each tortilla diagonally into 6 equal pieces.

1 serving: 380 Calories; 20 g Total Fat (6 g Mono, 1 g Poly, 9 g Sat); 40 mg Cholesterol; 43 g Carbohydrates (8 g Fibre, 12 g Sugar); 14 g Protein; 970 mg Sodium

Pictured on page 126.

Tasty Crab Bisque, page 192

Guacamole, page 205

ROOT BEER RIBS

MAKES: 12 SERVINGS   **DIFFICULTY: ★**

This rib recipe takes a bit of time. You cook the ribs in a roaster in water for 3 hours until they are fork tender, then let them stand while the juices are reabsorbed into the meat. Finally, you slather the sauce over top and reheat either by baking or barbecuing them.

5 lbs	2.2 kg	pork ribs
		salt and pepper to taste
2 Tbsp	30 mL	canola oil
2 cups	500 mL	roughly chopped onion
1 cup	250 mL	roughly chopped carrots
1 cup	250 mL	roughly chopped celery
10	10	cloves garlic
1 tsp	5 mL	dried thyme
2	2	bay leaves
1 tsp	5mL	dried rosemary
1 tsp	5 mL	ground cumin
3 cups	750 mL	chicken stock
3 cups	750 mL	good quality root beer

Place ribs in a roaster, leaving them whole if possible. Season with salt and pepper, then cover with boiling water. Cover tightly with foil and cook in a 300°F (150°C) oven for 3 hours. Remove from oven when ribs are fork tender. Let stand for 30 minutes (they will reabsorb liquid; if you remove them too quickly, the ribs will dry out). Place them on a baking sheet with parchment paper.

For the sauce, heat oil in a heavy saucepan and brown onions, carrots and celery until light golden brown. Add garlic, thyme, bay leaves, rosemary and cumin, and cook for another 5 minutes. If pan is a little dry, add a splash of oil. Add stock and deglaze the pan, scraping any brown bits off bottom. Strain sauce, and skim any fat from top. Add root beer and bring to a simmer. Reduce sauce by half, about 30 minutes.

Barbecue ribs until heated through, basting with sauce, about 10 minutes

1 serving: 990 Calories; 63 g Total Fat (27 g Mono, 22 g Poly, 12 g Sat); 100 mg Cholesterol; 96 g Carbohydrates (trace Fibre, 9 g Sugar); 28 g Protein; 1010 mg Sodium

Pictured on page 161.

STUFFED GAME DAY POTATO SKINS

MAKES: 5 SERVINGS
DIFFICULTY: ★

These easy potato skins will be all the rage on game day, so be prepared to buy a lot a potatoes and double the recipe at the last minute, depending on the group.

10	10	potatoes, cooked
1 cup	250 mL	cooking oil
1/4 cup	60 mL	real bacon pieces
10 ounces	285 g	shredded cheese
1 cup	250 mL	sour cream or ranch dressing

Cut potatoes in half and spoon out insides until only 1/4 inch (60 mL) shell remains (reserve potato innards for another use). Heat oil in a steep-sided cast iron skillet or saucepan. Place potato skins in oil and fry for 5 minutes. Transfer to plate lined with paper towel to drain, and pat with paper towel. Set aside until cool enough to handle.

Once cooled, fill each potato shell with bacon bits and cheese and place on a medium-sized baking pan sprayed with cooking spray. Bake in a 375°F (190°C) oven for 10 minutes until slightly brown and the cheese is melted. Serve hot with sour cream or ranch dressing.

1 serving: 500 Calories; 20 g Total Fat (7 g Mono, 1.5 g Poly, 11 g Sat); 50 mg Cholesterol; 66 g Carbohydrates (6 g Fibre, 3 g Sugar); 17 g Protein; 310 mg Sodium

Pictured on page 126.

SPICY JALAPEÑO POPPERS

MAKES: 5 SERVINGS
DIFFICULTY: ★

Most guy get-togethers at your local sports bar or roadhouse include a plate-ful of jalapeño poppers, so why not make them at home? It's not as hard as you might think.

12 ounces	340 g	whipped cream cheese
1 cup	250 mL	shredded Cheddar cheese
2 Tbsp	30 mL	real bacon pieces
10	10	jalapeño peppers, halved
1 cup	250 mL	milk
1 cup	250 mL	all-purpose flour
1 cup	250 mL	bread crumbs
1 quart	1 L	cooking oil

Mix cream cheese, Cheddar cheese and bacon pieces together in a bowl and spoon into jalapeño pepper halves.

Pour milk into a shallow bowl. Combine flour and breadcrumbs in a separate shallow bowl. Dip stuffed jalapeños into milk and then dredge in flour mixture, making sure to coat thoroughly. Allow coated jalapeños to dry for about 5 minutes.

Heat oil in a large steep-sided skillet. Gently place coated jalapeños in oil and fry until golden brown, turning once with a slotted spoon. Remove and let drain, and serve.

1 serving: 480 Calories; 23 g Total Fat (10 g Mono, 4 g Poly, 7 g Sat); 35 mg Cholesterol; 43 g Carbohydrates (2 g Fibre, 6 g Sugar); 24 g Protein; 730 mg Sodium

COLA CHICKEN WINGS

MAKES: 8 SERVINGS
DIFFICULTY: ★

Although there is no bad way to prepare chicken wings, this sticky sweet recipe can only be described as finger-licking good.

2 lbs	900 g	chicken wings, tips discarded
1/2 tsp	2 mL	garlic powder
1/2 tsp	2 mL	onion powder
1/2	1/2	12 oz (341 mL) can of cola
1/2 cup	125 mL	packed light brown sugar
1 Tbsp	15 mL	soy sauce

Place chicken wings in a shallow casserole dish. Season with garlic and onion powder.

Mix cola, brown sugar and soy sauce and pour over chicken wings. Bake, covered, at 325°F (160°C) for 1 hour, turning wings every 30 minutes. Uncover and bake for an additional 1 hour, turning wings every 30 minutes or so.

1 serving: 320 Calories; 18 g Total Fat (7 g Mono, 3.5 g Poly, 4.5 g Sat); 85 mg Cholesterol; 16 g Carbohydrates (0 g Fibre, 16 g Sugar); 21 g Protein; 210 mg Sodium

PARMESAN CHICKEN WINGS

MAKES: 24 DRUMETTES
DIFFICULTY: ★

Flavourful Parmesan cheese gives these wings a real lift.

3/4 cup	175 mL	golden Italian salad dressing
1 cup	250 mL	grated Parmesan cheese
1/2 cup	125 mL	fine dry bread crumbs
1 1/2 tsp	7 mL	paprika
3 lbs	1.4 kg	chicken drumettes

Measure salad dressing into a small bowl.

Combine next 3 ingredients in a separate small bowl.

Dip each drumette into salad dressing, then into cheese mixture until coated. Arrange in single layer on a greased foil-lined baking sheet with sides. Bake in 350°F (175°C) oven for about 45 minutes until tender and no longer pink inside.

1 drumette: 120 Calories; 5 g Total Fat (1 g Mono, 0.5 g Poly, 1.5 g Sat); 45 mg Cholesterol; 3 g Carbohydrates (0 g Fibre, trace Sugar); 14 g Protein; 250 mg Sodium

I wish my microwave had a "stealth mode" so the people I'm living with don't know I'm having a midnight snack.

—Anonymous

BONELESS BUFFALO CHICKEN STRIPS

MAKES: 6 SERVINGS   **DIFFICULTY:** ★

This delicious boneless chicken strip recipe rivals anything served in the best family restaurants in North America, and is much quicker than ordering in pizza!

1 cup	250 mL	all-purpose flour
1/2 tsp	2 mL	salt
1/2 tsp	2 mL	pepper
1/2 tsp	2 mL	cayenne pepper
1/2 tsp	2 mL	garlic powder
1	1	large egg
1 cup	250 mL	milk
3	3	4 oz (113 g) boneless, skinless chicken breasts, cut into 1 inch (2.5 cm) wide strips
1 quart	1 L	cooking oil
1/2 cup	125 mL	buffalo wing hot sauce

In a medium bowl, combine flour, salt, pepper, cayenne and garlic powder.

In a separate bowl, combine egg and milk.

Dip each piece of chicken individually in the mixture, and then dredge into flour bowl. In a large steep-sided skillet, or deep-fryer, heat oil until 375°F (190°C) degrees. Slowly place coated chicken pieces in pan and fry until golden brown. Use slotted spoon to turn once.

Brush cooked strips with buffalo wing hot sauce, and serve.

1 serving: 330 Calories; 12 g Total Fat (6 g Mono, 3 g Poly, 1.5 g Sat); 105 mg Cholesterol; 19 g Carbohydrates (trace Fibre, 3 g Sugar); 32 g Protein; 910 mg Sodium

Rule #1: There Are No Calories After Midnight
Technically, we are only supposed to eat so many calories per day; at 12:01 the calories don't count anymore (they go on the next day's total). You are absolved of all sin. Alternatively, turn this into a late night date night by making a healthy snack and winning some extra points. Don't go overboard, but try some kale chips or yogurt with stevia. Of course, if it's a really late snack it qualifies as breakfast.

HOME-STYLE POTATO CHIPS

MAKES: 6 SERVINGS   **DIFFICULTY: ★**

These crispy little taters take a bit of time to prepare but will likely be the best potato chips you've ever eaten. The potatoes need to be cut really thin, so you might want to use a mandolin to slice them. For added crispness, try experimenting a little with the frying time.

3 tbsp	45 mL	salt
6	6	large potatoes, peeled and sliced paper-thin
6 cups	1.5 L	cooking oil for deep frying

Stir salt into a large bowl of cold water and add potato slices as you slice them. Soak potatoes for 1 hour, then drain and rinse with cold water.

Heat oil in a deep-fryer (or deep saucepan) to 375°F (190°C). Fry potato slices until they start turning golden. Remove and drain on paper towels. Season with additional salt if desired.

1 serving: 390 Calories; 12 g Total Fat (7 g Mono, 3.5 g Poly, 1 g Sat); 0 mg Cholesterol; 64 g Carbohydrates (6 g Fibre, 3 g Sugar); 7 g Protein; 1190 mg Sodium

Pictured on page 71.

Helpful Tips

What guy doesn't enjoy snacks and munchies? Back in the day we all knew people who discovered little-known food groups contained in some of the most basic snacks, or at least that's what they claimed. If ever there was a universal food language it might be called Snackese, since every man appreciates this area of food. We all have our snack and munchie stand-bys and have even learned how to throw in our own personal twist or modification. Finding new ways to pickle eggs or that perfect chip dip recipe are all male-dominated activities.

CREAMY ARTICHOKE DIP

MAKES: 8 SERVINGS
DIFFICULTY: ★

This popular dip, served in many restaurants, is easily created at home and comes in handy when entertaining. There is something magical about the taste of artichoke in a cheesy dip. Finish it off with a garnish of chopped green onions and chopped tomato.

1	1	14 oz (398 mL) can of artichoke hearts, drained and chopped
1 cup	250 mL	mayonnaise
1 cup	250 mL	grated Parmesan cheese
1	1	4 oz (113 g) can of diced green chilis

Combine ingredients in a 2 quart (2 L) casserole dish. Bake in a 350°F (175°C) for 20 minutes or until lightly browned.

1 serving: 270 Calories; 24 g Total Fat (13 g Mono, 6 g Poly, 4 g Sat); 20 mg Cholesterol; 4 g Carbohydrates (2 g Fibre, 1 g Sugar); 6 g Protein; 600 mg Sodium

Pictured on page 126.

SEVEN LAYER TACO DIP

MAKES: 8 SERVINGS
DIFFICULTY: ★

This party favourite only gets better as you forage your way through the layers. The real trick, of course, is trying to balance all seven layers on a single tortilla.

1	1	1 1/4 oz (35 g) package of taco seasoning mix
1	1	16 oz (454 g) can of refried beans
1	1	16 oz (500 mL) container of sour cream
1	1	8 oz (250 g) package of cream cheese, softened
1	1	16 oz (500 mL) jar of salsa
1	1	large tomato, chopped
1	1	green pepper, chopped
1	1	bunch green onions
1	1	head iceberg lettuce, shredded
2 cups	500 mL	Cheddar cheese, shredded

Combine taco seasoning and refried beans and spread into bottom of a serving dish.

Combine sour cream and cream cheese and spread over refried beans. Top with salsa, then tomato, green pepper, onions and lettuce. Sprinkle with cheese. Refrigerate until ready to serve. Serve with tortilla chips.

1 serving: 460 Calories; 25 g Total Fat (6 g Mono, 1 g Poly, 14 g Sat); 55 mg Cholesterol; 39 g Carbohydrates (0 g Fibre, 8 g Sugar); 22 g Protein; 1320 mg Sodium

PUMPERNICKEL BREAD BOWL AND SPINACH DIP

MAKES: 6 SERVINGS
DIFFICULTY: ★ ★

This great snack might seem a little girly at first, but after 30 minutes of munching on the moist bread goodness and spinach accompaniment, most guys won't even care.

1	1	8 oz (225 g) container of sour cream
1	1	4 oz (113 g) package of cream cheese
2 Tbsp	30 mL	mayonnaise
1	1	1 oz (28 g) package dry dill dip mix
1/2	1/2	bunch spinach, rinsed and chopped
1	1	loaf round pumpernickel bread

In a large bowl, mix sour cream, cream cheese, mayonnaise, dip mix and spinach and stir until smooth.

Remove centre of pumpernickel loaf, creating a nice round bowl. Cut excavated bread into small bite-sized chunks.

Fill bread bowl with sour cream mixture. Serve with pumpernickel pieces arranged around outside of loaf, or place them in a separate bowl.

1 serving: 360 Calories; 15 g Total Fat (4.5 g Mono, 2 g Poly, 6 g Sat); 20 mg Cholesterol; 20 g Carbohydrates (7 g Fibre, 0 g Sugar); 14 g Protein; 1370 mg Sodium

---

GUACAMOLE

MAKES: 10 SERVINGS
DIFFICULTY: ★

Serve this spicy guacamole with sliced veggies for a guilt-free snacking experience. Or tortilla chips if you'd rather.

1 1/2 cups	375 mL	mashed avocado
1/2 cups	125 mL	chopped seeded tomato
1/4 cup	60 mL	finely chopped yellow pepper
3 Tbsp	45 mL	thinly sliced green onion
2 Tbsp	30 mL	lime juice
1 Tbsp	15 mL	chopped fresh cilantro (or parsley)
2 tsp	10 mL	cooking oil
1/4 tsp	1 mL	finely diced fresh hot chili pepper
1	1	clove garlic, minced
1/2 tsp	2 mL	salt
1/4 tsp	1 mL	pepper

Combine all 11 ingredients in a medium bowl, and serve.

1 serving: 60 Calories; 5 g Total Fat (3.5 g Mono, 1 g Poly, 0. g Sat); 0 mg Cholesterol; 4 g Carbohydrates (2 g Fibre, 0 g Sugar); trace Protein; 120 mg Sodium

Pictured on page 198.

NACHO DIP

MAKES: 6 SERVINGS
DIFFICULTY: ★

This tailgating standby never goes out of style. The level of heat will depend on the salsa you use. Serve with tortilla chips.

1	1	10 oz (284 mL) can of condensed Cheddar cheese soup
1/2 cup	125 mL	chunky salsa
1/2 cup	125 mL	chopped tomato
1	1	6 oz (170 g) can of sliced black olives, drained
1/2 cup	125 mL	shredded Cheddar cheese
6	6	green onions or shallots, finely chopped

In a microwave-safe bowl, combine soup and salsa. Heat in microwave on high (100%) until hot and bubbly, stirring occasionally to ensure even heating.

Add chopped tomato, olives and Cheddar cheese and return to microwave until cheese has melted.

Remove from microwave, sprinkle green onions on top and serve with tortilla chips.

1 serving: 460 Calories; 26 g Total Fat (13 g Mono, 2.5 g Poly, 6 g Sat); 10 mg Cholesterol; 49 g Carbohydrates (6 g Fibre, 3 g Sugar); 8 g Protein; 1150 mg Sodium

HOMEMADE SALSA

MAKES: 10 SERVINGS   DIFFICULTY: ★

This salsa recipe can be easily doubled or tripled and can be made well in advance.

1	1	8 oz (225 g) can of tomato sauce
1/4 tsp	1 mL	ground oregano
1 1/2 tsp	7 mL	crushed red pepper
1 Tbsp	15 mL	salt
1/4 cup	60 mL	cold water
6	6	medium tomatoes, diced, *divided*
4	4	jalapeño peppers, diced, *divided*
1/2	1/2	bunch green onions
1/2 cup	125 mL	fresh cilantro leaves
8	8	cloves garlic, peeled
1	1	medium onion, diced

In a large mixing bowl, combine tomato sauce, oregano, red pepper, salt and water and stir until well blended.

Put half of tomatoes and jalapeños in a food processor with green onions, cilantro and garlic and run at medium speed until veggies make a thick paste. Add tomato sauce mixture and run until well combined. Pour entire mixture back into mixing bowl.

Add onion, and remaining tomatoes and jalapeños, to mixing bowl, stirring until well combined. Cover and place in fridge for at least 1 hour so flavours can blend.

1 serving: 35 Calories; 0 g Total Fat (0 g Mono, 0 g Poly, 0 g Sat); 0 mg Cholesterol; 7 g Carbohydrates (2 g Fibre, 4 g Sugar); 1 g Protein; 830 mg Sodium

YUMMY PARTY MIX

MAKES: 12 SERVINGS
DIFFICULTY: ★

This mix is popular with all ages and can be set out for any event. It keeps for up to 2 weeks in an airtight container, and it freezes well, too, so you can make a double batch to always have some on hand.

2 cups	500 mL	rice squares cereal
2 cups	500 mL	"O"-shaped toasted oat cereal
1 cup	250 mL	fish-shaped crackers
1 cup	250 mL	pretzel twists
3 Tbsp	45 mL	butter
1 1/4 Tbsp	22 mL	hot sauce
1/2 x 1 oz	28 g	packet ranch dressing mix
1 tsp	5 mL	celery seed

In a large microwave-safe bowl, mix cereals, crackers and pretzels; set aside.

In a separate small microwave-safe bowl, heat butter, uncovered, on high (100%) for about 40 seconds or until melted. Stir in hot sauce and seasonings. Pour over cereal mixture and stir until evenly coated. Microwave, uncovered, on high (100%) for 4 to 5 minutes, thoroughly stirring every 2 minutes. Spread on paper towels to cool.

1 serving: 100 Calories; 4 g Total Fat (1 g Mono, 0 g Poly, 2 g Sat); 10 mg Cholesterol; 13 g Carbohydrates (trace Fibre, trace Sugar); 2 g Protein; 240 mg Sodium

SWEET AND SPICY NUT MIX

MAKES: 8 SERVINGS
DIFFICULTY: ★

Nuts are a great healthy snack with high levels of antioxidants and fibre to help lower cholesterol and prevent heart disease. The added sugar might reduce the health benefits of this recipe a little, but it is so good that who really cares!

2/3 cup	150 mL	walnut halves
2/3 cup	150 mL	pecan halves
2/3 cup	150 mL	whole almonds
1	1	egg white
2 Tbsp	30 L	water
1/2 cup	125 mL	granulated sugar
1 1/2 tsp	7 mL	ground cinnamon
1/4 tsp	60 mL	ground ginger
1/4 tsp	60 mL	nutmeg

Combine nuts in a medium bowl.

In a separate small bowl, beat egg white and water together until frothy. Pour over nuts and mix to coat, and then place in a colander to drain slightly.

Mix sugar and spices in a large resealable freezer bag. Add nuts and shake to coat. Spread nut mixture in a single layer on a microwave-safe plate; microwave on high (100%) for 1 1/2 minutes, or until mixture is bubbly. Stir and microwave for another 1 1/2 minutes. Stir to separate clumps and set aside to cool. Once nuts are cool, transfer to an airtight container.

1 serving: 290 Calories; 19 g Total Fat (8 g Mono, 8 g Poly, 1.5 g Sat); 0 mg Cholesterol; 17 g Carbohydrates (3 g Fibre, 13 g Sugar); 13 g Protein; 5 mg Sodium

PARTY TIME!

Entertaining is formally defined as a performance art, different from regular cooking and serving. It has much more to do with ritual. Think of those few traditional times a year when we are truly called upon to dig deep and draw upon our ancestral consciousness to prepare the BIG turkey for Thanksgiving or Christmas or ham for Easter (see chapter on Bigger is Better). It also means those few secret wow dishes and flourishes that make our party cuisine absolutely unique.

Entertaining also differs from game day dishes (see chapter on Game Day) in that this cuisine is meant to be done in a slow, patient manner and not served on the run—it's one of those rare chances to linger and get it just right. Which also means we are apparently so busy with our basting and quality control that we can't help with the other work in the house.

We have included some of our favourite seasonal classics as well as some great party dishes for all occasions. Cheers and enjoy.

PÂTE À CHOUX

MAKES: ABOUT 3 DOZEN **DIFFICULTY:** ★ ★ ★

These little balls of puff pastry also known as gougères, are really popular as appetizers. You can stuff them if you like, but they taste great as is.

1 cup	250 mL	milk
4 Tbsp	60 mL	butter
1/8 tsp	0.5 mL	salt
1 tsp	5 mL	granulated sugar
1 cup	250 mL	all-purpose flour
6	6	large eggs, *divided*
1/2 cup	125 mL	grated cheese (such as Parmesan or Asiago)
2 Tbsp	30 mL	water

Add milk, butter, salt and sugar in a small pan and bring to a boil. Immediately remove from heat and stir in flour until you have a paste. Place the pan over medium heat and cook until the dough forms a lump, and then cook another 2 minutes or until the dough begins to form a white cakish film. Place dough in bowl of a food processor fixed with a dough blade and allow to cool for 5 to 7 minutes.

Meanwhile, crack 5 eggs into a measuring bowl and set aside. Once dough is cool, pulse processor and add eggs, one at a time. Add cheese. To portion, use a pastry bag or ice cream scoop, and place 2 inches (5 cm) apart on baking sheets lined with parchment paper.

Lightly beat remaining egg with a fork. Brush pastry with egg wash, and bake in a 375°F (190°C) oven for 20 to 25 minutes or until golden brown.

1 pastry: 45 Calories; 2.5 g Total Fat (0.5 g Mono, 0 g Poly, 1.5 g Sat); 35 mg Cholesterol; 3 g Carbohydrates (0 g Fibre, 0 g Sugar); 2 g Protein; 55 mg Sodium

> Hors d'Oeuvres: A ham sandwich cut into forty pieces.
>
> —Jack Benny

CRAB CAKES WITH CREOLE SAUCE

MAKES: 8 SERVINGS   **DIFFICULTY: ★ ★**

Crab cakes and Creole sauce just go together. There won't be leftovers.

1 cup	250 mL	mayonnaise
2 Tbsp	30 mL	hot sauce
3 Tbsp	45 mL	olive oil, *divided*
1/4 cup	60 mL	finely diced onion
1/4 cup	60 mL	finely diced red pepper
1/4 cup	60 mL	mayonnaise
1 tsp	5 mL	Dijon mustard
2 tsp	10 mL	finely chopped green onion
1 tsp	5 mL	chopped dill
1	1	beaten egg
2/3 cup	150 mL	fresh bread crumbs
		salt and pepper to taste
1 lb	454 g	crabmeat
2 cups	500 mL	panko bread crumbs

For the sauce, combine mayonnaise and hot sauce with a whisk. Set aside.

In a small saucepan heat 1 Tbsp (15 mL) olive oil until just hot. Add onion and pepper and "sweat" until soft but no colour has been achieved. Set aside and allow to cool to room temperature.

Once cool, add to a large bowl with mayonnaise, Dijon mustard, green onions, dill, egg and bread crumbs and season with salt and pepper.

Add crabmeat and gently mix, trying not to break up the crabmeat. Shape mixture into flat patties, using an ice cream scoop to keep size consistent. Dredge in panko crumbs. Heat remaining 2 Tbsp (30 mL) oil in a frying pan over medium heat and, working in batches, fry patties until golden brown. Add more olive oil if necessary. Serve with Creole sauce on the side.

1 serving: 390 Calories; 30 g Total Fat (18 g Mono, 8 g Poly, 3 g Sat); 30 mg Cholesterol; 13 g Carbohydrates (trace Fibre, trace Sugar); 11 g Protein; 350 mg Sodium

Pictured on page 162.

SHRIMP LOLLIPOPS

MAKES: 12 SERVINGS
DIFFICULTY: ★ ★

Don't be put off by the long list of ingredients. Most grocery stores have plenty of Asian products and produce. Serve with Thai dipping sauce.

2 lbs	900 g	shrimp (peeled and deveined)
1/2	1/2	medium onion, diced
1/2	1/2	medium red pepper, diced
3	3	Thai chilies
1 cup	250 mL	unsweetened coconut
1 tsp	5 mL	brown sugar
1 Tbsp	15 mL	diced lemongrass
1	1	lime, zested and juiced
		salt and pepper to taste
1 cup	250 mL	all-purpose flour
1 cup	250 mL	canola oil
12	12	4 inch (10 cm) lemongrass stalks

Place shrimp, onions and peppers and chilies in bowl of food processor and pulse until mixture resembles ground meat.

Add next 8 ingredients and pulse until mixture resembles coarse ground meat. With wet hands, form shrimp mixture into balls and place on lemongrass stalks, leaving about 1 inch (2.5 cm) to hold on to. Flatten balls slightly and pan-fry in oil until golden brown.

1 serving: 180 Calories; 7 g Total Fat (3 g Mono, 2 g Poly, 1.5 g Sat); 115 mg Cholesterol; 12 g Carbohydrates (trace Fibre, 2 g Sugar); 0 g Protein; 220 mg Sodium

Pictured on page162.

THAI DIPPING SAUCE

MAKES: 2 CUPS (500 ML)
DIFFICULTY: ★

There is no limit to what can be dipped in this versatile sauce. Try it with the Pork Potstickers on page 134.

2 Tbsp	30 mL	cooking oil
2 Tbsp	30 mL	finely diced onion
2 tsp	10 mL	crushed garlic
2 tsp	10 mL	crushed ginger root
2 tsp	10 mL	finely diced lemongrass
1 cup	250 mL	chicken stock
3 Tbsp	45 mL	sambal olek
2 tsp	10 mL	soy sauce
2 tsp	10 mL	fish sauce
2 tsp	10 mL	granulated sugar
2 tsp	10 mL	cornstarch
1/4 cup	60 mL	cold water
1/4 cup	60 mL	shredded fresh basil

Heat oil in a small saucepan over medium. Add onion, garlic, ginger and lemongrass, and cook until soft. Add next 5 ingredients and bring to a simmer. Cook for 10 minutes. Dissolve cornstarch in water and add to saucepan. Cook until mixture has thickened. Remove from heat and add basil. Chill before serving.

3 Tbsp (45 mL): 30 Calories; 2.5 g Total Fat (1.5 g Mono, 0.5 g Poly, 0 g Sat); 0 mg Cholesterol; 2 g Carbohydrates (0 g Fibre, trace Sugar); 0 g Protein; 220 mg Sodium

CALAMARI

Preparing squid can be a messy and somewhat distasteful task. The faint of heart may, instead, want to take the easy way out and purchase prepared calamari rings. Serve with marinara sauce.

3 cups	750 mL	cooking oil
1/4 cup	60 mL	all-purpose flour
1 tsp	5 mL	salt
1 tsp	5 mL	dried oregano
1/2 tsp	2 m	pepper
12	12	squid, cleaned and sliced into rings

Preheat oil in a deep-fryer or heavy, deep frying pan to 375°F (190°C).

In a medium bowl, combine flour, salt, oregano and pepper and mix well. Dredge squid through flour and spice mixture. Cook squid in oil for 2 to 3 minutes or until light brown. Overcooking the squid will produce tough calamari, so try to remove it before it darkens. Dry squid on paper towels and serve.

1 serving: 100 Calories; 7 g Total Fat (4 g Mono, 2 g Poly, 0.5 g Sat); 65 mg Cholesterol; 4 g Carbohydrates (0 g Fibre, 0 g Sugar); 5 g Protein; 310 mg Sodium

DEEP-FRIED SHRIMP

One of the great things about deep-fried shrimp is that just about everyone enjoys eating it, be they seafood enthusiast or not. There's something unique about this meal that seems to draw dinner guests out of the woodwork.

1 lb	454 g	medium shrimp (peeled, deveined and tails removed
1/2 tsp	2 mL	salt
1/2 tsp	2 mL	pepper
1/2 tsp	2 mL	garlic powder
1 cup	250 mL	all-purpose flour
1 tsp	5 mL	paprika
2	2	large eggs, beaten
1 cup	250 mL	panko crumbs
1 quart	1 L	cooking oil for frying

Place shrimp in a bowl and season with salt, pepper and garlic powder.

In another small bowl, combine flour and paprika. Place eggs and panko crumbs into 2 other separate bowls.

Heat oil in a deep-fryer or deep skillet to 375°F (190°C). Dip each shrimp into flour mixture, then into egg, and finally into panko crumbs to coat. Fry a few at a time until golden brown, about 3 to 5 minutes.

Remove shrimp and place on paper towels to drain excess grease before serving.

1 serving: 580 Calories; 24 g Total Fat (13 g Mono, 6 g Poly, 2.5 g Sat); 320 mg Cholesterol; 48 g Carbohydrates (2 g Fibre, 0 g Sugar); 40 g Protein; 670 mg Sodium

GLAZED HAM

MAKES: 18 SERVINGS
DIFFICULTY: ★ ★

You might have to order a ham this large from a butcher or specialty food store. If you are cooking a smaller ham without the rind, halve the glaze recipe, brush it over the ham and proceed with cooking and basting as instructed. Choose from one of our two glazes.

20 lb	9 kg	leg of cooked ham with rind
		whole cloves, optional

Grease a wire rack and place it in a roasting pan. Cut through rind at shank end of leg. Run your fingers under rind to loosen it. Carefully pull rind away and discard it. Make shallow cuts, about 1 inch (2.5 cm) apart, in 1 direction diagonally across fat. Make sure cuts aren't too deep or you will lose decorative pattern. Then make shallow cuts in opposite direction to form a diamond pattern. Place 1 clove where each cut meets at tip of each diamond shape. Place ham in prepared pan. Wrap a piece of greased foil around bone-end. Brush ham with your choice of glaze. Bake, uncovered, in a 350°F (175°C) oven for about 1 hour, brushing frequently with glaze, until browned and glazed. Carve into thin slices. Serve hot or cold.

1 serving: 900 Calories; 63 g Total Fat (28 g Mono, 7 g Poly, 22 g Sat); 265 mg Cholesterol; 0 g Carbohydrates (0 g Fibre, 0 g Sugar); 76 g Protein; 250 mg Sodium

APRICOT GLAZE

1 cup	250 mL	pineapple juice
1/2 cup	125 mL	apricot jam
2 Tbsp	30 mL	grainy mustard

Stir all 3 ingredients in a small saucepan on medium heat until jam is melted.

1 serving: 30 Calories; 0 g Total Fat (0 g Mono, 0 g Poly, 0 g Sat); 0 mg Cholesterol; 7g Carbohydrates (0 g Fibre, 7 g Sugar); 7 g Protein; 25 mg Sodium

MAPLE ORANGE GLAZE

3/4 cup	175 mL	maple syrup
1/3 cup	75 mL	marmalade
1/3 cup	75 mL	orange juice
1 Tbsp	15 mL	Worcestershire sauce

Stir all 4 ingredients in a small saucepan on medium heat until marmalade is melted.

1 serving: 40 Calories; 0 g Total Fat (0 g Mono, 0 g Poly, 0 g Sat); 0 mg Cholesterol; 11 g Carbohydrates (0 g Fibre, 10 g Sugar); 0 g Protein; 15 mg Sodium

HERB BUTTER TURKEY

MAKES: 10 SERVINGS
DIFFICULTY: ★ ★ ★

Your Christmas feast will be a sure hit with this succulent turkey served with cranberry gravy. Serve with your favourite stuffing, cooked separately.

10 lb	4.5 kg	turkey
1/2 cup	125 mL	butter, softened
2 tsp	10 mL	chopped fresh thyme
1 tsp	5 mL	celery salt
1/4 tsp	1 mL	pepper
2	2	cloves garlic, minced
1/4 cup	60 mL	all-purpose flour
1/4 cup	60 mL	brandy (or chicken broth)
3 cups	750 mL	chicken (or turkey) broth
1/2 cup	125 mL	cranberry jelly
		salt and pepper to taste

Lightly grease a wire rack and place in a roasting pan. Remove and discard neck, giblets and any fat from turkey cavities. Rinse inside and out with cold water, then pat dry with paper towels. Combine next 5 ingredients in a small bowl. Using your fingers, carefully loosen turkey skin across breast and legs to separate skin from meat, trying not to pierce skin. Evenly spread butter mixture between skin and meat; smooth skin. Tuck wings under body. Secure body and neck cavity with toothpicks. Tie legs together. Place in prepared pan. Pour 1/2 cup (125 mL) water into pan. Cover turkey loosely with greased foil. Roast in a 325°F (160°C) oven for 2 1/2 hours until a meat thermometer inserted into thickest part of thigh reaches 180°F (82°C). Remove from oven, cover with foil and let stand for 20 minutes before carving. Reserve 1/2 cup (125 mL) pan drippings for gravy.

To make the gravy, heat reserved pan drippings in same roasting pan on medium until bubbling. Add flour and cook for about 1 minute until thickened. Stir in brandy. Slowly stir in chicken broth and cranberry jelly, whisking to remove any lumps. Boil gently for about 10 minutes, stirring occasionally, until thickened. Add salt and pepper. Strain to remove any lumps. Serve turkey with cranberry gravy.

1 serving: 700 Calories; 38 g Total Fat (13 g Mono, 8 g Poly, 14 g Sat); 270 mg Cholesterol; 9 g Carbohydrates (0 g Fibre, 5 g Sugar); 75 g Protein; 720 mg Sodium

Spicy Jack Chicken, page 239

Veal Chops with Morel Sauce, page 225

CIOPPINO

MAKES: 6 SERVINGS   **DIFFICULTY: ★**

Make the broth for this seafood stew a day ahead of time and then refrigerate it until needed. When ready to serve, remember to add the seafood that takes the longest to cook first, and the stuff that cooks the quickest last. This recipe makes a great dish for Christmas Eve because it is not too filling, is an easy to serve, one-pot meal, and it comes together quickly. Serve with salad and bread.

3 Tbsp	45 mL	olive oil
1/2 tsp	2 mL	crushed red chili flakes
1	1	medium onion, diced
6	6	cloves garlic
1	1	14 oz (398 mL) can of whole tomatoes
2 cups	500 mL	water
1/2 cups	125 mL	white wine
		salt and pepper to taste
1 lb	454 g	mussels
1/2 lb	225 g	shrimp (peeled and deveined)
1/2 lb	225 g	scallops
1/2 lb	225 g	assorted fish pieces (such as salmon, sole, sea bass or whitefish)
2 tsp	10 mL	chopped parsley
		salt and pepper to taste
4	4	lemon wedges

In a heavy stock pot, heat oil and chili flakes over medium for 3 to 5 minutes or until they begin to sizzle. Add onion, and cook for 5 minutes or until soft. Add garlic, tomatoes, water and white wine. Bring to a boil, and simmer for 5 to 10 minutes. Season with a little salt and pepper, but be careful not to over-season because some of the seafood may be quite salty.

To serve, simply reheat the broth, and add the seafood so that the product that is going to take the longest to cook is added first. Add mussels and cook for about 3 minutes, then add shrimp, then scallops and then fish, giving about 1 minute between each addition. The broth should just be simmering; you do not want a roiling boil. Once all seafood has been added, remove from heat, adjust seasoning and serve with lemon wedges.

1 serving: 270 Calories; 10 g Total Fat (6 g Mono, 1.5 g Poly, 1.5 g Sat); 110 mg Cholesterol; 10 g Carbohydrates (trace Fibre, 3 g Sugar); 31 g Protein; 470 mg Sodium

QUICK BROILED SCALLOPS

MAKES: 4 SERVINGS   **DIFFICULTY: ★**

Scallops are often compared to lobster and crab but with a lighter, creamier feel on the palate. They have gained popularity as one of the premiere items featured on TVs Hell's Kitchen.

2 lbs	1 kg	scallops
1 Tbsp	15 mL	garlic salt
2 Tbsp	30 mL	lemon juice
1/4 cup	60 mL	butter, melted

Preheat broiler. Rinse scallops with cold water, pat very dry with paper towel and place on a baking pan. Sprinkle with garlic salt and lemon juice.

Brush each scallop with melted butter. Broil for 5 to 8 minutes until scallops turn golden brown. Remove from oven, let stand for 5 minutes and serve.

1 serving: 300 Calories; 13 g Total Fat (3 g Mono, 1 g Poly, 7 g Sat); 105 mg Cholesterol; 62 g Carbohydrates (0 g Fibre, 0 g Sugar); 38 g Protein; 1730 mg Sodium

Food is not about impressing people. It's about making them feel comfortable.

—Ina Garten

MINI YORKSHIRE PUDDINGS

MAKES: 12 PUDDINGS
DIFFICULTY: ★ ★

You'll impress everyone with these mini yorkies. Serve with shaved roast beef and drizzle with horseradish mayo.

4	4	large eggs, at room temperature
1 1/2 cups	375 mL	milk, at room temperature
4 Tbsp	60 mL	melted butter, at room temperature
1 Tbsp	15 mL	prepared horseradish
2 Tbsp	30 mL	sliced green onion
1 Tbsp	15 mL	salt
1 1/3 cups	325 mL	all-purpose flour

Heat a mini muffin tin in a 450°F (230°C) oven. Mix first 3 ingredients together extremely well.

Combine horseradish, green onion, salt and flour in a small bowl. Add to milk mixture, scraping sides of bowl to incorporate all of flour. Remove empty muffin tin from oven and spray with cooking spray, then fill each cup half full. Bake for 25 minutes. DO NOT OPEN OVEN. Place puddings on a wire rack to cool.

1 pudding with 1 1/2 Tbsp (22 mL) horseradish mayo: 250 Calories; 19 g Total Fat (10 g Mono, 4.5 g Poly, 4.5 g Sat); 65 mg Cholesterol; 13 g Carbohydrates (trace Fibre, 2 g Sugar); 5 g Protein; 790 mg Sodium

---

HORSERADISH MAYO

Store this mayo in a squeeze bottle so you can easily control how much you add to your food. A little goes a long way.

1 Tbsp	15 mL	crushed pepper
1 Tbsp	15 mL	prepared horseradish
1 cup	250 mL	mayonnaise

Combine all 3 ingredients in a small bowl. Can be stored in fridge in an airtight container (or squeeze bottle) for up to 2 weeks.

COOKING
WITH BOOZE

Alcohol is not technically a food group, but it is the way that many of us men absorb most of our calories. Why not treat it as a cuisine rather than a bad habit? You can excuse all forms of sin if you have the right strategy for justification. Marinate the meat in beer or bourbon, or use the accent character of liquors or cognacs to highlight a dish. This exploration is endless and we intend to dedicate a large part of our life and liver exploring these well-watered paths.

BRAISED BEEF SHORT RIBS

MAKES: 8 SERVINGS   DIFFICULTY: ★ ★ ★

Either buy boneless beef short ribs, or remove the bones yourself.

1 1/4 cups	300 mL	cooking oil, *divided*
2 lbs	900 g	boneless beef short ribs, cut into 4 portions
		salt and pepper to taste
1	1	onion, diced
1	1	carrot, peeled and diced
4	4	garlic cloves
2 cups	500 mL	red wine
8 cups	2 L	chicken stock
2	2	black cardamom pods
2	2	star anise
1	1	cinnamon stick
10	10	black peppercorns
1	1	bay leaf
7/8 cup	200 mL	rice wine vinegar
3 1/2 oz	100 g	granulated sugar
1	1	sprig of thyme
1	1	shallot, diced
30	30	chanterelle mushrooms, cleaned
10	10	morel mushrooms, cut in half and cleaned
3 Tbsp	45 mL	white wine
3 Tbsp	45 mL	butter

Drizzle 1/4 cup (60 mL) oil on ribs and season with salt and pepper. Heat 3/4 cup (175 mL) oil over medium-high; sear ribs until golden. Remove meat from pot. Cook onion, carrot and garlic until golden. Deglaze pot with wine and reduce until almost dry. Place short ribs back in pot and cover with stock. Add next 4 ingredients and simmer for 3 hours. Remove short ribs and place in a small pot with 7/8 cup (200 mL) braising liquid. Season remaining braising liquid with salt and pepper and reserve, keeping warm.

Heat vinegar and sugar in a pot over high and reduce to one-quarter. Add reserved braising liquid and reduce by another to one-quarter. Strain through a fine-mesh strainer; sauce should be slightly thick. If too thin, thicken it with a cornstarch slurry (equal parts cold water and cornstarch mixed in a small bowl). Add thyme and steep for 5 minutes. Strain and set aside.

Heat remaining 1/4 cup (60 mL) oil on medium in a large pan. Add shallots and cook until translucent. Turn heat to high and add all mushrooms; sauté for 1 minute. Add wine and butter; sauté for 1 minute. Season to taste with salt and pepper. Serve short ribs with natural reduction and mushrooms atop mashed potatoes.

1 serving: 940 Calories; 79 g Total Fat (42 g Mono, 11 g Poly, 21 g Sat); 85 mg Cholesterol; 26 g Carbohydrates (trace Fibre, 19 g Sugar); 19 g Protein; 630 mg Sodium

Pictured on page 252.

PORCHETTA

MAKES: 12 SERVINGS   **DIFFICULTY: ★ ★**

This savoury rolled pork dish is Italian in origin. The pork cooks slowly so it's moist and tasty when it's done. Serve with polenta, roasted vegetables and bread for sopping up the juices.

1/2 cup	125 mL	crushed garlic
1/2 cup	125 mL	chopped parsley
1/4 cup	60 mL	chopped sage
1/4 cup	60 mL	chopped rosemary
1/2 cup	125 mL	chopped onions
1/2 tsp	2 mL	chili flakes
2/3 cup	150 mL	olive oil, *divided*
1	1	5 lb (2.2 kg) pork shoulder
		salt and pepper to taste
1/2 cup	125 mL	sweet wine

Combine first 6 ingredients and 1/2 cup (250 mL) olive oil in a large bowl.

Butterfly pork by cutting horizontally through middle not quite to other side. Spread open and pound with flat side of meat mallet until about 1 inch (2.5 cm) thick. Season with salt and pepper generously. Splash wine onto meat and massage it in. Spread herb mixture evenly over pork, pressing down to make it stick. Roll up as tight as possible, then secure with kitchen string.

Rub outside with 2 Tbsp (30 mL) olive oil and season again with salt and pepper. Place in fridge for 4 hours. Place on rack in a 400°F (200°C) oven and turn down to 350°F (175°C). After 1 hour turn oven down to 300°F (150°C). After 1 more hour turn oven down to 275°F (135°C) and let cook for 3 hours or until fork tender.

1 serving: 560 Calories; 44 g Total Fat (4.5 g Mono, 22 g Poly, 13 g Sat); 110 mg Cholesterol; 3 g Carbohydrates (trace Fibre, 0 g Sugar); 35 g Protein; 125 mg Sodium

> I cook with wine, sometimes I even add
> it to the food.
> —W.C. Fields

MEDITERRANEAN CHICKEN

MAKES: 8 SERVINGS   DIFFICULTY: ★

Prunes, sundried apricots, olives and capers combine to make a flavour combination you've gotta try. Boneless, skinless chicken thighs can dry out if they're not cooked properly, but they are very versatile. Serve this dish over a bed of rice with salad on the side.

4 lbs	1.8 kg	boneless, skinless chicken thighs
1/4 cup	60 mL	dried oregano
1/2 cup	125 mL	red wine vinegar
1/2 cup	125 mL	olive oil
1 cup	250 mL	pitted prunes
1 cup	250 mL	pitted green olives
1/2 cup	125 mL	capers
1 cup	250 mL	sundried apricots
2	2	bay leaves
3	3	cloves garlic, crushed
1 cup	250 mL	white wine
		salt and pepper to taste
1 cup	250 mL	brown sugar

Combine chicken, oregano, red wine vinegar, olive oil, prunes, olives, capers, apricots, bay leaves, garlic and white wine. Season with salt and pepper, and refrigerate overnight.

Place in a roasting pan, sprinkle with brown sugar and bake in a 350°F (175°C) oven for 60 minutes, or until juices run clear.

1 serving: 660 Calories; 24 g Total Fat (14 g Mono, 3.5 g Poly, 4 g Sat); 190 mg Cholesterol; 60 g Carbohydrates (4 g Fibre, 35 g Sugar); 47 g Protein; 770 mg Sodium

Alcohol is necessary for a man so that
he can have a good opinion of himself,
undisturbed by the facts.

—Finley Peter Dunne

ITALIAN MINESTRONE SOUP

MAKES: 12 SERVINGS   **DIFFICULTY: ★ ★**

Here's another bean soup recipe where you can substitute canned beans if you're short on time. Feel free to add whatever veggies you like to this soup—zucchini, pearl onions, mushrooms are good choices.

4 cups	1 L	white beans, soaked overnight
16 cups	4 L	chicken stock
1/4 cup	60 mL	olive oil
1 lb	454 g	sliced Italian sausage
1/4 cup	60 mL	diced pancetta
1 cup	250 mL	diced onion
1 cup	250 mL	diced celery
1 cup	250 mL	diced carrots
1 cup	250 mL	shredded cabbage
1 cup	250 mL	diced or quartered potatoes
1	1	28 oz (796 mL) can of tomatoes, roughly chopped
1 Tbsp	15 mL	dried oregano
1 cup	250 mL	red wine
1 tsp	5 mL	red chili flakes
2 cups	500 mL	chopped spinach
1 cup	250 mL	grated Parmesan cheese

Bring pre-soaked beans and chicken stock to a boil and simmer until beans are soft. If you do not soak beans overnight, you will have to cook them longer in chicken stock. Once beans are cooked, drain and purée half. Combine whole beans and puréed beans and set aside.

While beans are simmering, heat oil and cook sausage and pancetta until they start to render their fat.

Add next 5 ingredients, stirring to make sure vegetables are well coated with fat. Add next 4 ingredients and puréed beans, and simmer over low heat for 1 hour, stirring frequently.

Once all vegetables are cooked, remove from heat and stir in spinach and cheese. Cover with a lid and let soup steep for 10 minutes. If soup is too thick, add a little chicken stock or water. Stir and serve.

1 serving: 530 Calories; 22 g Total Fat (9 g Mono, 2.5 g Poly, 7 g Sat); 40 mg Cholesterol; 54 g Carbohydrates (20 g Fibre, 3 g Sugar); 26 g Protein; 760 mg Sodium

VEAL CHOPS WITH MOREL SAUCE

MAKES:: 6 SERVINGS   **DIFFICULTY:** ★ ★ ★

Some people have issues with eating veal, but it's really worth a try. Milk-fed is best—ask your butcher to source it out if you can't find it. Armagnac, a French brandy, adds a certain je ne sais quoi to *the dish.*

3 Tbsp	45 mL	butter, *divided*
1 Tbsp	15 mL	minced shallot
1 Tbsp	15 mL	minced garlic
1 lb	500 g	fresh morel mushrooms, cleaned and halved
1 Tbsp	15 mL	parsley, chopped
6	6	thick-cut veal chops
2 cup	500 mL	flour, seasoned with salt and pepper
1 Tbsp	15 mL	cooking oil
1/2 cup	125 mL	Armagnac
1 Tbsp	15 mL	Dijon mustard
3 Tbsp	45 mL	crème fraîche
		salt and pepper to taste

Heat 2 Tbsp (30 mL) butter in a large frying pan over medium. Cook shallots and garlic for 2 minutes. Add morels and cook for about 3 minutes until tender. Add parsley and set aside.

Dredge veal chops in flour and shake off excess. Heat oil and remaining 1 Tbsp (15 mL) butter in a large ovenproof frying pan over high. Sear chops for 3 to 4 minutes per side until golden brown. Transfer to 375°F (190°C) oven for 5 to 6 minutes to finish cooking. Transfer chops to a plate.

Deglaze pan with Armagnac. Add Dijon mustard and stir to incorporate. Add crème fraîche, morel mixture and any juices from resting chops, and bring to a simmer. Adjust seasoning with salt and pepper to taste. Serve veal chops with morel sauce.

1 serving: 900 Calories; 31 g Total Fat (12 g Mono, 2.5 g Poly, 13 g Sat); 215 mg Cholesterol; 63 g Carbohydrates (1 g Fibre, 0 g Sugar); 66 g Protein; 510 mg Sodium

Pictured on page 216.

> He was a wise man who invented beer.
> —Plato

DIFFERENT TYPES OF BEER

PALE ALES

Medium-bodied pale ales balance the flavour of hops and barley. India pale ales tend to be slightly more bitter than regular pale ales. Ales generally have a stronger flavour than traditional beers.

LAMBIC BEERS

Lambic beers are made from a combination of wheat and malted barley, with fruit sometimes added during aging. They are aged in casks and can be slightly sour when aged for a short time. Varieties with longer aging times are more mellow.

BROWN AND AMBER ALES

Brown ales are full-bodied, slightly sweet and lightly hopped. The darker brown or amber colour comes from the caramelized malts used to produce these ales. Scotch ale, a form of brown ale, has a strong malty flavour.

PORTERS AND STOUTS

These heavy, dark, and strongly flavoured beers include roasted malt, which gives them their characteristic colour and flavour. Most porters have balanced flavour, both slightly bitter and sweet. Stouts and porters tend to be higher in alcohol than other beers.

LAGERS AND PILSNERS

Lagers tend to be light and bubbly with a golden colour. Pilsners are a light, pale variety of lager, generally with milder flavours and a slightly hoppy taste.

BRAISED CHUCK WITH BARASSICA MUSTARD

MAKES: 10 SERVINGS   **DIFFICULTY: ★ ★**

The beer in this recipe helps tenderize the meat. A long cooking time also helps.
After three hours or so, it just falls apart. Yummy. Serve over mashed potatoes.

3 lbs	1.4 kg	beef chuck
1/2 cup	125 mL	grainy mustard, *divided*
		salt and pepper to taste
2 Tbsp	30 mL	cooking oil
2 cups	500 mL	sliced onion
2	2	cloves garlic, minced
1	1	12 oz (341 mL) bottle of dark beer
2 cups	500 mL	beef stock
1 Tbsp	15 mL	chopped thyme
1 Tbsp	15 mL	chopped rosemary
1	1	bay leaf

Trim chuck of excess fat (but not all fat; fat equals flavour). Cut chuck into 2 x 2 inch (5 x 5 cm) pieces.

In a large bowl mix meat with 1/4 cup (60 mL) grainy mustard to coat well. Season with salt and pepper.

Heat oil in a large Dutch oven until just about smoking and brown beef on all sides, in batches if necessary. Set aside. Drain excess fat from pan.

Over medium heat, brown onions, then add garlic and beer, scraping bottom to loosen any brown bits.

Stir in stock and herbs. Place Dutch oven in a 300°F (150°C) oven and cook for 3 hours. Remove from oven and allow to rest for 15 minutes. Remove meat and excess fat from pan and cook beer mixture over high heat to reduce liquid by half. Stir in remaining 1/4 cup (60 mL) mustard and adjust seasoning.

1 serving: 430 Calories; 30 g Total Fat (14 g Mono, 1.5 g Poly, 11 g Sat); 115 mg Cholesterol; 6 g Carbohydrates (0 g Fibre, 1 g Sugar); 29 g Protein; 390 mg Sodium

EASY DEEP-FRIED FISH

MAKES: 4 SERVINGS   **DIFFICULTY: ★**

Although there's nothing fancy about fried fish, it sure hits the spot after a long day. Complement your fish fry with a tangy tartar sauce on the side.

1	1	large egg
1 1/2 cups	375 mL	beer
1 cup	250 mL	all-purpose flour
1 tsp	5 mL	garlic powder
1/2 tsp	2 mL	salt
1/2 tsp	2 mL	pepper
1 lb	454 g	pike or walleye fillets
2 cups	500 mL	dry bread crumbs
1 tsp	5 mL	Cajun seasoning
1 quart	1 L	cooking oil for frying

In a medium bowl, beat together egg, beer, flour, garlic powder, salt and pepper. Place fish in bowl, and thoroughly coat all pieces with mixture.

In a separate medium bowl, mix bread crumbs and Cajun seasoning. Dip cod in crumb mixture and thoroughly coat all sides.

In a large, heavy skillet or deep-fryer, heat oil to 375°F (190°C). Fry fish until golden brown and flesh flakes easily with a fork. Place fish on paper towel to drain excess fat before serving.

1 serving: 600 Calories; 18 g Total Fat (9 g Mono, 5 g Poly, 2 g Sat); 80 mg Cholesterol; 66 g Carbohydrates (3 g Fibre, 4 g Sugar); 34 g Protein; 1010 mg Sodium

Milk is for babies. When you grow up, you have to drink beer.

—Arnold Schwarzenegger

FLAMISH CHICKEN IN DARK BEER

MAKES: 8 SERVINGS   **DIFFICULTY:** ★ ★ ★

This recipe, from Canadian Culinary Olympic Chefs Cook at Home, *has superb flavouring.*

2	2	4 1/2 lb (2 kg) chickens, each cut into 8 portions
2 Tbsp	30 mL	all-purpose flour, seasoned with salt and pepper
1 oz	28 g	butter
1 Tbsp	15 mL	canola oil
1/2 cup	125 mL	Holland or Dutch gin (Genievre)
1 cup	250 mL	diced celery
1 cup	250 mL	peeled and diced carrots
2	2	shallots, chopped
3	3	juniper berries, crushed
1/2 lb	225 g	mushrooms, halved
1	1	bouquet garni of 1 parsley stem, 2 bay leaves and 1 sprig of thyme
2 cups	500 mL	dark beer
1/2 cup	125 mL	crème fraîche
		salt and pepper to taste
1 Tbsp	15 mL	chopped fresh flat-leaf parsley for garnish

Dredge chicken pieces in flour and shake well to remove excess. Heat butter and oil in a large pan over high. Add chicken; cook for 5 minutes on each side to get a nice colour. Add gin and carefully bring edge of pan over flame to flambé, or use a lighter. Be very careful, as there will be at least 1 foot (30 cm) of flame. Remove chicken from pan and keep warm.

Add celery, carrots, shallots and juniper berries to pan; cook for 5 minutes until vegetables are tender, stirring occasionally. Add mushrooms and bouquet garni to pan. Return chicken to pan. Stir in beer and bring to a simmer. Cover, reduce heat and simmer for 35 to 45 minutes until chicken is cooked.

When done, remove chicken from pan and keep warm. Discard bouquet garni. Place pan over medium heat and stir in crème fraîche. Cook for 5 minutes. Remove from heat and adjust seasoning with salt and pepper. Pour sauce over chicken and sprinkle with parsley.

1 serving: 960 Calories; 66 g Total Fat (27 g Mono, 13 g Poly, 20 g Sat); 340 mg Cholesterol; 8 g Carbohydrates (1 g Fibre, 2 g Sugar); 67 g Protein; 310 mg Sodium

Pictured on page 234.

A bouquet garni is a collection of flavourful herbs such as parsley, bay leaves and thyme tied together in cheesecloth or just tied together. It is removed once the dish is cooked.

FRESH BAKED BEER BREAD

MAKES: 1 LOAF   **DIFFICULTY:** ★

This recipe gives new meaning to the old expression "going for a barley sandwich."

3 cups	750 mL	self-rising flour
1/3 cup	75 mL	granulated sugar
1 tsp	5 mL	salt
1	1	12 oz (341 mL) bottle of beer
2 Tbsp	30 mL	butter, melted

In a large bowl, combine flour, sugar, salt and beer and mix well. The mixture will be sticky. Pour into a buttered loaf pan. Bake in a 375°F (190°C) oven for about 55 minutes.

Before last 3 minutes of baking, remove from oven, brush top of loaf with melted butter and return to oven for final minutes of baking. Cuts into 12 slices.

1 slice: 150 Calories; 2 g Total Fat (0 g Mono, 0 g Poly, 1 g Sat); 5 mg Cholesterol; 28 g Carbohydrates (trace Fibre, 5 g Sugar); 3 g Protein; 590 mg Sodium

> Alcohol is a good preservative for everything but brains.
>
> —Mary Pettibone Poole

IF IT'S NOT ON THE LABEL IT'S NOT WHISKY

SCOTCH WHISKY

Scotch, produced from malted barley, is often thought too precious to be used in cooking, though its diverse spectrum of flavours makes it ideal for enhancing a variety of dishes. Some chefs consider it the alcoholic equivalent of salt because it brings out the flavor of whatever food it is added to. It works well in stir-fries or other Asian dishes, or as a marinade. Scotch can also be used to finish a dish such as sautéed scallops or add flavour to fruit salads or fruitcakes. Finally, you can use it in place of brandy to flambé.

BOURBON WHISKY

Bourbon, distilled from corn and considered the whisky of the American South, adds a sweet, smoky flavour to dishes and can be used in place of brandy in most recipes. Although typically used in desserts, it is frequently used in barbecue sauces. It will add a subtle flavour of caramel, vanilla and a very slight woody taste to your recipes, and works well in both sweet and savoury dishes.

RYE WHISKY

Rye whisky, sometimes called Canadian whisky, is generally thought of as being less full-bodied than bourbon but not as smoky as Scotch. It is more popular in cocktails than in cooking, but can be used in place of bourbon in most recipes. Rye whisky is not as sweet or as smooth as bourbon, and will add a deeper, slightly fruiter spicy flavour to dishes. It works best in marinades and in desserts.

BOURBON STREET STEAK WITH CITRUS BUTTER

MAKES: 4 SERVINGS   **DIFFICULTY: ★**

A dash of the French Quarter adds flair to your dinner. Zesty citrus butter complements the Cajun-spiced steak—all you need is a little New Orleans jazz playing in the background.

1/2 cup	125 mL	bourbon
2 Tbsp	30 mL	minced onion
1/4 cup	60 mL	butter, softened
1 Tbsp	15 mL	chopped fresh chives
1/2 tsp	2 mL	chopped fresh thyme
1/2 tsp	2 mL	grated lemon zest
1/2 tsp	2 mL	grated orange zest
1 Tbsp	15 mL	brown sugar, packed
1 Tbsp	15 mL	onion powder
1 Tbsp	15 mL	smoked sweet paprika
2 tsp	10 mL	salt
1 1/2 tsp	7 mL	dried thyme
1 1/2 tsp	7 mL	garlic powder
1/2 tsp	2 mL	chili powder
1/2 tsp	2 mL	pepper
1/4 tsp	1 mL	cayenne pepper
4	4	6 oz (170 g) beef strip loin steaks, about 3/4 inch (2 cm) thick

Combine bourbon and onion in a frying pan. Cook on medium for about 5 minutes until liquid is almost all evaporated. Remove from heat, leaving onion in pan to cool completely.

Stir in next 5 ingredients and spoon onto a sheet of waxed paper. Form into a 3 inch (7.5 cm) long cylinder. Wrap tightly and freeze for about 1 hour until firm.

Combine next 9 ingredients and rub over steaks. Grill on direct medium-high heat for about 5 minutes per side for medium-rare or until steak reaches desired doneness. Cover with foil and let stand for 10 minutes. Serve with sliced citrus butter medallions.

1 serving: 490 Calories; 23 g Total Fat (8 g Mono, 1 g Poly, 11 g Sat); 105 mg Cholesterol; 5 g Carbohydrates (trace Fibre, 3 g Sugar); 33 g Protein; 930 mg Sodium

Pictured on page 233.

Bourbon Street Steak with Citrus Butter, page 232

Flamish Chicken in Dark Beer, page 229

SWEET BOURBON RIBS

MAKES: 6 SERVINGS　　　**DIFFICULTY:** ★

Real bourbon really brings out the tangy sweetness in this recipe while providing some added kick, but go easy on it. Don't eat too many ribs and then drive! Serve with your favourite barbecue sauce and a baked potato on the side.

3/4 cup	175 mL	Kentucky Bourbon
1 cup	250 mL	brown sugar
3/4 cup	175 mL	soy sauce
3	3	cloves garlic, minced
3 lbs	1.4 kg	pork back ribs

Mix bourbon, brown sugar, soy sauce and garlic in a blender. Pour into a large bowl. Place ribs in bowl and marinate in fridge overnight.

Preheat non-stick grill to medium-low. Place ribs on grill and cook for 20 minutes, turning often.

1 serving: 850 Calories; 53 g Total Fat (24 g Mono, 4.5 g Poly, 20 g Sat); 185 mg Cholesterol; 36 g Carbohydrates (0 g Fibre, 35 g Sugar); 37 g Protein; 300 mg Sodium

Other ideas for incorporating booze: deglaze the pan with the same wine you are drinking. Combine bourbon with bacon—we already know that everything is better with bacon. Okay, everything is better with bourbon as well. Use whisky in your cream sauce, but make sure it doesn't split. And don't forget: Robbie Burns and Athol Bros are an inseparable combination.

SPICY BOURBON WINGS

MAKES: 10 WINGS   **DIFFICULTY:** ★

Wild Turkey is a popular brand of bourbon, but there are other Kentucky bourbons on the market that would work just as well. Serve wings with celery, carrots and ranch or blue cheese dressing.

2 Tbsp	30 mL	smoked paprika
4 tsp	20 mL	cayenne pepper, *divided*
2 Tbsp	30 mL	garlic powder
2 Tbsp	30 mL	onion powder
3 tsp	15 mL	salt, *divided*
1 Tbsp	15 mL	pepper, *divided*
10	10	chicken wings
6 Tbsp	90 mL	butter, melted
1 cup	250 mL	hot sauce
2 Tbsp	30 mL	Kentucky bourbon
1 Tbsp	15 mL	pepper

In a mixing bowl, combine paprika, 3 tsp (15 mL) cayenne, garlic powder, onion powder, 2 Tbsp (30 mL) salt and 1/2 Tbsp (7 mL) pepper and mix well.

Rinse wings and pat dry. Rub wings with dry spice rub and refrigerate at least 6 hours and up to overnight.

In a bowl, combine butter, hot sauce, bourbon, remaining 1 tsp (5 mL) cayenne, remaining 1 Tbsp salt (15 mL) and remaining 1/2 Tbsp (7 mL) pepper and whisk until combined. Set aside half of mixture. Toss chicken with remaining half of marinade and place on a rimmed baking sheet. Bake in a 400°F (200°C) oven for 60 minutes, checking at the 50-minute mark.

Once wings are cooked, brush them with reserved marinade right before serving.

1 wing: 200 Calories; 15 g Total Fat (4.5 g Mono, 2 g Poly, 7 g Sat); 55 mg Cholesterol; 5 g Carbohydrates (1 g Fibre, 1 g Sugar); 10 g Protein; 2330 mg Sodium

BOURBON PEPPER-CRUSTED SALMON

MAKES: 6 SERVINGS   **DIFFICULTY: ★ ★**

Entertaining has never been easier—toss some lightly oiled bell pepper pieces onto the grill next to the cedar-planked salmon, then join your guests for pre-dinner drinks. Have a spray bottle of water handy to douse any flames if the plank happens to catch fire.

1 1/2 lbs	680 g	salmon fillet, skin-on
1	1	cedar plank, soaked in water for 4 hours
3 Tbsp	45 mL	fine dry bread crumbs
2 Tbsp	30 mL	brown sugar, packed
1 Tbsp	15 mL	bourbon
2 tsp	10 mL	thick teriyaki sauce
1 tsp	5 mL	coarsely ground pepper

Place salmon, skin side down, on cedar plank.

Combine next 5 ingredients and spread over salmon. Prepare grill for direct medium-high heat. Place salmon and plank on grill. Reduce heat to medium-low and cook salmon for about 14 minutes until fish flakes easily when tested with a fork.

1 serving: 200 Calories; 7 g Total Fat (2.5 g Mono, 3 g Poly, 1 g Sat); 60 mg Cholesterol; 8 g Carbohydrates (0 g Fibre, 5 g Sugar); 23 g Protein; 161 mg Sodium

Helpful Tips

Salmon is often cooked on cedar, but other kinds of wood, such as alder, hickory, maple and oak may also be used. Using the oak staves of old wine barrels can infuse the fish with wine flavour as it cooks. Make sure whatever plank you use is clean, unvarnished and comes from non-resinous wood.

WHISKY BAKED BEANS

MAKES: ABOUT 5 CUPS (1.25 L)   **DIFFICULTY: ★**

A simple and quick version of slow-baked beans, with an interesting addition of whisky in the sauce.

1/4 cup	60 mL	bourbon
1/4 cup	60 mL	hickory barbecue sauce
1/4 cup	60 mL	maple syrup
1 Tbsp	15 mL	apple cider vinegar
1 Tbsp	15 mL	dry mustard
1/4 tsp	1 mL	salt
1/4 tsp	1 mL	pepper
2	2	19 oz (540 mL) cans of navy beans, rinsed and drained
1	1	14 oz (398 mL) can of diced tomatoes (with juice)
1 cup	250 mL	finely chopped onion

Combine first 7 ingredients in a large bowl. Stir in remaining 3 ingredients. Transfer to ungreased 2 quart (2 L) casserole. Bake, covered, in 375°F (190°C) oven for 1 hour. Bake, uncovered, for about 10 minutes until sauce is thickened.

1 cup (250 mL): 200 Calories; 0 g Total Fat (0 g Mono, 0 g Poly,0 g Sat); 0 mg Cholesterol; 30 g Carbohydrates (10 g Fibre, 12 g Sugar); 7 g Protein; 760 mg Sodium

Love makes the world go round? Not at all. Whisky makes it go round twice as fast.

—Compton Mackenzie

SPICY JACK CHICKEN

MAKES: 4 SERVINGS   **DIFFICULTY: ★ ★ ★**

Crispy seasoned chicken baked with much less fat than popular fast-food varieties.
A perfect combination of sweet and spicy with a splash of whisky to boot, this dish
is ridiculously easy to prepare and pairs well with polenta. If you don't have quinoa
flour, use whole wheat flour instead. Having your pan and oven hot before adding
your ingredients makes a significant difference in the quality of this entrée.

2	2	large eggs
1 tsp	5 mL	lemon juice
1/2 cup	125 mL	quinoa flour
1 tsp	5 mL	dried oregano
1/4 tsp	1 mL	paprika
		salt and pepper to taste
4	4	4 oz (113 g) boneless, skinless chicken breasts
3 oz	85 g	jalapeño havarti cheese, cut into 4 skinny rectangles
4 tsp	20 mL	butter, *divided*
1/2 cup	125 mL	canned kernel corn
3/4 cup	175 mL	southern whisky (such as Jack Daniels)
1/4 cup	60 mL	Louisiana hot sauce
1/4 cup	60 mL	water

Mix egg and lemon juice on a large plate. In a medium bowl, combine flour, oregano,
paprika, salt and pepper, and pour half of mixture onto a second large plate.

Cut a small horizontal slit in top of chicken breasts and stuff in 1 cheese slice per breast.
Dredge chicken first in flour mixture, then egg mixture, then back in flour mixture, adding
more flour mixture to the second plate as needed.

Add 3 tsp (15 mL) butter to a large heavy bottomed cast iron pan over medium-high
heat. Sear chicken until browned on bottom, then flip each breast over and place pan in
a 400°F (200°C) oven. Bake for 10 minutes. Flip chicken over and continue to bake for
another 8 to 10 minutes, until internal temperature of chicken is 165°F (74°C). Remove
from pan, set on a cooling rack and cover with foil.

Return pan to heat and add remaining 1 tsp (5 mL) butter. Add corn and toss vigorously.
Pour in whisky, hot sauce and water. Reduce by half. Sauce should be thick enough to
coat the back of a spoon. To serve, cut each breast into thirds and drizzle with sauce.

1 serving: 620 Calories; 19 g Total Fat (4.5 g Mono, 1.5 g Poly, 10 g Sat); 295 mg Cholesterol; 15 g Carbohydrates
(3 g Fibre, trace Sugar); 69 g Protein; 580 mg Sodium

Pictured on page 215.

VEGETABLES WITH PANACHE:
DECORATING WITH COLOUR

Consider the vegetable. Many people will have you believe it provides an important nutritional element on a plate, but really, it's just there to add colour. An entire group of people chooses to eat meatless foods either all the time or when they want to eat more healthy, which means their entire plate has no meat on it.

VEGETARIAN STEW

MAKES: 6 SERVINGS   **DIFFICULTY: ★**

Perhaps the best thing about vegetable stew is, much like a good scotch, it only gets better with age.

1 Tbsp	15 mL	butter
1/2	1/2	large onion, chopped
6	6	shallots, chopped
1/2	1/2	clove garlic, chopped
2	2	stalks celery, chopped
2	2	medium carrots, chopped
3 cups	750 mL	vegetable broth
1/2	1/2	29 oz (823 g) can of tomato sauce
1/2	1/2	15 oz (425 g) can of black beans
1/4	1/4	head cabbage, cored and shredded
2	2	large potatoes, peeled, cooked and diced
1 1/2 tsp	7 mL	dried oregano
1 tsp	5 mL	dried basil
1/2 tsp	2 mL	salt
1/2 tsp	2 mL	pepper
1/8 tsp	0.5 mL	cayenne pepper
1/2 cup	125 mL	Parmesan cheese

Heat butter in a large pot and add onion, shallots and garlic. Cook until tender, then add celery and carrots. Stir in broth, tomato sauce, black beans, cabbage and potatoes.

Season with oregano, basil, salt, pepper and cayenne. Bring to a boil. Reduce heat to low and cover. Simmer for 25 minutes, stirring occasionally, until vegetables are tender. Top with Parmesan and serve.

1 serving: 240 Calories; 4.5 g Total Fat (1 g Mono, 0 g Poly, 3 g Sat); 10 mg Cholesterol; 42 g Carbohydrates (7 g Fibre, 10 g Sugar); 10 g Protein; 950 mg Sodium

SUNDRIED TOMATO AND SPINACH PIZZA

MAKES: 4 SERVINGS   **DIFFICULTY:** ★

You don't have to be a vegetarian to appreciate this yummy pizza. Feel free to add or replace veggies as you wish. Some great options are red peppers, green olives or arugula.

1 cup	250 mL	tomato sauce
1	1	12 inch (30 cm) prebaked pizza crust
1 cup	250 mL	shredded mozzarella cheese
1 cup	250 mL	goat cheese, crumbled
1 cup	250 mL	chopped sundried tomatoes
1 cup	250 mL	chopped spinach

Spread tomato sauce evenly over pizza crust. Arrange mozzarella, goat cheese and tomatoes on pizza crust.

Bake in a 350°F (175°C) oven until cheese is bubbly, about 20 minutes. Remove from oven and top with chopped spinach.

1 serving: 470 Calories; 15 g Total Fat (2 g Mono, 0 g Poly, 9 g Sat); 30 mg Cholesterol; 60 g Carbohydrates (4 g Fibre, 13 g Sugar); 22 g Protein; 1830 mg Sodium

Vegetarians are cool. All I eat
are vegetarians – except for the
occasional mountain lion steak.

—Ted Nugent

GRILLED EGGPLANT

MAKES: 4 SERVINGS   **DIFFICULTY: ★**

According to the statistics, 4% of Canadians are proclaimed vegetarians (compared to 2.8% of Americans), which means that eventually you may have a friend or relative over who does not eat meat. This recipe is perfect to pull from your bag of tricks on those occasions.

2	2	large eggplants cut into 1 inch (2.5 cm) slices
1/3 cup	60 mL	extra virgin olive oil
1/2 tsp	2 mL	salt
1/2 tsp	2 mL	pepper
1	1	loaf thick-sliced Italian bread
1 cup	250 mL	fresh mozzarella cheese
1 lb	500 g	sliced tomatoes
3 Tbsp	45 mL	balsamic vinegar

Preheat barbecue grill to medium-low. Brush eggplant slices with olive oil and season with salt and pepper. Place eggplant on grill. Cook slices until brown on bottom, then flip over. Brush other side with olive oil and cook until brown. Remove from heat.

Grill bread slices with same technique, brushing each side with oil and cooking until lightly browned.

Arrange toasted bread on platter with cheese, eggplant and tomato slices. Drizzle with balsamic vinegar and serve.

1 serving: 310 Calories; 16 g Total Fat (10 g Mono, 1.5 g Poly, 4 g Sat); 10 mg Cholesterol; 34 g Carbohydrates (8 g Fibre, 8 g Sugar); 9 g Protein; 350 mg Sodium

Let my words, like vegetables, be tender and sweet, for tomorrow I may have to eat them.

—Author Unknown

CLASSIC CAESAR SALAD

MAKES: 6 SERVINGS   **DIFFICULTY: ★**

The king of all salads, the classic Caesar complements just about any dish and is hearty enough to be a meal all on its own. To add your own personal touch to this salad, try creating your own croutons.

1/4 cup	60 mL	olive oil
3 Tbsp	45 mL	grated Parmesan cheese
1 Tbsp	15 mL	white wine vinegar
2 tsp	10 mL	Dijon mustard
3	3	cloves garlic, minced
1/2 tsp	2 mL	salt
1/2 tsp	2 mL	pepper
3 Tbsp	45 mL	mayonnaise
6	6	prewashed Romaine hearts
2 1/2 cups	625 mL	croutons
1/4 cup	60 mL	grated Parmesan cheese

Whisk first 8 ingredients in a bowl until smooth.

Cut romaine hearts lengthwise into 1 inch (2.5 cm) strips and place in an extra large salad bowl. Add dressing, croutons and Parmesan cheese and toss to combine.

1 serving: 220 Calories; 17 g Total Fat (11 g Mono, 2.5 g Poly, 3 g Sat); 10 mg Cholesterol; 12 g Carbohydrates (1 g Fibre, 1 g Sugar); 5 g Protein; 470 mg Sodium

Salads are a decorative element meant to impress you girlfriend or wife, mother, grandmother and doctor. To make them actually taste good and transform them into guy cuisine, smother the evil lettuce and veggies with cheese, meat and a vinaigrette or cream sauce. Caesar salad is performance art at its best. Make it tableside (and if you flub it, just take it back to the kitchen and serve it in individual portions).

ROMANO CIABATTA VEGETABLE SALAD

MAKES: 12 CUPS (3 L)   **DIFFICULTY: ★**

Quartering the onion with the stem still on helps the pieces stay intact during grilling. The core of the fennel serves the same stabilizing purpose.

2	2	large fennel bulbs (white part only), cut into 4 wedges each
1	1	large red onion, cut into 4 wedges
1	1	large eggplant, cut into 3/4 inch (2 cm) slices
2	2	medium zucchini, quartered lengthwise
1	1	large red pepper, halved
1	1	large yellow pepper, halved
7/8 cup	200 mL	extra virgin olive oil, *divided*
2	2	multigrain ciabatta buns, split
1	1	19 oz (540 mL) can of romano beans, rinsed and drained
2 cups	500 mL	grape tomatoes
4	4	cloves garlic, roasted and mashed
2/3 cup	150 mL	balsamic vinegar
2 tsp	10 mL	granulated sugar
1/2 tsp	2 mL	salt
1/2 tsp	2 mL	pepper

Brush first 6 ingredients with 3 Tbsp (45 mL) olive oil. Grill fennel and onion on direct medium heat for about 25 minutes, turning occasionally, until tender. Grill eggplant, zucchini and peppers for about 15 minutes, turning occasionally, until tender-crisp and browned. Let stand until cool enough to handle. Cut fennel and onion into 1 inch (2.5 cm) pieces. Cut eggplant, zucchini and peppers into 1 1/2 inch (3.8 cm) pieces.

Brush bun halves with 1 Tbsp (15 mL) olive oil. Grill for 1 to 2 minutes until toasted. Cut into 1 inch (2.5 cm) pieces.

Combine beans and tomatoes with vegetables and bread cubes in a large bowl.

Combine remaining 2/3 cup (150 mL) olive oil with remaining 5 ingredients. Drizzle over salad and toss until coated.

1 serving: 500 Calories; 36 g Total Fat (27 g Mono, 3 g Poly, 5 g Sat); 0 mg Cholesterol; 44 g Carbohydrates (11 g Fibre, 11 g Sugar); 11 g Protein; 270 mg Sodium

Helpful Tips

To roast garlic, trim 1/4 inch (6 mm) from each bulb to expose tops of cloves, leaving bulbs intact. Wrap bulbs individually in greased foil and bake in a 350°F (175°C) oven for about 45 minutes until tender. Let stand until cool enough to handle. Squeeze garlic bulb to remove cloves from skins. Excess roasted garlic can be wrapped and stored in the freezer.

ROASTED ASPARAGUS WITH FETA AND OREGANO

MAKES: 6 SERVINGS   **DIFFICULTY: ★**

Asparagus lends an air of elegance to any dish it's in, and it is so easy to cook.

2 lbs	1 kg	**trimmed asparagus**
4 Tbsp	60 mL	**cold pressed canola oil, *divided***
		salt and pepper to taste
1/2 lb	225 g	**feta cheese**
2 Tbsp	30 mL	**fresh oregano**

Toss 2 Tbsp (30 mL) canola oil over asparagus and season with salt and pepper. Roast in a 350°F (175°C) oven for 10 minutes. To serve, lay out asparagus and drizzle remaining canola oil over top, then crown with feta and fresh oregano.

1 serving: 220 Calories; 17 g Total Fat (7 g Mono, 2.5 g Poly, 6 g Sat); 35 mg Cholesterol; 9 g Carbohydrates (4 g Fibre, 4 g Sugar); 9 g Protein; 430 mg Sodium

Helpful Tips

To trim asparagus, snap off the tough ends. Peel stalks if they are thick.

GRILLED BALSAMIC VEGETABLES

MAKES: 8 SERVINGS   **DIFFICULTY:** ★

Serve these sweet, balsamic-glazed veggies on skewers for a more novel approach to dining.

1/3 cup	75 mL	orange juice
1/4 cup	60 mL	balsamic vinegar
1/4 cup	60 mL	maple syrup
1 Tbsp	15 mL	Dijon mustard
1/4 tsp	1 mL	salt
1/4 tsp	1 mL	pepper
16	16	red pepper pieces, about 1 inch (2.5 cm)
16	16	yellow pepper pieces, about 1 inch (2.5 cm)
16	16	fresh whole white mushrooms
8	8	zucchini slices (with peel), about 1/2 inch (12 mm), cut in half
8	8	cherry tomatoes
8	8	bamboo skewers (8 inch, 20 cm, each), soaked in water for 10 minutes

For the glaze, combine first 6 ingredients in a small saucepan and bring to a boil. Reduce heat to medium and boil gently, uncovered, for about 10 minutes until slightly thickened.

Thread next 5 ingredients alternately onto skewers. Preheat barbecue to medium. Cook skewers on a greased grill for 10 to 15 minutes, turning occasionally and brushing with glaze, until vegetables are tender.

1 serving: 60 Calories; 0 g Total Fat (0 g Mono, 0 g Poly,0 g Sat); 0 mg Cholesterol; 13 g Carbohydrates (2 g Fibre, 8 g Sugar); 2 g Protein; 105 mg Sodium

Pictured on page 251.

> Vegetables are interesting but lack a sense of purpose when unaccompanied by a good cut of meat.
>
> —Fran Lebowitz

ANTIPASTO SALAD

MAKES: 8 SERVINGS   **DIFFICULTY: ★**

This quick salad can be very impressive depending on the garnishes you serve with it—feta cheese, bocconcini cheese and pine nuts are excellent choices. The dressing is quite practical—you can use it to marinate chicken or lamb for the barbecue. If you like it a lot, double the recipe and keep it on hand. It can be stored for two to three weeks in the fridge.

1/3 cup	75 mL	red wine vinegar
1 cup	250 mL	extra virgin olive oil
1 Tbsp	15 mL	lemon juice
1 Tbsp	15 mL	dried oregano
1 tsp	5 mL	thyme
1 Tbsp	15 mL	liquid honey
		salt and pepper to taste
1	1	head of lettuce
1/2	1/2	sliced red onion
1	1	14 oz (398 mL) can of artichoke hearts
1/2 cup	125 mL	roasted peppers, chopped
1/4 cup	60 mL	olives
1 cup	250 mL	diced tomatoes or cherry tomatoes
1/4 cup	60 mL	hot peppers

For the dressing, mix first 8 ingredients together in a jar with a lid and set aside. Shake well before using.

Tear lettuce into bite-sized pieces, and place on chilled platter. Mix remaining ingredients together in a large bowl and add 2 Tbsp (30 mL) dressing. Top lettuce with mixture and drizzle dressing over top. Serve with your choice of garnishes.

1 serving: 290 Calories; 29 g Total Fat (22 g Mono, 2 g Poly, 4 g Sat); 0 mg Cholesterol; 10 g Carbohydrates (4 g Fibre, 5 g Sugar); 2 g Protein; 250 mg Sodium

BROCCOLI AND CORN SALAD

MAKES: 4 SERVINGS   **DIFFICULTY:** ★

Here's another nice vegetable salad blending the classic combination of fresh honey and mustard. Makes an excellent side or a healthy snack on its own.

1	1	**corncob, cooked and cooled**
1	1	**bunch of broccoli florets**
1/2 cup	125 mL	**diced onion**
1/2 cup	125 mL	**diced orange pepper**
3/4 cup	175 mL	**mayonnaise**
2 Tbsp	30 mL	**lemon juice**
2 Tbsp	30 mL	**mustard**
2 Tbsp	30 mL	**liquid honey**
1/2 tsp	2 mL	**salt**
1/2 tsp	2 mL	**pepper**

Using a knife, remove kernels from cob of corn and place in a large salad bowl. Mix in broccoli, diced onions and peppers.

In a small bowl, combine mayonnaise, lemon juice, mustard, honey, salt and pepper and mix well. Toss with vegetables. Refrigerate for at least 1 hour before serving.

1 serving: 380 Calories; 31 g Total Fat (18 g Mono, 9 g Poly, 3 g Sat); 15 mg Cholesterol; 19 g Carbohydrates (1 g Fibre, 0 g Sugar); 3 g Protein; 680 mg Sodium

> It is my view that the vegetarian manner of living, by its purely physical effect on the human temperament, would most beneficially influence the lot of mankind.
>
> —Albert Einstein

SUMMER CARROT SALAD

MAKES: 4 SERVINGS   **DIFFICULTY:** ★

Every garden party or gathering on the deck requires a mitt-full of good salads. This summer carrot blend is sweet and creamy and a guaranteed hit.

2 cups	500 mL	grated carrots
1 cup	250 mL	crushed pineapple
1/2 cup	125 mL	raisins
1 Tbsp	15 mL	liquid honey
3 Tbsp	45 mL	mayonnaise or salad dressing
1/4 tsp	60 mL	lemon juice

Mix carrots, pineapple and raisins together in a large salad bowl. Stir in honey, mayonnaise and lemon juice. Refrigerate for 1 hour before serving.

1 serving: 240 Calories; 8 g Total Fat (4.5 g Mono, 2.5 g Poly, 1 g Sat); trace Cholesterol; 42 g Carbohydrates (5 g Fibre, 33 g Sugar); 2 g Protein; 160 mg Sodium

Even as a junkie I stayed true to vegetarianism. I shall have heroin but I shan't have a hamburger. What a sexy little paradox.

—Russell Brand

Grilled Balsamic Vegetables, page 247

Braised Beef Short Ribs, page 221

QUICK SLAW

MAKES: 4 SERVINGS   **DIFFICULTY:** ★

This slaw is so easy it's destined to be a favourite in your arsenal of salads.

1	1	small head green cabbage, thinly sliced
1/4 cup	60 mL	red cabbage, thinly sliced
1	1	medium carrot, shredded
2/3 cup	150 mL	mayonnaise
3 Tbsp	45 mL	granulated sugar
3/4 tsp	4 mL	salt
3/4 tsp	4 mL	celery seed
3 Tbsp	45 mL	white vinegar
3/4 tsp	4 mL	mustard
		dash of white pepper

Combine green and red cabbage and carrot in a large bowl and set aside.

Combine remaining ingredients in a small bowl and mix well. Pour part of dressing into cabbage mixture to moisten. Refrigerate until ready to serve. Serve additional dressing on the side.

1 serving: 370 Calories; 27 g Total Fat (16 g Mono, 8 g Poly, 2.5 g Sat); 15 mg Cholesterol; 27 g Carbohydrates (5 g Fibre, 18 g Sugar); 4 g Protein; 800 mg Sodium

Pictured on page 71.

Vegetables are a must on a diet.
I suggest carrot cake, zucchini
bread, and pumpkin pie.
—Jim Davis

FRUIT

THE FORGOTTEN FOOD

There are too many recipes with fruit in them to include even the most significant here. Nevertheless, here's just a friendly reminder that fruit smoothies, BBQ fruits, a morning apple snack and a grape and cheese platter go a long way to covering a whole food group.

FRUITED LAMB CURRY

MAKES: 6 SERVINGS **DIFFICULTY:** ★

Delectably tender lamb with the sweetness of banana and pineapple.

1 Tbsp	15 mL	cooking oil
2 lbs	900 g	boneless lamb shoulder, trimmed of fat and cut into 1 1/2 inch (3.8 cm) cubes
1 tsp	5 mL	seasoned salt
		pepper to taste
1 1/2 cups	375 mL	coarsely chopped onion
2 tsp	10 mL	curry paste
2	2	cloves garlic, crushed
1/4 tsp	1 mL	ground coriander
1/4 tsp	1 mL	ground ginger
1	1	14 oz (398 mL) can of coconut milk
1	1	14 oz (398 mL) can of pineapple tidbits, drained and juice reserved
2	2	underripe bananas, cut into 1/2 inch (12 mm) slices
2 Tbsp	30 mL	water
1 Tbsp	15 mL	lemon juice
1 Tbsp	15 mL	cornstarch
1/4 cup	60 mL	slivered almonds, toasted

Heat cooking oil in a large frying pan on medium-high. Cook lamb in batches, turning occasionally, until browned. Sprinkle with seasoned salt and pepper. Transfer to plate lined with paper towel to drain.

Add next 5 ingredients to same frying pan. Cook, stirring occasionally, until onion is softened. Stir in coconut milk and reserved pineapple juice. Add lamb and simmer, covered, for 1 to 1 1/2 hours until lamb is tender.

Stir in pineapple and banana.

Stir water and lemon juice into cornstarch in a small bowl. Add to lamb mixture and cook, stirring, for about 5 minutes until boiling and slightly thickened. Sprinkle with almonds and serve.

1 serving: 460 Calories; 25 g Total Fat (5 g Mono, 1.5 g Poly, 16 g Sat); 95 mg Cholesterol; 30 g Carbohydrates (3 g Fibre, 18 g Sugar); 33 g Protein; 540 mg Sodium

GRILLED TILAPIA WITH MANGO SALSA

MAKES: 4 SERVINGS   **DIFFICULTY:★**

Mild-flavoured tilapia, basted with a zesty sauce and grilled to perfection, is topped with a fresh mango salsa.

1 cup	250 mL	diced fresh (or frozen, thawed) mango
3/4 cup	175 mL	diced kiwi fruit
2/3 cup	150 mL	diced Roma (plum) tomatoes
1 Tbsp	15 mL	finely chopped red onion
1 Tbsp	15 mL	finely chopped jalapeño pepper, seeds and membranes removed
1 Tbsp	15 mL	chopped fresh cilantro
1 Tbsp	15 mL	chopped fresh mint
1/3 cup	75 mL	tomato sauce
2 Tbsp	30 mL	lime juice
1 Tbsp	15 mL	cooking oil
1	1	clove garlic, minced
1 tsp	5 mL	liquid honey
1/2 tsp	2 mL	grated lime zest
1/2 tsp	2 mL	hot pepper sauce
1/4 tsp	1 mL	salt
1 lb	454 g	tilapia fillets, any small bones removed

Combine first 7 ingredients in medium bowl.

Combine next 8 ingredients in small bowl. Stir 1/3 cup (75 mL) into mango mixture. Chill, covered, for 30 minutes.

Preheat barbecue to medium-high. Place fillets on greased sheet of heavy duty foil and brush with remaining tomato sauce mixture. Place on a greased grill. Close lid and cook for 2 to 4 minutes per side, brushing with tomato sauce mixture, until fish flakes easily when tested with a fork. Transfer to a serving plate. Serve with mango salsa.

1 serving: 210 Calories; 6 g Total Fat (2 g Mono, 1 g Poly, 1.5 g Sat); 60 mg Cholesterol; 17 g Carbohydrates (2 g Fibre, 11 g Sugar); 24 g Protein; 340 mg Sodium

STRAWBERRY PECAN SALAD

MAKES: 6 SERVINGS   **DIFFICULTY: ★**

Simple yet elegant and sure to impress. Warming up the strawberry jam infuses the dressing with a wonderful berry flavour.

2/3 cup	150 mL	pecan pieces
1/2 cup	125 mL	granulated sugar
1/4 cup	60 mL	water
6 cups	1.5 L	fresh spinach leaves, lightly packed
2 cups	500 mL	sliced fresh strawberries
3 oz	85 g	goat (chèvre) cheese, cut up, optional
3 Tbsp	45 mL	olive (or cooking) oil
2 Tbsp	30 mL	balsamic vinegar
2 Tbsp	30 mL	strawberry jam, warmed
1/8 tsp	0.5 mL	pepper

Spread pecans evenly on an ungreased baking sheet with sides. Bake in a 350°F (175°C) oven for 5 to 10 minutes, stirring or shaking often, until golden.

Combine sugar and water in a small saucepan on low and cook, stirring, until sugar is dissolved. Bring to a boil on medium-high. Boil, uncovered, for 5 to 10 minutes, without stirring, until golden. Drizzle over pecans. Let stand for about 20 minutes until cool and hard, then chop pecans.

Arrange spinach on 6 salad plates. Scatter pecans, strawberries and cheese over top.

For the dressing, combine last 4 ingredients in a jar with a tight-fitting lid. Shake well. Drizzle over each salad.

1 serving: 340 Calories; 19 g Total Fat (11 g Mono, 3.5 g Poly, 4 g Sat); 5 mg Cholesterol; 35 g Carbohydrates (6 g Fibre, 24 g Sugar); 8 g Protein; 770 mg Sodium

Technically, men are not allowed to claim spinach as a guy food, but if you need to convince your family that they are eating healthy, here is a way to make it palatable.

FRESH FRUIT SALAD

MAKES: 10 SERVINGS   **DIFFICULTY:** ★

One nice thing about fruit salad is that you can use whatever fruits you have at your disposal, or whatever is in season. Another nice thing is that it will stay fresh for a couple of days in the fridge and can be enjoyed anytime.

2/3 cup	175 mL	**fresh orange juice**
1/3 cup	75 mL	**fresh lemon juice**
1/3 cup	75 mL	**packed brown sugar**
1 tsp	5 mL	**orange zest**
1/2 tsp	2 mL	**lemon zest**
1 tsp	5 mL	**vanilla extract**
2 cups	500 mL	**cubed fresh pineapple**
2 cups	500 mL	**strawberries, sliced**
2	2	**kiwi fruit, peeled and sliced**
2	2	**bananas, sliced**
2	2	**oranges, peeled and sectioned**
1	1	**grapefruit, peeled and sectioned**
1 cup	250 mL	**seedless grapes**
1 cup	250 mL	**apple, cored and diced**
1 cup	250 mL	**blueberries**

Bring juices, brown sugar and both zests to a boil in a saucepan over medium-high heat. Reduce heat to medium-low, and simmer until slightly thickened, about 5 minutes. Remove from heat, and stir in vanilla extract. Set aside to cool.

Add fruit to a large bowl and pour the cooled sauce over the fruit. Cover and refrigerate for at least 2 hours before serving.

1 serving: 150 Calories; 0.5 g Total Fat (0 g Mono, 0 g Poly, 0 g Sat); 0 mg Cholesterol; 37 g Carbohydrates (4 g Fibre, 28 g Sugar); 2 g Protein; 5 mg Sodium

BALSAMIC PEACHES

MAKES: 6 SERVINGS   DIFFICULTY: ★

Fresh, glazed peaches with visible grill marks. Delicious served with grilled croissants and ice cream.

6	6	fresh peaches (with skin), cut in half and pits removed
1/3 cup	75 mL	balsamic vinegar
1/4 cup	60 mL	liquid honey, warmed
3	3	croissants, cut in half horizontally
2 Tbsp	30 mL	butter (or hard margarine), melted
1 1/2 cups	375 mL	vanilla ice cream, *divided*
1/2 cup	125 mL	fresh raspberries

Put peaches into a large non-metal bowl. Add vinegar and toss gently. Cover and chill for 1 hour, stirring occasionally. Drain and discard liquid.

Preheat barbecue to medium. Cook peaches on greased grill for 5 minutes per side, brushing with honey, until browned and grill marks appear.

Brush cut sides of croissants with butter. Cook croissants on greased grill for about 2 minutes per side until crisp and grill marks appear.

Place 1 croissant half, 2 peach halves and 1/4 cup (60 mL) ice cream (about 1 scoop) on each of 6 individual plates. Sprinkle raspberries over top of each.

1 serving: 340 Calories; 14 g Total Fat (3.5 g Mono, 1 g Poly, 8 g Sat); 45 mg Cholesterol; 512 g Carbohydrates (5 g Fibre, 37 g Sugar); 5 g Protein; 270 mg Sodium

TEQUILA GRILLED PINEAPPLE

MAKES: 6 SERVINGS
DIFFICULTY: ★

A delicious way to end to any grilled meal, this healthy sweet is delicious on its own…but if you want to be more decadent, top with a scoop of lime sherbet. Because of the alcohol in the marinade, be prepared for a brief flare-up when adding the pineapple to the grill.

1/2 cup	125 mL	tequila
1/4 cup	60 mL	lime juice
1 tsp	5 mL	grated lime zest
1	1	small fresh pineapple, cut into 1/2 inch (12 mm) slices
2 Tbsp	30 mL	granulated sugar

Combine first 3 ingredients in a large resealable freezer bag. Add pineapple and seal. Let stand for 30 minutes, turning at halftime. Drain, reserving 1/2 cup (125 mL) tequila mixture in a small bowl. Add sugar and stir until dissolved. Preheat barbecue to medium. Place pineapple on greased grill and cook for 3 to 4 minutes per side, bushing often with sugar mixture, until grill marks appear.

1 serving: 100 Calories; 0 g Total Fat (0 g Mono, 0 g Poly, 0 g Sat); 0 mg Cholesterol; 15 g Carbohydrates (1 g Fibre, 12 g Sugar); 0 g Protein; 0 mg Sodium

FROZEN BANANAS ON A STICK

MAKES: 8 SERVINGS   **DIFFICULTY:** ★

Kids go crazy for this recipe and enjoy getting involved. It's fun to show them how yummy things are made, and it goes a long way toward making them more self-sufficient.

8	8	**lollipop sticks**
4	4	**bananas cut in half (horizontally)**
1/3 cup	75 mL	**peanut butter**
1 cup	250 mL	**chocolate chips**
1/2 cup	125 mL	**chopped peanuts or candy sprinkles, optional**

Insert a lollipop stick into each half banana and lay on a cookie sheet lined with wax paper. Put sheet in freezer until bananas are frozen through (about 2 hours).

Remove bananas from freezer and spread a layer of peanut butter on each banana. Return the bananas to the freezer for about 45 minutes.

Before removing bananas from freezer, place chocolate chips in a microwave-safe container and cook on medium (50%) in the microwave, 1 minute at a time, stirring every minute until chocolate is completely melted.

Dip each frozen banana into chocolate and roll it in the chopped peanuts or candy sprinkles. Freeze again until chocolate is firm.

1 banana: 260 Calories; 14 g Total Fat (0 g Mono, 0 g Poly, 16 g Sat); 0 mg Cholesterol; 38 g Carbohydrates (4 g Fibre, 25 g Sugar); 5 g Protein; 55 mg Sodium

Every now and then, I'll run into someone who claims not to like chocolate, and while we live in a country where everyone has the right to eat what they want, I want to say for the record that I don't trust these people, that I think something is wrong with them, and that they're probably - and this must be said - total duds in bed.

—Steve Almond

ESSENTIAL SIDES

Most guys tend to scrimp on side dishes, opting to focus instead on the main course. You don't need to be a foodie or Michelin star chef to realize that a balanced meal requires a good side to make your "main" really shine. In this section, we have compiled some top-notch and tasty side dishes you may have enjoyed as a child and have since forgotten all about. Today's standard table fare calls for something substantial on the plate other than pure protein to serve as an accent point for an aesthetic standpoint, but also from a gastronomic standpoint. Some men may need to force themselves when tackling these the first time around, however you will quickly discovered these sensible sides to be a required element. Fear not—"side" is no longer a scary four-letter word!

BUDDY BOB'S RICE PILAF

MAKES: 6 SERVINGS   **DIFFICULTY: ★**

Men, as a whole, enjoy rice pretty much anyway at all. This pilaf recipe is sure to become a ubiquitous side dish of North American male rice connoisseurs.

2 Tbsp	30 mL	butter
1/2 cup	125 mL	risoni pasta
1/2 cup	125 mL	diced onion
2	2	cloves garlic, minced
1/2 cup	125 mL	uncooked long grain rice
2 cups	500 mL	chicken broth

Melt butter in a medium skillet over medium heat. Add pasta and cook, stirring, until golden brown.

Stir in onion and cook until onion becomes translucent, then add garlic and cook for another 2 minutes.

Mix in rice and chicken broth. Turn heat to high and bring to a boil. Turn heat to low. Cover skillet and simmer for 20 minutes.

1 serving: 120 Calories; 3 g Total Fat (1 g Mono, 0 g Poly, 2 g Sat); 10 mg Cholesterol; 20 g Carbohydrates (trace Fibre, 1 g Sugar); 1 g Protein; 300 mg Sodium

A good side dish can make your main dish better. Or at least bigger. It also shows versatility and a multi-talented capacity, and it can sometimes be used to mop up the juices from the main dish.

TRADITIONAL FRIED RICE

MAKES: 4 CUPS   **DIFFICULTY:** ★

Fried rice is one of those homey, comforting dishes liked by just about everybody.
Prepare the rice ahead of time so it's cold—it fries much better that way.

5 tsp	25 mL	cooking oil, *divided*
2	2	large eggs, fork-beaten
1 cup	250 mL	thinly sliced fresh white mushrooms
1/2 cup	125 mL	finely chopped celery
1/2 cup	125 mL	finely chopped onion
3 cups	750 mL	cold cooked long grain white rice (about 1 cup, 250 mL, uncooked),
1/2 cup	125 mL	frozen peas, thawed
1/4 cup	60 mL	chopped green onion
2 Tbsp	30 mL	soy sauce

Heat 2 tsp (10 mL) cooking oil in a large frying pan or wok on medium-high. Add egg. Cook for about 30 seconds, without stirring, until almost set. Turn and cook for about 30 seconds until set. Transfer to a cutting board. Roll-up, jelly-roll style, and cut into thin slices. Set aside.

Heat remaining 3 tsp (15 mL) oil in same frying pan on medium. Add next 3 ingredients. Stir-fry for 2 to 4 minutes until onion is softened and liquid is evaporated.

Add rice and stir-fry for about 1 minute until heated through, then add remaining 3 ingredients and egg. Stir-fry for about 1 minute until heated through.

1 cup (250 mL): 270 Calories; 9 g Total Fat (4.5 g Mono, 2 g Poly, 1.5 g Sat); 105 mg Cholesterol; 39 g Carbohydrates (2 g Fibre, 3 g Sugar); 9 g Protein; 530 mg Sodium

ROASTED POTATOES

MAKES: 4 SERVINGS   **DIFFICULTY:** ★

Roasted potatoes have long been a North American male staple, and a dash of chili powder brings a little more heat to the game.

5	5	large red potatoes, peeled and diced
1	1	medium onion, chopped
2 tsp	10 mL	chili powder
1 Tbsp	15 mL	garlic powder
2 tsp	10 mL	salt
1/4 cup	60 mL	extra virgin olive oil
1 cup		shredded Cheddar cheese

Spread potatoes and onions out on a large greased baking dish. Season with chili powder, garlic powder and salt. Drizzle with olive oil and stir well.

Bake for about 40 minutes, until potatoes are tender and slightly crisp. Remove dish from oven and sprinkle with cheese. Return to oven for another 5 minutes to melt cheese, then remove from oven and let stand 5 minutes before serving.

1 serving: 500 Calories; 11 g Total Fat (3.5 g Mono, 0.5 g Poly, 6 g Sat); 30 mg Cholesterol; 86 g Carbohydrates (8 g Fibre, 6 g Sugar); 17 g Protein; 1390 mg Sodium

What I say is that, if a man really likes potatoes, he must be a pretty decent sort of fellow.

—A.A. Milne

EXTRA-SWEET SWEET POTATO FRIES

MAKES: 4 SERVINGS
DIFFICULTY: ★

If you think conventional fries are good, you'll think these sweet potato fries are a little slice of heaven. The combination of sweetness from the yams and savoury from the seasonings will have you gobbling them up like they're going out of style.

4	4	sweet potatoes
1/2 tsp	2 mL	ground cinnamon
1/2 tsp	2 mL	ground ginger
2 Tbsp	30 mL	brown sugar
3 Tbsp	45 mL	extra virgin olive oil
1 Tbsp	15 mL	salt

Wash and rinse sweet potatoes and cut into long 1/4 inch (6 mm) French fry strings. Spread out on a large cookie sheet.

In a bowl, mix cinnamon, ginger and brown sugar and then sprinkle over fries. Drizzle olive oil over fries and bake in a 350°F (175°C) oven until tender inside and golden brown outside, usually about 30 minutes. Season with salt and serve.

1 serving: 230 Calories; 11 g Total Fat (8 g Mono, 1 g Poly, 1.5 g Sat); 0 mg Cholesterol; 33 g Carbohydrates (4 g Fibre, 12 g Sugar); 2 g Protein; 1830 mg Sodium

Pictured on page 36.

DEEP-FRIED ZUCCS

MAKES: 8 SERVINGS   DIFFICULTY: ★

Deep friend zuccs are one of the tastiest ways for a guy to get his veggie requirement. Certainly not as nutritious as zucchini cooked by other methods, but man are they ever good!

2 quarts	2 L	oil
3	3	medium zucchinis, quartered
4	4	large eggs
1/4 cup	60 mL	whole cream (30%)
1/2 tsp	2 mL	pepper
1/4 tsp	1 mL	salt
3/4 cup	175 mL	Italian-style dry bread crumbs

Preheat oil in your deep-fryer or heavy, deep frying pan or pot to 375°F (190°C).

Slice zucchini quarters into pieces about 3 inches (7.5 cm) long.

In a large bowl, combine eggs, cream, pepper and salt and mix with whisk until well blended. Dip zucchini pieces into egg mixture, then coat with bread crumbs.

Carefully place battered pieces in oil and fry 3 to 4 minutes, until brown and crispy. Drain on a paper towel. Repeat until the slices have been fried. Serve with your favourite dip.

1 serving: 150 Calories; 11 g Total Fat (5 g Mono, 2.5 g Poly, 2 g Sat); 75 mg Cholesterol; 10 g Carbohydrates (1 g Fibre, 2 g Sugar); 5 g Protein; 105 mg Sodium

TRADITIONAL POTATO SALAD WITH EGG

MAKES: 8 SERVINGS   **DIFFICULTY:** ★

Nothing beats traditional potato salad with egg as a summertime side. This terrific cold side dish is perfect for a deck party or as a tail-gating side. Always serve chilled and be sure to season with a dash of salt and pepper.

4 lbs	1.8 kg	potatoes, peeled and chopped
8	8	large eggs, hard-boiled, chopped and chilled
1	1	medium onion, chopped
2 cups	500 mL	sweet pickles, chopped
2 cups	500 mL	mayonnaise

Boil potatoes until slightly tender, about 10 to 12 minutes. Drain and place in fridge for 1 hour.

Place eggs in a large salad bowl. Stir in onion, sweet pickles and mayonnaise, and chill mixture in fridge for 1 hour. Add cooked, chilled chopped potatoes to bowl with mayonnaise mixture. Stir and refrigerate for at least 1 hour before serving.

1 serving: 700 Calories; 52 g Total Fat (13 g Mono, 28 g Poly, 8 g Sat); 210 mg Cholesterol; 47 g Carbohydrates (5 g Fibre, 4 g Sugar); 12 g Protein; 770 mg Sodium

SLOW COOKER SCALLOPED POTATOES

MAKES: 11 CUPS (2.75 ML)   **DIFFICULTY:** ★

Traditional scalloped potatoes are always welcome at a hearty feast, but you usually need chisel to clean the dish. And because these are made in your slow cooker, your oven will be free to cook other dishes, plus it's easier to clean.

1/4 cup	60 mL	butter (or hard margarine)
1/4 cup	60 mL	all-purpose flour
3 cups	750 mL	milk
1 Tbsp	15 mL	parsley flakes
1 tsp	5 mL	dried rosemary, crushed
1/2 tsp	2 mL	garlic powder
1 tsp	5 L	salt
1/2 tsp	2 mL	pepper
5 lbs	2.3 kg	potatoes, peeled and thinly sliced
2 cups	500 mL	thinly sliced onion
1/4 cup	60 mL	grated Parmesan cheese
1/4 tsp	1 mL	paprika

Melt butter in a medium saucepan on medium. Add flour. Heat and stir for 1 minute. Slowly add 1 cup (250 mL) milk, stirring constantly, until boiling and thickened. Add remaining milk. Cook and stir until heated through.

Add next 5 ingredients. Stir.

Put half of potato and onion into greased 5 quart (5 L) slow cooker. Pour half of sauce over top and stir. Add remaining potato and onion, then pour remaining sauce over top and stir. Cook, covered, on Low for 8 hours or on High for 4 hours.

Sprinkle with cheese and paprika. Let stand, covered, for 5 minutes before serving.

1 serving: 220 Calories; 6 g Total Fat (1 g Mono, 0 g Poly, 3.5 g Sat); 15 mg Cholesterol; 34 g Carbohydrates (4 g Fibre, 6 g Sugar); 8 g Protein; 330 mg Sodium

BAKED POTATO CASSEROLE

MAKES: 8 SERVINGS   **DIFFICULTY:** ★

One of nature's most versatile vegetables, the stupendous spud is an integral part of any guy's repertoire. Potatoes can be prepared in countless ways. This recipe takes the classic baked potato and gives it a little twist—and a crispy cornflake crust.

1 cup	250 mL	sour cream
1	1	10 oz (284 mL) can of condensed cream of chicken soup
4 cups	1 L	thinly sliced white potatoes
2 cups	500 mL	shredded Cheddar cheese
1/2 cup	125 mL	chopped green onions
1/2 cup	125 mL	melted butter
1 cup	250 mL	cornflakes cereal

Mix sour cream and soup together in a large bowl. Add potatoes, cheese and onions, and mix until smooth. Pour mixture into a greased 9 x 13 inch (23 x 33 cm) casserole dish and cover with foil. Bake in a 350°F (175°C) oven for 30 minutes.

In a small bowl, mix melted butter and cornflakes without breaking cornflakes. Quickly remove casserole dish from oven, pull back and remove foil and then sprinkle cornflake mixture over potatoes. Return casserole dish to oven and bake, uncovered, for 15 minutes more until bubbly and golden brown on top.

1 serving: 410 Calories; 29 g Total Fat (8 g Mono, 1.5 g Poly, 18 g Sat); 75 mg Cholesterol; 28 g Carbohydrates (2 g Fibre, 2 g Sugar); 11 g Protein; 600 mg Sodium

Helpful Tips

How on earth were we coerced to peel a potato? Oven-roasted potatoes, mashed potatoes, baked potatoes, stuffed potatoes: just leave the peeler in the drawer. Don't forget rice: rice pilaf is easy, and wild rice is a nice variation.

Philippine Chicken Stew, page 167 • Traditional Slow Cooker Chili, page 73 •
Black Bean Soup, page 168

Panzanella Salad, page 271

PANZANELLA SALAD

MAKES: 6 SERVINGS   **DIFFICULTY:** ★

This salad is delicious with grilled meats. The capers add briny little pops of flavour. Don't cheap out and use canned black olives—many stores have a variety of fresh olives in their deli departments. Wildflower honey is outstanding in the dressing.

2 Tbsp	30 mL	liquid honey
2 Tbsp	30 mL	red wine vinegar
1/2 cup	125 mL	extra virgin olive oil
1	1	clove garlic, optional
		salt and pepper to taste
1	1	loaf of good quality artisan bread
1 1/2 lbs	680 g	vine-ripened tomatoes
2 Tbsp	30 mL	capers
1/4 cup	60 mL	roughly chopped, pitted black olives
1/3 cup	75 mL	bunch of fresh basil or oregano, or a mix

For the vinaigrette, add first 6 ingredients to a small glass container, cover and shake well. Taste to make sure that seasoning and balance are correct, and adjust to your liking, if necessary. Set aside.

For the salad, chop bread and tomatoes into 1 inch (2.5 cm) cubes. Place in a large bowl, including any tomato juice left on your cutting board. Add remaining 3 ingredients and toss well. Drizzle dressing over top and toss well, allowing dressing to absorb into bread.

1 serving: 320 Calories; 20 g Total Fat (15 g Mono, 2 g Poly, 3 g Sat); 0 mg Cholesterol; 33 g Carbohydrates (3 g Fibre, 9 g Sugar); 6 g Protein; 140 mg Sodium

Pictured on page 270.

ROASTED BRUSSELS SPROUTS

MAKES: 8 SERVINGS   **DIFFICULTY: ★**

Brussels sprouts tend to get a bad rap as little green blobs of hell, but when properly cooked, they are delicious.

2 lbs	900 g	Brussels sprouts
2 Tbsp	30 mL	extra virgin olive oil
2 cups	500 mL	mixed greens
		salt and pepper to taste
1/4 cup	60 mL	pure maple syrup
1/4 cup	60 mL	toasted pine nuts

Clean and trim Brussels sprouts, then cut in half and toss with olive oil. Place on a baking sheet lined with parchment paper and bake in a 400°F (200°C) oven for 10 to 12 minutes or until golden brown.

Meanwhile spread greens on a platter and season with salt and pepper. Once Brussels sprouts are done, place them on top of mixed greens, drizzle with maple syrup and pine nuts and serve.

1 serving: 130 Calories; 7 g Total Fat (3.5 g Mono, 2 g Poly, 1 g Sat); 0 mg Cholesterol; 16 g Carbohydrates (5 g Fibre, 7 g Sugar); 5 g Protein; 35 mg Sodium

Pictured on page 143.

We kids feared many things in those days - werewolves, dentists, North Koreans, Sunday School - but they all paled in comparison with Brussels sprouts.

—Dave Barry

CREAMED LEEKS

MAKES: 8 SERVINGS   **DIFFICULTY: ★ ★**

Simple but decadent, this dish is an excellent accompaniment for chicken or steak, but it really shines alongside a sautéed fillet of fish.

2 Tbsp	30 mL	butter
4 cups	1 L	leeks, white part only, chopped
1/4 cup	60 mL	vegetable stock
3/4 cup	175 mL	whipping cream
		salt and pepper to taste
2 tsp	10 mL	fresh thyme

In a large pan, melt butter until foam subsides, then add leeks and cook for about 5 minutes just until they begin to soften, without adding any colour. Add stock and cook for another 5 to 7 minutes, or until stock has reduced by about two-thirds.

Add cream and cook until reduced and thickened, 5 to 10 minutes, then season with salt, pepper and thyme. Serve or chill quickly, then reheat when needed.

1 serving: 90 Calories; 7 g Total Fat (2 g Mono, 0 g Poly, 4.3 g Sat); 25 mg Cholesterol; 7 g Carbohydrates (1 g Fibre, 2 g Sugar); trace Protein; 70 mg Sodium

Eat leeks in March and wild garlic in May
And all year after physicians may play.

—proverb of unknown origin

MOM'S CREAMED CORN CASSEROLE

MAKES: 6 SERVINGS   **DIFFICULTY: ★**

This delicious meal is a Morrison male favourite. It goes great with baked ham, pork or as another side dish with steak and potatoes. Try it once and you will be hooked.

1/2 cup	125 mL	melted butter
2	2	large eggs, beaten
1	1	8 oz (225 g) package of corn bread mix
2	2	15 oz (425 g) cans of creamed corn
1 cup	250 mL	sour cream

Combine ingredients in a large mixing bowl. Stir until well blended. Spoon mixture into a greased 9 x 13 inch (23 x 33 cm) casserole dish and bake in a 350°F (175°C) oven for 45 minutes or until golden brown and bubbly on top.

1 serving: 500 Calories; 30 g Total Fat (9 g Mono, 1.5 g Poly, 16 g Sat); 130 mg Cholesterol; 49 g Carbohydrates (4 g Fibre, 16 g Sugar); 8 g Protein; 1020 mg Sodium

After a good dinner one can forgive anybody, even one's own relations.
—Oscar Wilde

PARMESAN POLENTA

Very little effort with outstanding results. This creamy, cheesy polenta is a perfect match for roasted pork, pork chops or grilled chicken.

1 Tbsp	15 mL	butter
1 tsp	5 mL	olive oil
1/2	1/2	medium onion, diced
6 cups	1.5 mL	chicken stock
1 1/2 cups	375 mL	cornmeal
1 cup	250 mL	grated Parmesan cheese
1/2 cup	125 mL	cream
		salt and pepper to taste

Melt butter and olive oil in a medium frying pan over medium heat. Cook onion until soft and translucent. Add chicken stock and bring to a rolling boil, then slowly whisk in cornmeal. Lower temperature and cook for 10 to 15 minutes or until very thick.

Add cheese and cream, season with salt and pepper and serve.

1 serving: 290 Calories; 11 g Total Fat (3.5 g Mono, 0 g Poly, 7 g Sat); 35 mg Cholesterol; 36 g Carbohydrates (trace Fibre, 1 g Sugar); 9 g Protein; 830 mg Sodium

CAJUN CORNBREAD

MAKES: 24 PIECES   **DIFFICULTY:** ★

Slightly sweet thanks to the addition of corn kernels, this quickbread is a great side for chilies, soups and stews. Slathered with butter or jam, it also makes a tasty breakfast.

2 cups	500 mL	all-purpose flour
1 1/2 cups	375 mL	cornmeal
1 Tbsp	15 mL	baking powder
1 tsp	5 mL	baking soda
1 Tbsp	15 mL	salt
1/4 cup	60 mL	diced red pepper
1/4 cup	60 mL	chopped chives
1 cup	250 mL	fresh or frozen corn kernels
4 oz	115 g	melted butter
2 1/2 cups	625 mL	buttermilk
1/4 cup	60 mL	liquid honey
2 Tbsp	30 mL	hot sauce
6	6	large eggs

Combine flour, cornmeal, baking powder, baking soda and salt in a large mixing bowl. Stir in peppers, chives and corn.

Add remaining 5 ingredients, making sure to scrape bottom of bowl. Mix only until all ingredients are combined. Bake in a 9 x 13 inch (23 x 33 cm) pan in a 325°F (160°C) oven for 1 hour. Cool and cut into squares.

1 piece: 150 Calories; 5 g Total Fat (1.5 g Mono, 0 g Poly, 3 g Sat); 50 mg Cholesterol; 22 g Carbohydrates (trace Fibre, 3 g Sugar); 3 g Protein; 450 mg Sodium

Pictured on page 161.

Helpful Tips

For a tasty variation, line 2 baking pans with parchment paper and spray well with cooking spray. Prepare recipe as above and divide it among both pans. Bake for about 20 minutes or until golden brown. The cornbread will now resemble a wafer or cracker and can be used as a base for meat or shellfish.

WORKOUT FOOD

The human body needs to be treated well when it's in the midst of an exercise regime. Whether you're training for the Boston Marathon or just interested in losing a few pesky ounces before that trip to the beach, you need to consider what you're eating to make sure it provides the fuel needed to power your well-oiled machine.

HEALTHY BANANA COOKIES

MAKES: 14 COOKIES   **DIFFICULTY: ★**

No need to feel guilty about eating these cookies before a workout! With no added fat or sugar, these moist morsels are more like a solid, hand-held bowl of oatmeal than a cookie. Oats, walnuts, dates, banana—there is not one unhealthy ingredient in the mix!

3	3	ripe bananas
2 cups	500 mL	rolled oats
1 cup	250 mL	pitted and chopped dates
1/3 cup	75 mL	unsweetened applesauce
1 tsp	5 mL	vanilla extract
1 tsp	5 mL	ground cinnamon
1/4 cup	60 mL	chopped walnuts
1/2 cup	125 mL	dried cranberries (optional)

Mash bananas in a large bowl. Stir in oats, dates, applesauce, vanilla, cinnamon, walnuts and cranberries. Mix well and let stand for 15 minutes. Drop by teaspoonfuls onto an ungreased cookie sheet. Bake in a 350°F (175°C) oven for about 20 minutes, until lightly brown. Store in an airtight container for up to a week, or freeze for up to 3 months.

1 cookie: 120 Calories; 2.5 g Total Fat (0 g Mono, 1.5 g Poly, 0 g Sat); 0 mg Cholesterol; 24 g Carbohydrates (3 g Fibre, 11 g Sugar); 2 g Protein; 0 mg Sodium

> Never make eye contact while eating a banana.
>
> —Anonymous

SEED AND FRUIT GRANOLA BARS

MAKES: 12 BARS   **DIFFICULTY: ★**

Full of protein and complex carbohdrates, these bars are a great on-the-go sack and will give you the energy you need to fuel your workout.

2 cups	500 mL	large flake rolled oats
1/2 cup	125 mL	raw pumpkin seeds
1/2 cup	125 mL	raw sunflower seeds
1/3 cup	75 mL	chopped dried cherries
1/3 cup	75 mL	dried blueberries
1/3 cup	75 mL	golden raisins
1/3 cup	75 mL	wheat germ
1 Tbsp	15 mL	flaxseed
1 Tbsp	15 mL	sesame seeds
1/3 cup	75 mL	butter
1/4 cup	60 mL	muscovado sugar, packed (or 2 tsp [10 mL] stevia powder)
1/4 cup	60 mL	liquid honey
1/4 cup	60 mL	maple syrup

Spread rolled oats on an ungreased rimmed baking sheet. Bake in a 350°F (175°C) oven for about 18 minutes, stirring occasionally, until golden. Transfer to a large bowl. Stir in pumpkin seeds, sunflower seeds, cherries, blueberries, raisins, wheat germ, flaxseed and sesame seeds.

Combine butter, sugar (or stevia), honey and maple syrup in a small saucepan. Heat and stir on medium for about 5 minutes until starting to boil. Drizzle over rolled oat mixture and stir until coated. Press into a greased 9 x 13 inch (23 x 33 cm) pan. Bake for about 15 minutes until golden. Let stand for 15 minutes to cool slightly. Run knife around inside edge of pan to loosen. Cut into bars while still warm. Let cool in pan on wire rack.

1 bar: 230 Calories; 11 g Total Fat (2.5 g Mono, 3 g Poly, 4 g Sat); 15 mg Cholesterol; 31 g Carbohydrates (3 g Fibre, 17 g Sugar); 5 g Protein; 40 mg Sodium

MANGO ALMOND SMOOTHIE

MAKES: 6 CUPS (1.5 L)
DIFFICULTY: ★

Super simple and full of protein. Frozen fruit adds a creamy element to this power-packed smoothie.

3 cups	750 mL	frozen mango pieces
1 tsp	5 mL	vanilla extract
2 cups	500 mL	skim milk, chilled
1	1	14 oz (398 mL) can of sliced peaches (in juice)
1/4 cup	60 mL	almond butter

Process all 5 ingredients in a blender or food processor until smooth.

1 cup (250 mL): 190 Calories; 7 g Total Fat (4 g Mono, 1.5 g Poly, 0.5 g Sat); 0 mg Cholesterol; 30 g Carbohydrates (3 g Fibre, 27 g Sugar); 6 g Protein; 55 mg Sodium

CHOCOLATE BANANA PROTEIN SHAKE

MAKES: 4 CUPS (1 L)
DIFFICULTY: ★

Chocolate milk is touted as one of the best post-workout beverages—it has carbs and protein for building muscle, water for rehydration and sodium and sugar for providing energy. Use well-ripened bananas to make this creamy, chocolatey drink even better!

2	2	medium bananas
3 Tbsp	45 mL	protein powder
2/3 cup	150 mL	vanilla Greek yogurt
2 cups	500 mL	chocolate milk cocoa, sifted if lumpy, sprinkle

Put first 4 ingredients into a blender and process until smooth. Sprinkle cocoa over individual servings.

1 cup (250 mL): 200 Calories; 6 g Total Fat (0 g Mono, 0 g Poly, 3.5 g Sat); 20 mg Cholesterol; 29 g Carbohydrates (2 g Fibre, 22 g Sugar); 9 g Protein; 105 mg Sodium

Life is half delicious yogurt, half crap, and your job is to keep the plastic spoon in the yogurt.

—Scott Adams

CREAMY COUSCOUS PARFAITS

MAKES: 4 PARFAITS   **DIFFICULTY:** ★

This blend of fruit, Greek yogurt and whole grains makes for a hearty post-workout snack. It is also great for breakfast or as a healthy dessert.

2/3 cup	150 mL	**skim milk**
		salt to taste
1/3 cup	75 mL	**whole wheat couscous**
1	1	**14 oz (398 mL) can of pineapple tidbits, drained and juice reserved**
1 cup	250 mL	**coarsely chopped kiwifruit**
1 cup	250 mL	**coarsely chopped strawberries**
1/4 cup	60 mL	**reserved pineapple juice**
2 Tbsp	30 mL	**chopped fresh mint**
1 cup	250 mL	**peach Greek yogurt**
1 Tbsp	15 mL	**liquid honey**
1 tsp	5 mL	**minced crystallized ginger**
1/2 tsp	2 mL	**grated orange zest**

Combine milk and salt in a small saucepan. Bring to a boil and stir in couscous. Remove from heat and let stand, covered, for about 5 minutes until tender. Fluff with a fork. Spread on rimmed baking sheet. Freeze for 5 minutes.

Meanwhile, combine next 5 ingredients in medium bowl. Let stand for 15 minutes, stirring occasionally.

Combine remaining 5 ingredients in a separate medium bowl. Stir in chilled couscous. Spoon half of fruit mixture into 4 parfait glasses or small bowls. Spoon couscous mixture over fruit. Top with remaining fruit mixture.

1 parfait: 310 Calories; 9 g Total Fat (0 g Mono, 0 g Poly, 6 g Sat); 25 mg Cholesterol; 54 g Carbohydrates (4 g Fibre, 27 g Sugar); 8 g Protein; 80 mg Sodium

EASY HOMEMADE HUMMUS

MAKES: 4 SERVINGS   **DIFFICULTY: ★**

After a strenuous workout, your body needs foods high in protein and carbohydrates to build muscle and replace glucose lost from muscle as you were exercising. Hummus fits the bill nicely, especially when paired with whole wheat pita chips, though fresh veggies are also a good option.

1	1	15 oz (425 g) can of garbanzo beans (chick peas), drained, liquid reserved
1	1	clove garlic, crushed
2 tsp	10 mL	ground cumin
1/2 tsp	2 mL	salt
1 Tbsp	15 mL	olive oil

In a blender or food processor combine garbanzo beans, garlic, cumin, salt and olive oil and blend for a minute or less. Once mixture is blended, gradually add reserved bean liquid, a little at a time, blending with each addition, until hummus reaches your desired consistency.

1 serving: 100 Calories; 4 g Total Fat (1 g Mono, 0 g Poly, 2 g Sat); 10 mg Cholesterol; 13 g Carbohydrates (trace Fibre, trace Sugar); 2 g Protein; 240 mg Sodium

Helpful Tips

For a more traditional hummus replace the reserved bean water with tahini.

ALMOND BUCKWHEAT GRANOLA

MAKES: 6 CUPS (1.5 L)　　　　　**DIFFICULTY:** ★

Whole grain breakfast cereals are a great way to refuel your body after a workout. Bypass the commercially produced variety with this hearty, sweet, nutty breakfast staple. Try it with skim milk or sprinkled over Greek yogurt.

2 cups	500 mL	large flake rolled oats
2 cups	500 mL	whole buckwheat
1 cup	250 mL	sliced natural almonds
1/4 cup	60 mL	raw sunflower seeds
1/4 cup	60 mL	sesame seeds
1/4 cup	60 mL	brown sugar, packed
1/4 cup	60 mL	canola oil
1/4 cup	60 mL	liquid honey
1 tsp	5 mL	almond extract
1 tsp	5 mL	ground cinnamon

Combine first 5 ingredients in a large bowl.

Combine remaining 5 ingredients in small saucepan. Heat, stirring, on medium for about 2 minutes until brown sugar is dissolved. Add to oat mixture and stir until coated. Spread evenly on 2 ungreased rimmed baking sheets. Bake on separate racks in a 325°F (160°C) oven for about 20 minutes, stirring occasionally and switching positions of baking sheets at halftime, until golden. Let stand on baking sheet until cool. Store in an airtight container for up to 1 month.

1 cup (250 mL): 630 Calories; 28 g Total Fat (14 g Mono, 9 g Poly, 2.5 g Sat); 0 mg Cholesterol; 86 g Carbohydrates (10 g Fibre, 23 g Sugar); 16 g Protein; 150 mg Sodium

Variation: Add 2 cups (500 mL) puffed wheat cereal to granola after baking.

Pictured on page 287.

PEPPERED EGG QUESADILLA

MAKES: 2 QUESADILLAS   **DIFFICULTY:** ★

Quesadillas aren't just for dinner anymore! Eggs are packed with protein, which is necessary for muscle growth and recovery, and so are a perfect post-workout food. You could use whole wheat or whole grain tortillas for this nutritious, delicious handheld snack.

2	2	whole grain flour tortillas (9 inch, 23 cm, diameter)
4 Tbsp	60 mL	grated jalapeño Monterey Jack cheese, *divided*
1/2 tsp	2 mL	canola oil
1/2 cup	125 mL	sliced fresh white mushrooms
1/4 cup	60 mL	chopped red pepper
2	2	large eggs, fork-beaten
2 Tbsp	30 mL	chopped green onion
1/8 tsp	0.5 mL	pepper

Place 1 tortilla on an ungreased baking sheet and sprinkle with 2 Tbsp (30 mL) cheese. Set aside.

Heat canola oil in a medium non-stick frying pan on medium. Add mushrooms and red pepper. Cook for about 3 minutes, stirring occasionally, until red pepper is softened.

Add eggs. Sprinkle with green onion and pepper. Reduce heat to medium-low. Cook, covered, for about 2 minutes, without stirring, until eggs are set. Slide egg mixture onto tortilla on baking sheet. Sprinkle with remaining 2 Tbsp (30 mL) cheese. Place remaining tortilla on top. Bake in a 400°F (200°C) oven for about 3 minutes until cheese is melted. Cut into wedges.

1 quesadilla: 320 Calories; 17 g Total Fat (8 g Mono, 2 g Poly, 5 g Sat); 225 mg Cholesterol; 30 g Carbohydrates (6 g Fibre, 2 g Sugar); 16 g Protein; 670 mg Sodium

DESSERTS TO WOW

Although not every guy has a sweet tooth, a delectable well thought-out dessert will go a long way to pleasing others in your life. For many men, putting a decent dessert on the table includes an eight-inch apple pie from the corner store, and then opening a container of ice cream. Come on guys, we can do better than that! The ability to fine-tune a world-class after-dinner treat doesn't make you any less of a man. The ability to make dessert will garner more brownie points than you will need in a lifetime. Trust us; every man owes it to himself to have a few good dessert ideas in the old tackle box.

DARK CHOCOLATE CAKE WITH CREAM CHEESE ICING

MAKES: 10 WEDGES   **DIFFICULTY: ★ ★**

Who doesn't love chocolate cake? This elegant three-layer cake is as impressive to look at as it is to eat. If you prefer a darker icing, add more cocoa or some melted chocolate. For icing that is less sweet, reduce the amount of icing sugar.

2 cups	500 mL	boiling water
1 1/2 cups	375 mL	cocoa, sifted if lumpy, *divided*
2 3/4 cups	675 mL	all-purpose flour
2 tsp	10 mL	baking soda
1/2 tsp	2 mL	baking powder
1/2 tsp	2 mL	salt
1 1/4 cups	300 mL	butter (or hard margarine), softened, *divided*
2 1/4 cups	550 mL	granulated sugar
4	4	large eggs
2 1/2 tsp	12 mL	vanilla extract, *divided*
1 x 8 oz	250 g	block of cream cheese, softened
4 cups	1 L	icing (confectioner's) sugar

For the cake, pour boiling water over 1 cup (250 mL) cocoa in a medium bowl. Whisk until smooth, then set aside to cool.

Sift flour, baking soda, baking powder and salt onto a plate.

In a mixing bowl cream 1 cup (250 mL) butter and sugar together well. Beat in eggs 1 at a time, beating until light coloured. Add 1/2 tsp (2 mL) vanilla.

Add flour mixture to butter mixture in 3 parts alternately with cocoa mixture in 2 parts, beginning and ending with flour. Spread into 3 greased 9 inch (23 cm) round pans. Bake in a 350°F (175C) oven for 25 to 30 minutes until an inserted wooden pick comes out clean. Set aside to cool.

For the icing, put cream cheese, icing sugar, remaining 1/2 cup (125 mL) cocoa, remaining 1/4 cup (60 mL) butter and remaining 2 tsp (10 mL) vanilla into a mixing bowl. Beat slowly at first to combine, then beat at medium speed until light and fluffy. Ice cake.

1 wedge: 670 Calories; 29 g Total Fat (6 g Mono, 1 g Poly, 18 g Sat); 140 mg Cholesterol; 99 g Carbohydrates (4 g Fibre, 71 g Sugar); 9 g Protein; 540 mg Sodium

Pictured on page 288.

Almond Buckwheat Granola, page 283

Dark Chocolate Cake with Cream Cheese Icing, page 286

BLACK AND WHITE CHEESECAKE

MAKES: 12 WEDGES   **DIFFICULTY: ★ ★**

This classy white chocolate cheesecake is nothing short of perfection.

3/4 cup	175 mL	**all-purpose flour**
1/4 cup	60 mL	**cocoa, sifted if lumpy**
1/8 tsp	0.5 mL	**salt**
2	2	**large eggs**
1 1/2 cups	375 mL	**granulated sugar,** *divided*
1/2 cup	125 mL	**butter (or hard margarine), melted**
1	1	**1/4 oz (7 g) envelope of unflavoured gelatin (about 2 1/4 tsp, 11 mL)**
1/4 cup	60 mL	**cold water**
1 cup	250 mL	**white chocolate chips**
1	1	**8 oz (250 g) block cream cheese, cut up and softened**
1 1/4 cups	300 mL	**whipping cream,** *divided*
3 1/2 oz	100 g	**dark chocolate, chopped**

Combine first 3 ingredients in a small bowl. Beat eggs, 1 cup (250 mL) sugar and butter in a medium bowl. Add flour mixture and stir until just moistened. Spread evenly in greased 9 inch (23 cm) springform pan. Bake in a 350°F (175°C) oven for about 18 minutes until wooden pick inserted in centre comes out moist but not wet with batter. Do not overbake. Let stand in pan on wire rack until cool.

Sprinkle gelatin over water in small saucepan. Let stand for 1 minute. Heat, stirring, on medium-low until gelatin is dissolved. Put chocolate chips into a small microwave-safe bowl. Microwave on medium (50%) for about 2 minutes, stirring every 30 seconds, until almost melted. Do not overheat. Stir until smooth.

Beat cream cheese and remaining 1/2 cup (125 mL) sugar in a separate medium bowl until combined. Add melted white chocolate and gelatin mixture. Beat until smooth.

Beat 1 cup (250 mL) whipping cream in a small bowl until soft peaks form. Fold into cream cheese mixture. Spread evenly over base in pan. Chill, covered, for about 2 hours until set.

Heat remaining 1/4 cup (60 mL) whipping cream in a small saucepan on medium until hot, but not boiling. Remove from heat. Add dark chocolate. Stir until smooth and let stand for 5 minutes. Spread evenly over cheesecake. Chill for about 30 minutes until firm.

1 serving: 470 Calories; 30 g Total Fat (4 g Mono, 0.5 g Poly, 19 g Sat); 85 mg Cholesterol; 51 g Carbohydrates (1 g Fibre, 39 g Sugar); 4 g Protein; 170 mg Sodium

CHOCOLATE FLOURLESS CAKE

MAKES: 12 SERVINGS   **DIFFICULTY: ★ ★**

Delicious but unbelievably rich. You need only a thin slice of this cake. Perfect for sharing.

8 oz	225 g	dark chocolate
1 cup	250 mL	butter
4	4	large eggs, separated
1 cup	250 mL	granulated sugar, *divided*

Melt chocolate and butter together over hot water until melted and smooth. Beat yolks with 1/2 cup (125 mL) sugar. Fold in chocolate.

Beat whites until frothy, then add remaining 1/2 cup (125 mL) sugar and beat until stiff peaks form. Fold whites into chocolate mixture and pour into a greased 9 inch (23 cm) cake pan lined with parchment paper. Bake in a 325°F (160°C) oven for 40 to 50 minutes, or until a toothpick inserted into centre comes out clean. Serve warm or cold—it's a very sticky cake.

1 serving: 460 Calories; 38 g Total Fat (9 g Mono, 1.5 g Poly, 24 g Sat); 155 mg Cholesterol; 28 g Carbohydrates (2 g Fibre, 26 g Sugar); 3 g Protein; 240 mg Sodium

Helpful Tips

You want desserts that are easy to make yet still have a huge wow factor. Chocolate. Sauce. That's it. Saucepan brownies, a cobbler, maybe a healthy option (yogurt and stevia is simplest). Some guys might want to incorporate some molecular gastronomy and do ice cream with liquid nitrogen, but it's safer to stick with chocolate.

APPLE PIE

If you prefer a sweeter pie, serve with a scoop of ice cream and lay on ribbons of caramel sauce.

1	1	pastry for 9 inch double-crust (22 cm) pie
1 cup	250 mL	granulated sugar, plus more for sprinkling
2 Tbsp	30 mL	all-purpose flour
1/2 tsp	2 mL	ground cinnamon
5 cups	1.25 L	chopped or sliced, peeled cooking apples (such as McIntosh)
2 tsp	10 mL	lemon juice

Divide pastry into 2 portions, making 1 portion slightly larger than the other. Shape each portion into slightly flattened disc. Roll out larger portion on lightly floured surface to about 1/8 inch (3 mm) thickness. Line 9 inch (22 cm) pie plate.

Combine 1 cup (250 mL) sugar, flour and cinnamon in a small bowl.

Stir apples and lemon juice in large bowl. Sprinkle with flour mixture and stir well. Spread in pie shell. Roll out smaller portion of pastry on lightly floured surface to about 1/8 inch (3 mm) thickness. Dampen edge of pastry shell with water. Cover with remaining pastry. Trim and crimp decorative edge to seal. Sprinkle with 1/2 tsp (2 mL) sugar. Cut several small vents in top to allow steam to escape. Bake on bottom rack in a 350°F (175°C) oven for 45 to 55 minutes until golden and apples are tender. If top crust browns too quickly, lay sheet of foil over top of pie and allow bottom crust to finish baking.

1 serving: 450 Calories; 23 g Total Fat (5 g Mono, 1 g Poly, 14 g Sat); 55 mg Cholesterol; 60 g Carbohydrates (2 g Fibre, 32 g Sugar); 4 g Protein; 290 mg Sodium

FLAKY PIE CRUST

Use this easy recipe for making a pie, tarts or even a savoury chicken pot pie. The key is to use a rolling pin after the dough has come out of the food processor.

2 cups	500 mL	all-purpose flour
1/2 tsp	2 mL	salt
1/2 tsp	2 mL	granulated sugar
7/8 cup	200 mL	butter
1 Tbsp	15 mL	shortening
1/3 cup	75 mL	ice water

In a food processor, mix together first 3 ingredients, then add butter and shortening and pulse 8 to 9 times. Small pea-size shapes of butter should be visible. Add water then pulse about 4 to 5 times just until it begins to adhere. Transfer to counter. It will look like wet sand. With a rolling pin, roll back and forth gently pressing, and pretty soon the "sheets" of dough will start coming together. If they stick to your rolling pin, scrape off with a knife. Once dough has come together enough, shape into a flat disc, wrap in plastic wrap and place in fridge until ready to use.

1/8 of pie crust: 310 Calories; 22 g Total Fat (5 g Mono, 1 g Poly, 14 g Sat); 55 mg Cholesterol; 24 g Carbohydrates (trace Fibre, trace Sugar); 3 g Protein; 290 mg Sodium

CHERRY COBBLER

MAKES: 6 SERVINGS   **DIFFICULTY:** ★ ★ ★

A great dessert that taste like summer. If you don't have a cherry pitter, get creative! Use a chopstick to push out the pit or even a small inverted funnel. Make sure you have a bowl underneath to catch all the pits. Or if all else fails, you can always use two 19 oz (540 mL) cans of cherry pie filling. Serve with ice cream.

6 cups	1.5 L	red cherries, pitted
1/4 tsp	1 mL	ground cinnamon
1/4 cup	60 mL	water
4 tsp	20 mL	cornstarch
1 1/2 cups	375 mL	granulated sugar, *divided*
1 tsp	5 mL	almond extract
1 cup	250 mL	flour
3 Tbsp	45 mL	brown sugar
1 tsp	5 mL	baking powder
4 Tbsp	60 mL	butter
1	1	egg, beaten
2 Tbsp	30 mL	milk
1 Tbsp	15 mL	evaporated milk

In a saucepan over medium heat combine first 4 ingredients and 1 1/4 cups (300 mL) sugar until bubbling and thickened, about 6 to 8 minutes, making sure it doesn't burn. Stir in almond extract and pour into a greased 2 quart (2 L) baking dish.

Mix next 3 ingredients and 1/4 cup (60 mL) sugar in a large bowl. Cut in butter until crumbly. Combine egg and both milks. Add to flour mixture and stir with a fork until just combined. If mixture is too dry add 1 tsp (5 mL) milk at a time until it combines. Drop topping by tablespoonful onto filling. Bake in a 400°F (200°C) oven for 25 minutes until brown and bubbly.

1 serving: 460 Calories; 8 g Total Fat (2 g Mono, 0 g Poly, 4.5 g Sat); 20 mg Cholesterol; 95 g Carbohydrates (4 g Fibre, 73 g Sugar); 4 g Protein; 120 mg Sodium

APPLE CRISP

MAKES: 8 SERVINGS   **DIFFICULTY: ★**

Tender apples smothered in a sweet crumbly topping. This is comfort food at its best, especially when served piping hot and topped with a generous scoop of vanilla ice cream.

6	6	**fresh apples, peeled and cored**
1 cup	250 mL	**brown sugar**
3/4 cup	175 mL	**all-purpose flour**
1 tsp	5 mL	**ground cinnamon**
1/4 tsp	1 mL	**salt**
1/3 cup	75 mL	**butter, softened**

Dice apples and place them in a greased 10 inch (25 cm) baking dish.

In a small bowl, combine brown sugar, flour, cinnamon and salt. Blend in softened butter until mixture is about pea-sized. Sprinkle mixture over apples. Bake in a 350°F (175°C) for 30 to 45 minutes or until top is crisp and apples are bubbling.

1 serving: 260 Calories; 8 g Total Fat (2 g Mono, 0 g Poly, 4.5 g Sat); 20 mg Cholesterol; 48 g Carbohydrates (2 g Fibre, 36 g Sugar); 2 g Protein; 140 mg Sodium

Stressed spelled backwards is desserts.
Coincidence? I think not!
—Anonymous

APPLE RAISIN PECAN BREAD PUDDING

MAKES: 8 SERVINGS   **DIFFICULTY: ★ ★ ★**

Traditional bread pudding gets a stylish makeover with the addition of apples, raisins and pecans. Serve at room temperature with vanilla ice cream and caramel sauce.

1	1	loaf of crusty bread
5	5	large eggs
2 cups	500 mL	whipping cream
1 cup	250 mL	granulated sugar
1 Tbsp	15 mL	vanilla
1 Tbsp	15 mL	ground cinnamon
1/4 lb	115 g	melted butter
2 Tbsp	30 mL	maple syrup
1 cup	250 mL	raisins
1 cup	250 mL	roughly chopped pecans
1 cup	250 mL	chopped apple

Cut bread into 2 inch (5 cm) cubes and place in a bowl. Set aside.

In bowl of mixer whip eggs until lightly and fluffy, then add next 5 ingredients. Continue to mix until well incorporated. Pour mixture over bread cubes and allow it to soak for 30 minutes.

Add raisins and pecans and stir well to evenly distribute. Pour into a 2 quart (2 L) baking dish and bake in a 300°F (150°C) oven for 1 1/2 hours, or until light golden brown. Cool to room temperature before serving.

1 serving: 570 Calories; 31 g Total Fat (13 g Mono, 4 g Poly, 13 g Sat); 190 mg Cholesterol; 65 g Carbohydrates (4 g Fibre, 45 g Sugar); 10 g Protein; 140 mg Sodium

WHITE CHOCOLATE CRÈME BRÛLÉE

MAKES: 8 SERVINGS   **DIFFICULTY: ★ ★ ★**

To make this dish really decadent, pour 1 cup (250 mL) melted white chocolate over the custard in place of the sugar, then broil for 2 to 3 minutes. It will blow your mind.

4 cups	1 L	whipping cream
1 cup	250 mL	melted white chocolate
2 oz	60 mL	crème de cacao
6	6	egg yolks
2	2	large eggs
7/8 cup	200 mL	granulated sugar, *divided*
1 Tbsp	15 mL	vanilla
1/8 tsp	0.5 mL	salt

In a medium saucepan scald cream, then remove from heat. Add cream into melted chocolate and whisk to combine. Add crème de cacao.

Beat eggs, 3/4 cup (175 mL) sugar, vanilla and salt together in a small bowl. Slowly temper eggs by adding a little of hot cream mixture at a time until all mixture has been added. Mix until well combined. Pour slowly into 3/4 cup (175 mL) ramekins so that you do not create any air pockets. Put ramekins in a large baking pan, then place pan on middle shelf of oven. Pour hot water into baking pan until it reaches half way up sides of ramekins. Bake in a 300°F (150°C) oven for 45 minutes and check for doneness. Crème brulée can take anywhere from 45 minutes to 1 1/2 hours. When it's done, just the middle of the custard should have a slight jiggle. Refrigerate until firm.

For the topping, dust with 3 Tbsp (45 mL) sugar and place under the broiler for 2 to 3 minutes. Or use your blowtorch.

1 serving: 510 Calories; 35 g Total Fat (8 g Mono, 1.5 g Poly, 22 g Sat); 290 mg Cholesterol; 43 g Carbohydrates (0 g Fibre, 35 g Sugar); 7 g Protein; 115 mg Sodium

Coffee makes it possible to get out of bed.
Chocolate makes it worthwhile.

—Author Unknown

BOARDWALK-STYLE FUNNEL CAKES

MAKES: 4 SERVINGS   **DIFFICULTY: ★ ★**

No matter if you call them beaver tails or fried dough, there is something magical about funnel cakes that brings out the little boy in all of us. The best part is you can top them off with anything you like.

8 cups	2 L	cooking oil for frying
1 1/2	3 75 mL	cups milk
2	2	large eggs
2 cups	500 mL	all-purpose flour
1 tsp	5 mL	baking powder
1/2 tsp	2 mL	ground cinnamon
1/2 tsp	2 mL	salt
3/4 cup	175 mL	icing (confectioner's) sugar

Preheat oil in a deep-fryer, frying pan or pot to 375ºF (190ºC). In a large bowl, beat milk and eggs together.

In a separate bowl, combine flour, baking powder, cinnamon and salt. Stir into egg mixture and mix until smooth.

Pour 1 cup (250 mL) of batter into funnel while covering funnel hole with a finger. Remove finger from bottom of funnel so batter pour into oil, starting from centre of pan and moving in a swirling motion until all batter is in oil. Fry cake on both sides until golden brown. Remove and drain on paper towels. Sprinkle with powdered sugar and serve warm.

1 serving: 490 Calories; 17 g Total Fat (9 g Mono, 4 g Poly, 2.5 g Sat); 75 mg Cholesterol; 72 g Carbohydrates (2 g Fibre, 24 g Sugar); 13 g Protein; 450 mg Sodium

NO-BAKE PEANUT BUTTER BARS

MAKES: 12 SQUARES **DIFFICULTY: ★**

The genius who discovered the miracle combination of chocolate and peanut butter must an astrophysicist, or at the very least, a rocket scientist!

1 cup	250 mL	butter or margarine, melted
2 cups	500 mL	graham cracker crumbs
2 cups	500 mL	icing (confectioners') sugar
1 1/4 cups	300 mL	smooth peanut butter, divided
1 1/2 cups	375 mL	semi-sweet chocolate chips

In a medium bowl, mix together butter, graham cracker crumbs, icing sugar and 1 cup (250 mL) peanut butter until well blended. Press evenly into bottom of an ungreased 9 x13 inch (23 x 33 cm) pan.

Place chocolate chips and remaining 1/4 cup (60 mL) peanut butter in a microwave-safe bowl and melt on high (100%) in 30 second increments, stirring occasionally, until smooth. Spread over prepared crust. Refrigerate for at least 1 hour before cutting into squares.

1 bar: 530 Calories; 38 g Total Fat (4 g Mono, 0.5 g Poly, 18 g Sat); 40 mg Cholesterol; 48 g Carbohydrates (4 g Fibre, 36 g Sugar); 8 g Protein; 300 mg Sodium

> Seize the moment. Remember all those women on the *Titanic* who waved off the dessert cart.
>
> —Erma Bombeck

TART LEMON SQUARES

MAKES: 24 SQUARES   **DIFFICULTY: ★**

This easy homemade recipe for lemon squares will put the store-bought variety to shame. The fabulous tartness of these squares makes them one of the most addictive desserts you will ever try.

1 cup	250 mL	**butter, softened**
2 cups	500 mL	**granulated sugar**
2 1/4 cups	550 mL	**all-purpose flour,** *divided*
4	4	**large eggs**
3/4 cup	175 mL	**fresh squeezed lemon juice, about 2 lemons**
1/4 cup	60 mL	**powdered sugar**

In a medium mixing bowl, blend together butter, 2 cups (500 mL) flour and 1/2 cup (125 mL) sugar. Press into bottom of an ungreased 9 x13 inch (23 x 33 cm) pan until bottom of pan is covered completely. Bake in a 350°F (175°C) oven or 15 to 20 minutes or until crust starts to brown.

Meanwhile, in another bowl, whisk together the remaining 1 1/2 cups (375 mL) sugar and 1/4 cup (60 mL) flour. Whisk in eggs and lemon juice. Pour lemon mixture over baked crust. and bake for an additional 20 minutes or until the lemon top has firmed up and started to brown slightly. Remove from oven and allow to cool. The bars will firm up as they cool.

Cut into 24 squares and sprinkle with powdered sugar.

1 square: 190 Calories; 9 g Total Fat (2.5 g Mono, 0 g Poly, 5 g Sat); 55 mg Cholesterol; 27 g Carbohydrates (0 g Fibre, 18 g Sugar); 2 g Protein; 65 mg Sodium

Life is uncertain. Eat dessert first.

—Ernestine Ulmer

INDEX